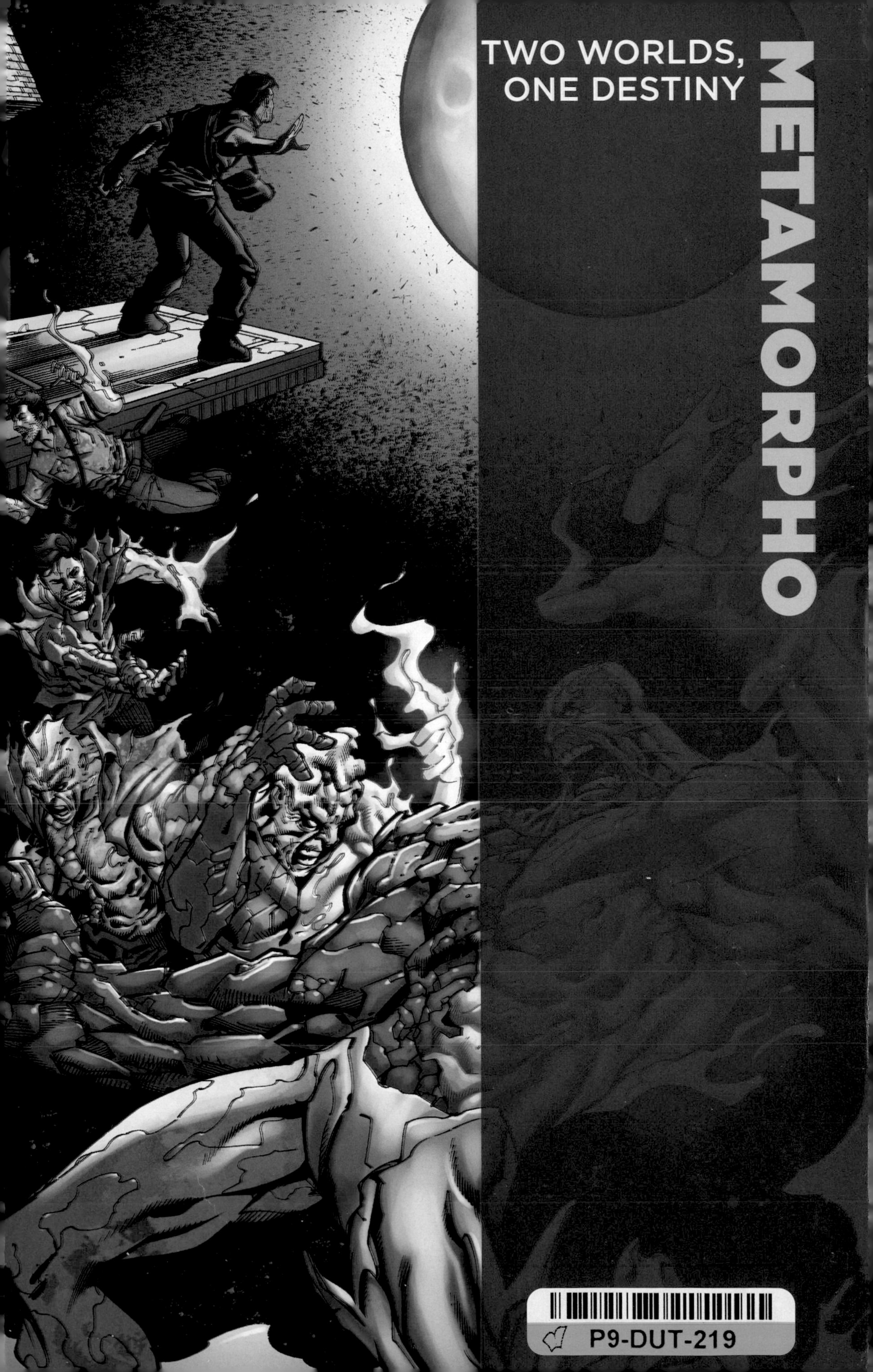
TWO WORLDS,
ONE DESTINY
METAMORPHO

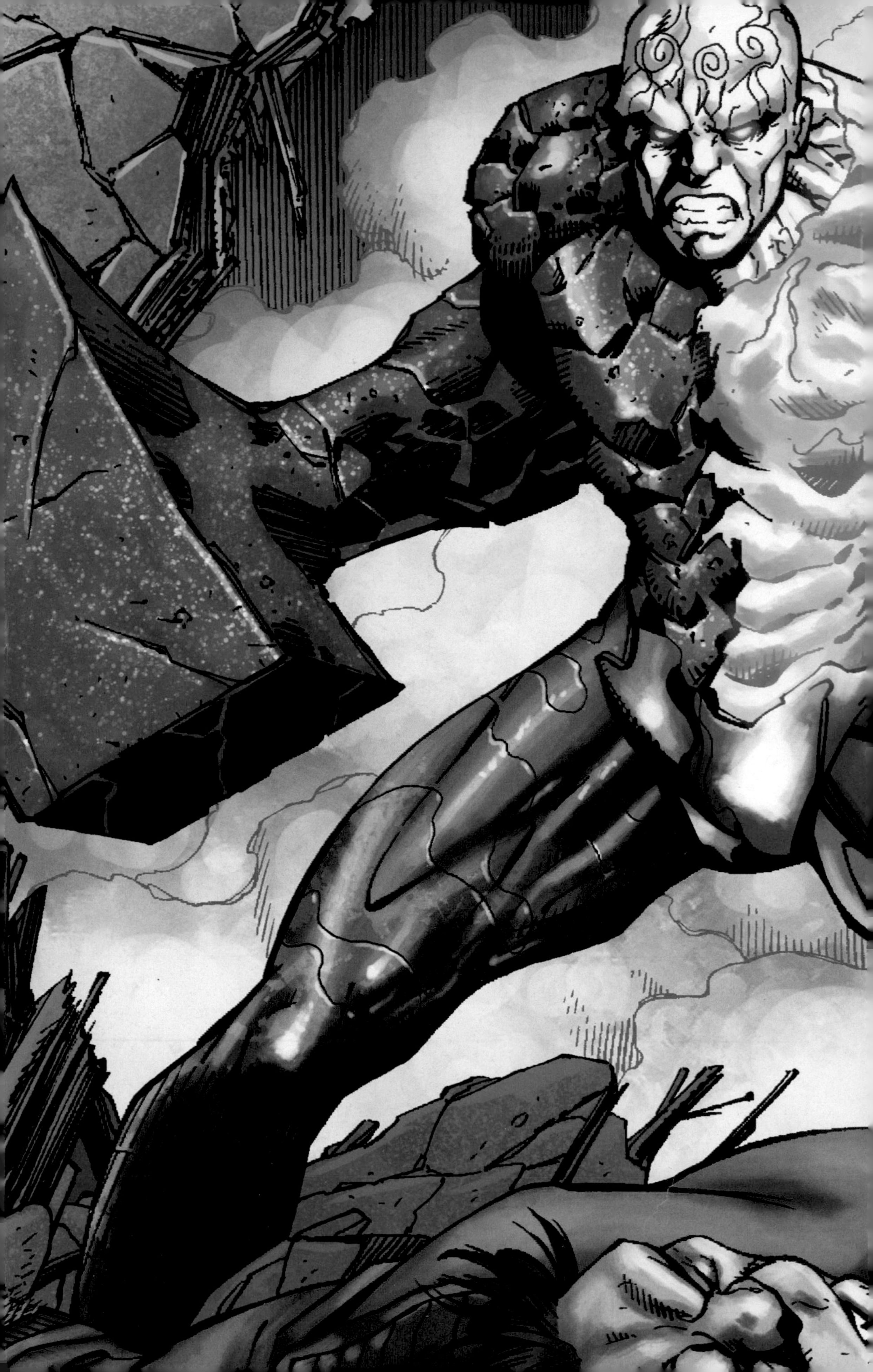

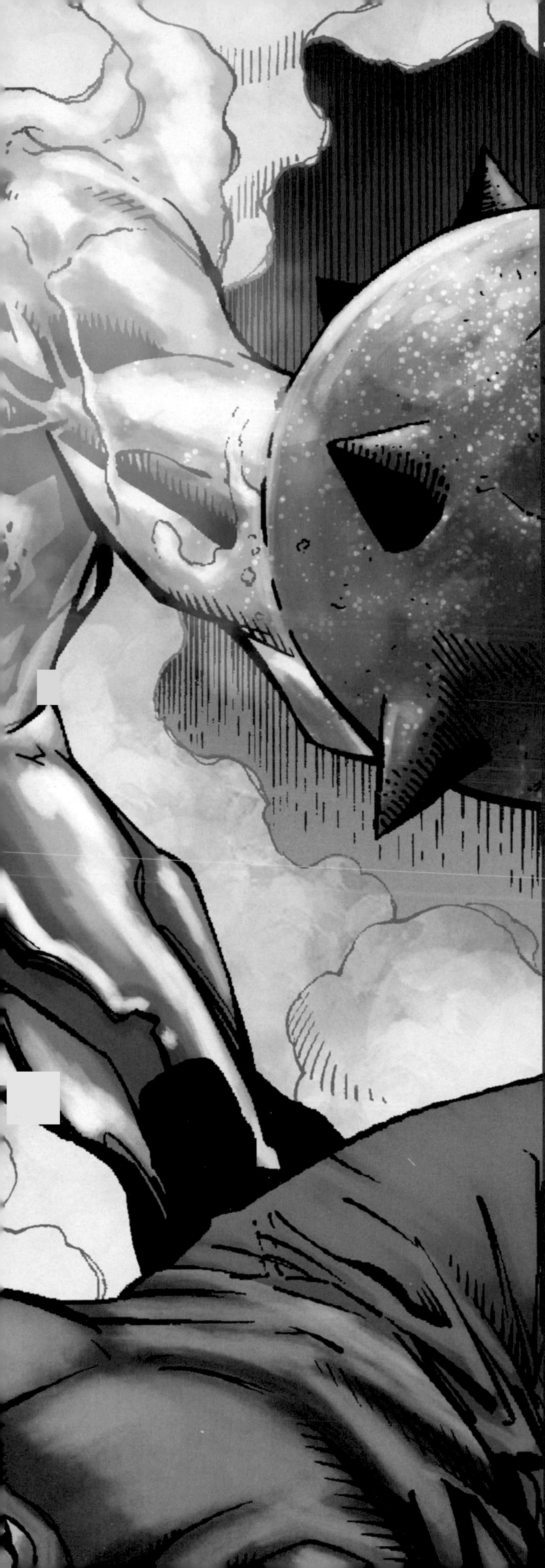

TWO WORLDS,
ONE DESTINY

METAMORPHO

WRITTEN BY
AARON LOPRESTI

PENCILS BY
AARON LOPRESTI

INKS BY
MATT BANNING
JONATHAN GLAPION
AARON LOPRESTI
LIVESAY

COLOR BY
CHRIS SOTOMAYOR

LETTERS BY
MICHAEL HEISLER

COLLECTION COVER ART BY
AARON LOPRESTI,
MATT BANNING &
CHRIS SOTOMAYOR

METAMORPHO
CREATED BY
BOB HANEY AND
RAMONA FRADON

DAVE WIELGOSZ Editor - Original Series
JEB WOODARD Group Editor - Collected Editions
SUZANNAH ROWNTREE Editor - Collected Edition
STEVE COOK Design Director - Books
DAMIAN RYLAND Publication Design

BOB HARRAS Senior VP - Editor-in-Chief, DC Comics

DIANE NELSON President
DAN DiDIO Publisher
JIM LEE Publisher
GEOFF JOHNS President & Chief Creative Officer
AMIT DESAI Executive VP - Business & Marketing Strategy, Direct to Consumer & Global Franchise Management
SAM ADES Senior VP - Direct to Consumer
BOBBIE CHASE VP - Talent Development
MARK CHIARELLO Senior VP - Art, Design & Collected Editions
JOHN CUNNINGHAM Senior VP - Sales & Trade Marketing
ANNE DePIES Senior VP - Business Strategy, Finance & Administration
DON FALLETTI VP - Manufacturing Operations
LAWRENCE GANEM VP - Editorial Administration & Talent Relations
ALISON GILL Senior VP - Manufacturing & Operations
HANK KANALZ Senior VP - Editorial Strategy & Administration
JAY KOGAN VP - Legal Affairs
THOMAS LOFTUS VP - Business Affairs
JACK MAHAN VP - Business Affairs
NICK J. NAPOLITANO VP - Manufacturing Administration
EDDIE SCANNELL VP - Consumer Marketing
COURTNEY SIMMONS Senior VP - Publicity & Communications
JIM (SKI) SOKOLOWSKI VP - Comic Book Specialty Sales & Trade Marketing
NANCY SPEARS VP - Mass, Book, Digital Sales & Trade Marketing

METAMORPHO: TWO WORLDS, ONE DESTINY

DC Comics, 2900 West Alameda Ave., Burbank, CA 91505
Printed by LSC Communications, Salem, VA, USA. 11/25/16. First Printing.
ISBN: 978-1-4012-6518-2

Library of Congress Cataloging-in-Publication Data is available.

PEFC Certified
Printed on paper from sustainably managed forests, controlled sources
www.pefc.org
PEFC/29-31-337

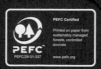

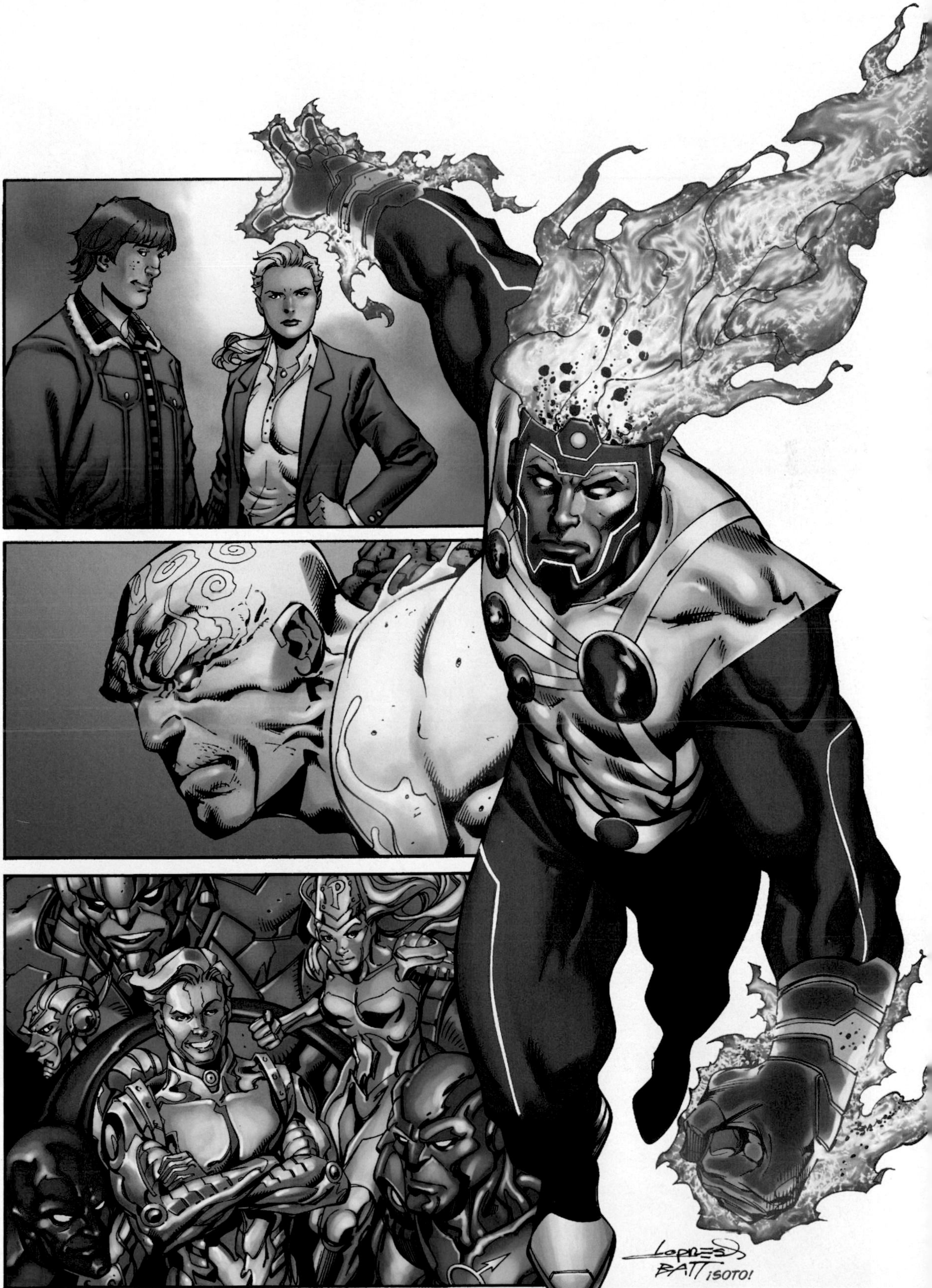
BATT ¡SOTO!

BOUND BUT NOT BROKEN

AARON LOPRESTI writer/penciller MATT BANNING inker CHRIS SOTOMAYOR colorist MICHAEL HEISLER letterer
AARON LOPRESTI with CHRIS SOTOMAYOR cover

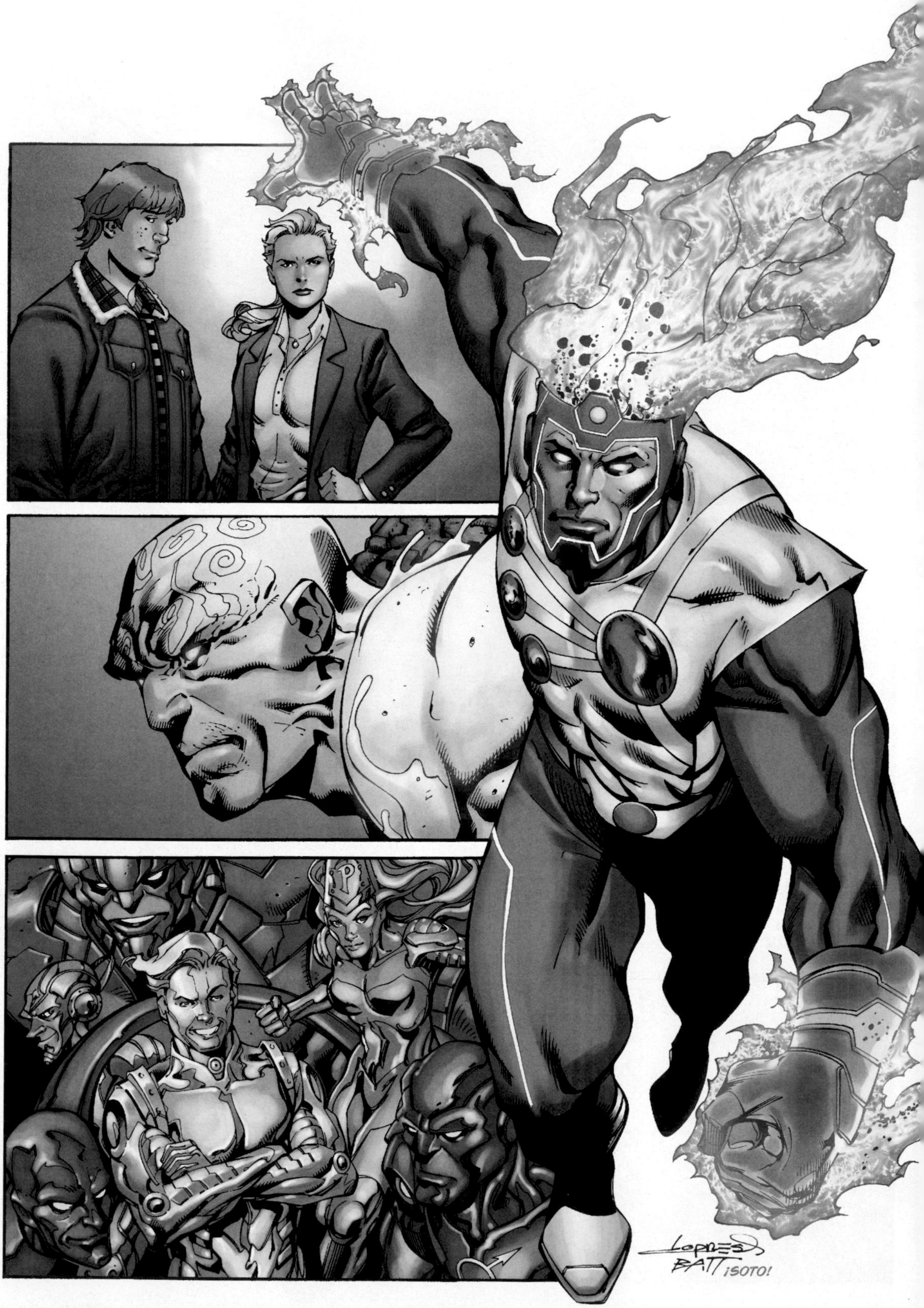
LOPRESTI
BATT ¡SOTO!

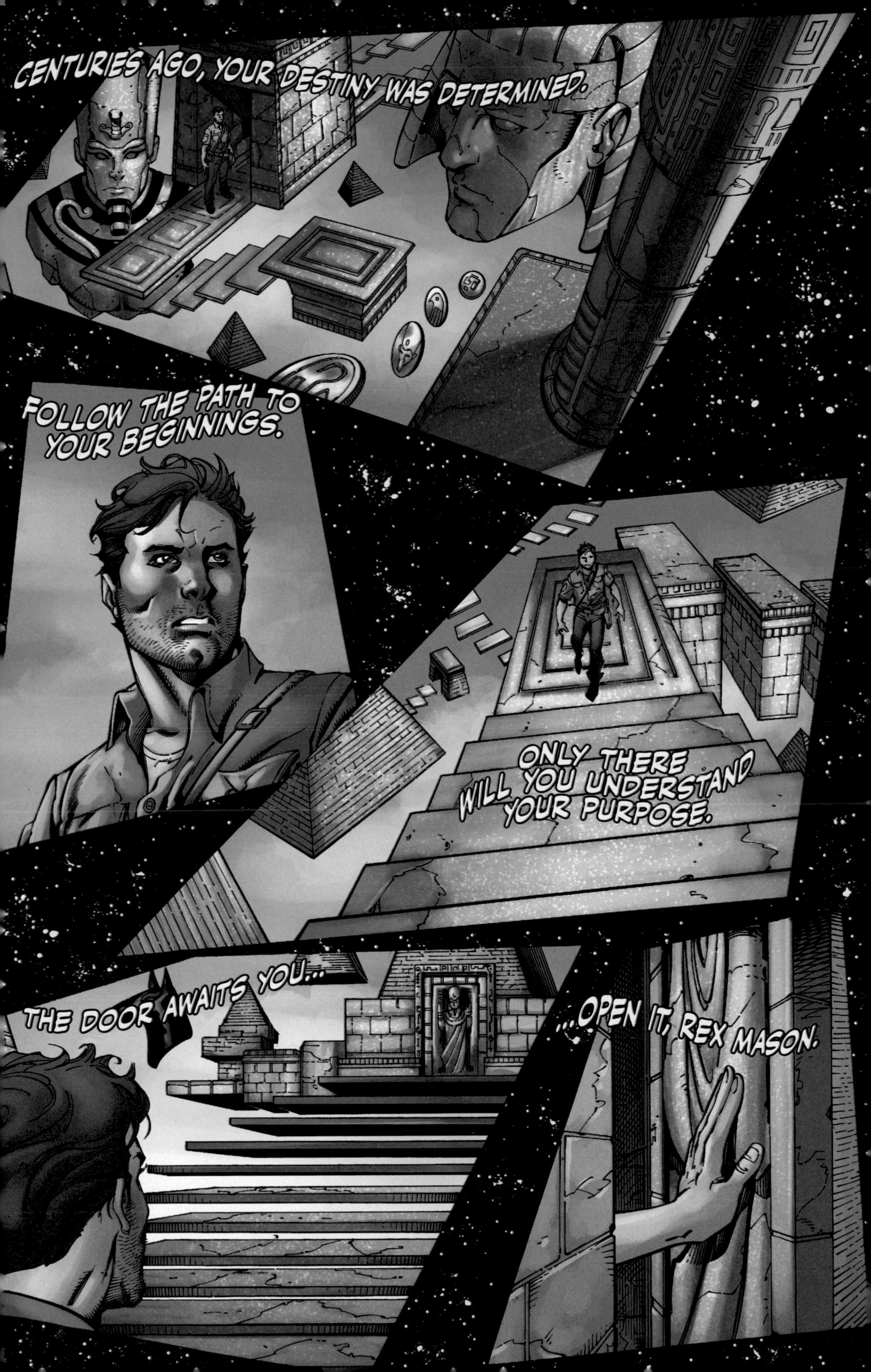
CENTURIES AGO, YOUR DESTINY WAS DETERMINED.
FOLLOW THE PATH TO YOUR BEGINNINGS.
ONLY THERE WILL YOU UNDERSTAND YOUR PURPOSE.
THE DOOR AWAITS YOU...
...OPEN IT, REX MASON.

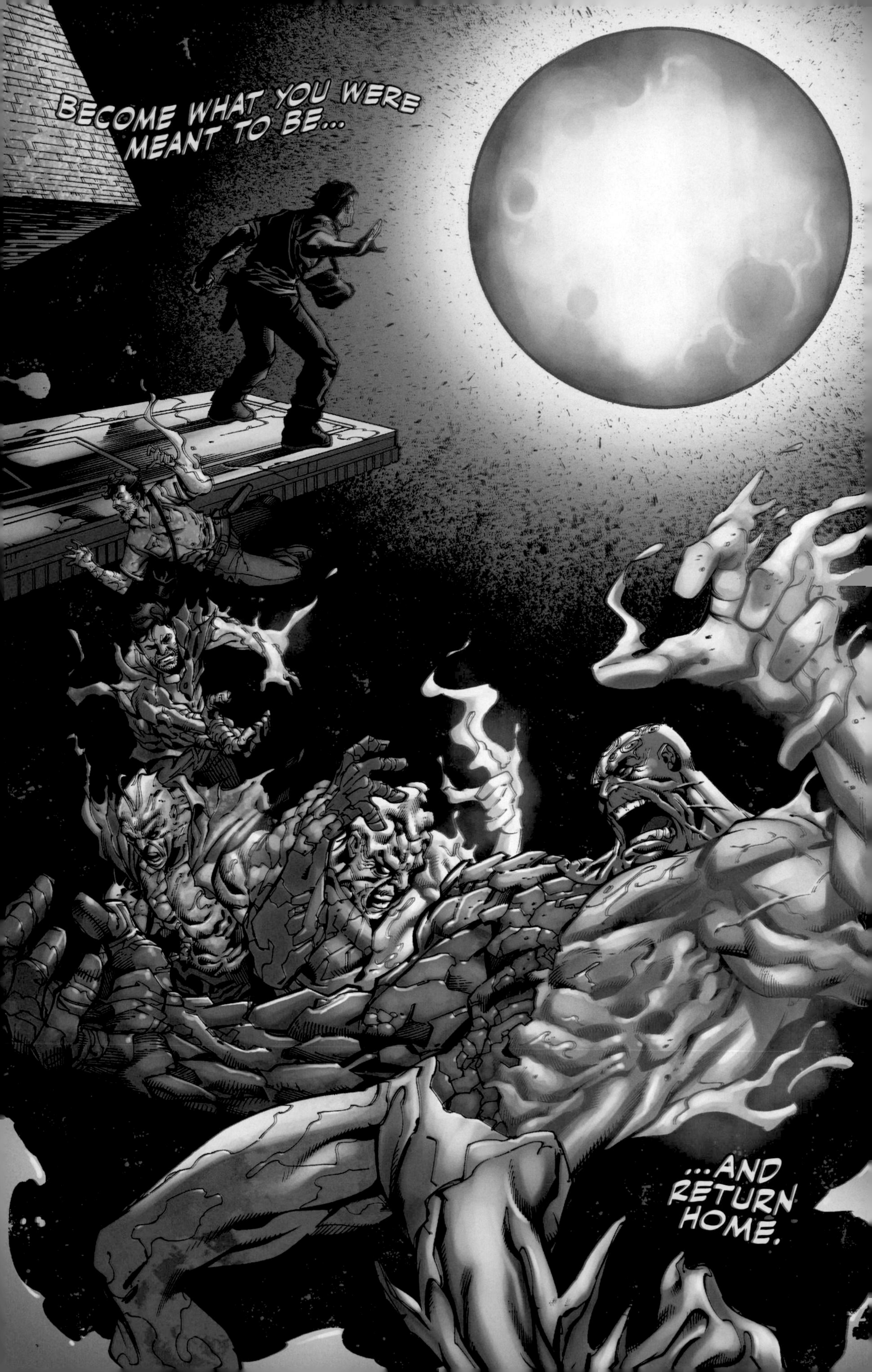
BECOME WHAT YOU WERE MEANT TO BE...
...AND RETURN HOME.

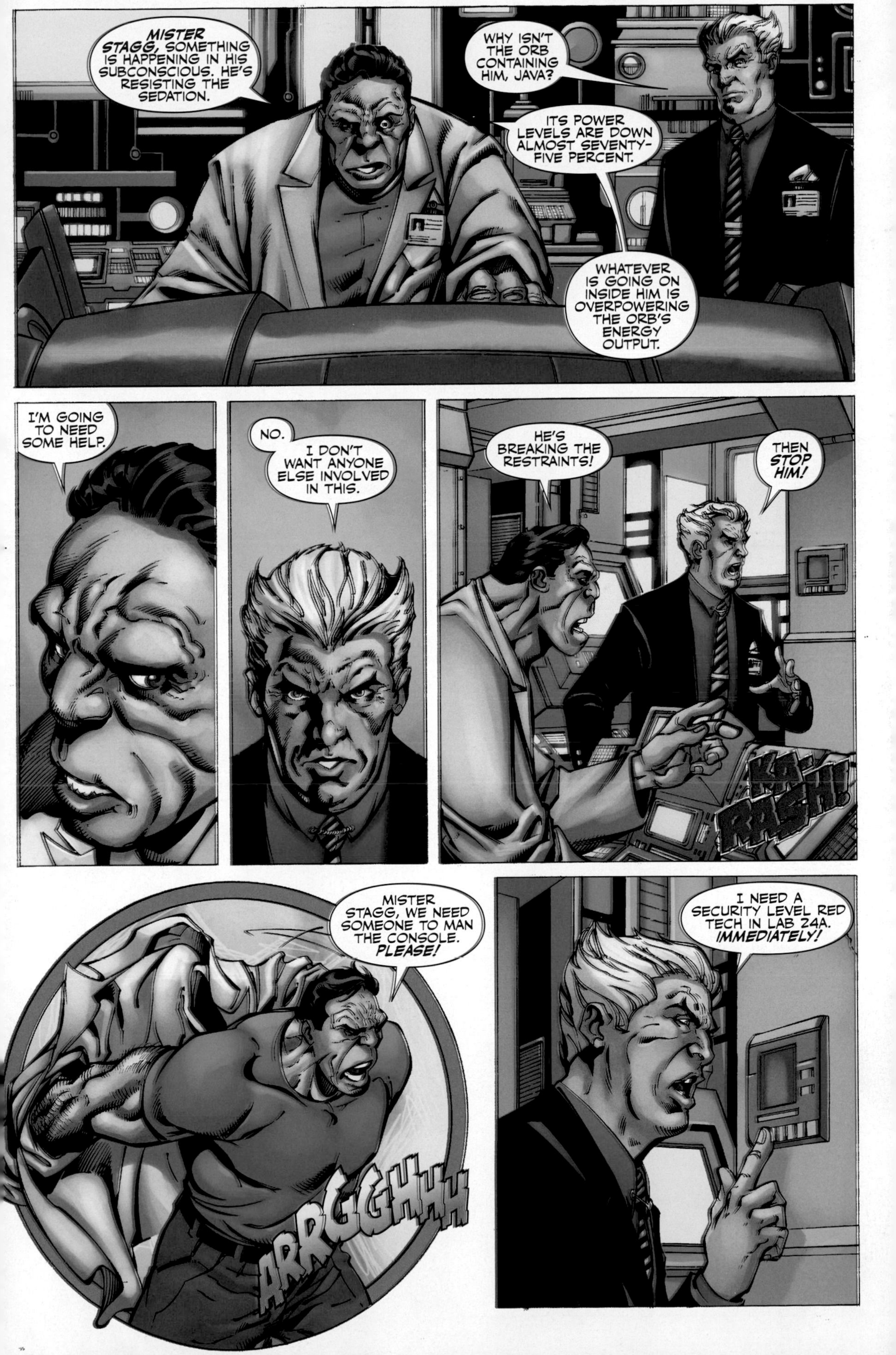
MISTER STAGG, SOMETHING IS HAPPENING IN HIS SUBCONSCIOUS. HE'S RESISTING THE SEDATION.
WHY ISN'T THE ORB CONTAINING HIM, JAVA?
ITS POWER LEVELS ARE DOWN ALMOST SEVENTY-FIVE PERCENT.
WHATEVER IS GOING ON INSIDE HIM IS OVERPOWERING THE ORB'S ENERGY OUTPUT.
I'M GOING TO NEED SOME HELP.
NO.
I DON'T WANT ANYONE ELSE INVOLVED IN THIS.
HE'S BREAKING THE RESTRAINTS!
THEN STOP HIM!
KA-RASH!
MISTER STAGG, WE NEED SOMEONE TO MAN THE CONSOLE. PLEASE!
ARRGGHHH
I NEED A SECURITY LEVEL RED TECH IN LAB 24A. IMMEDIATELY!

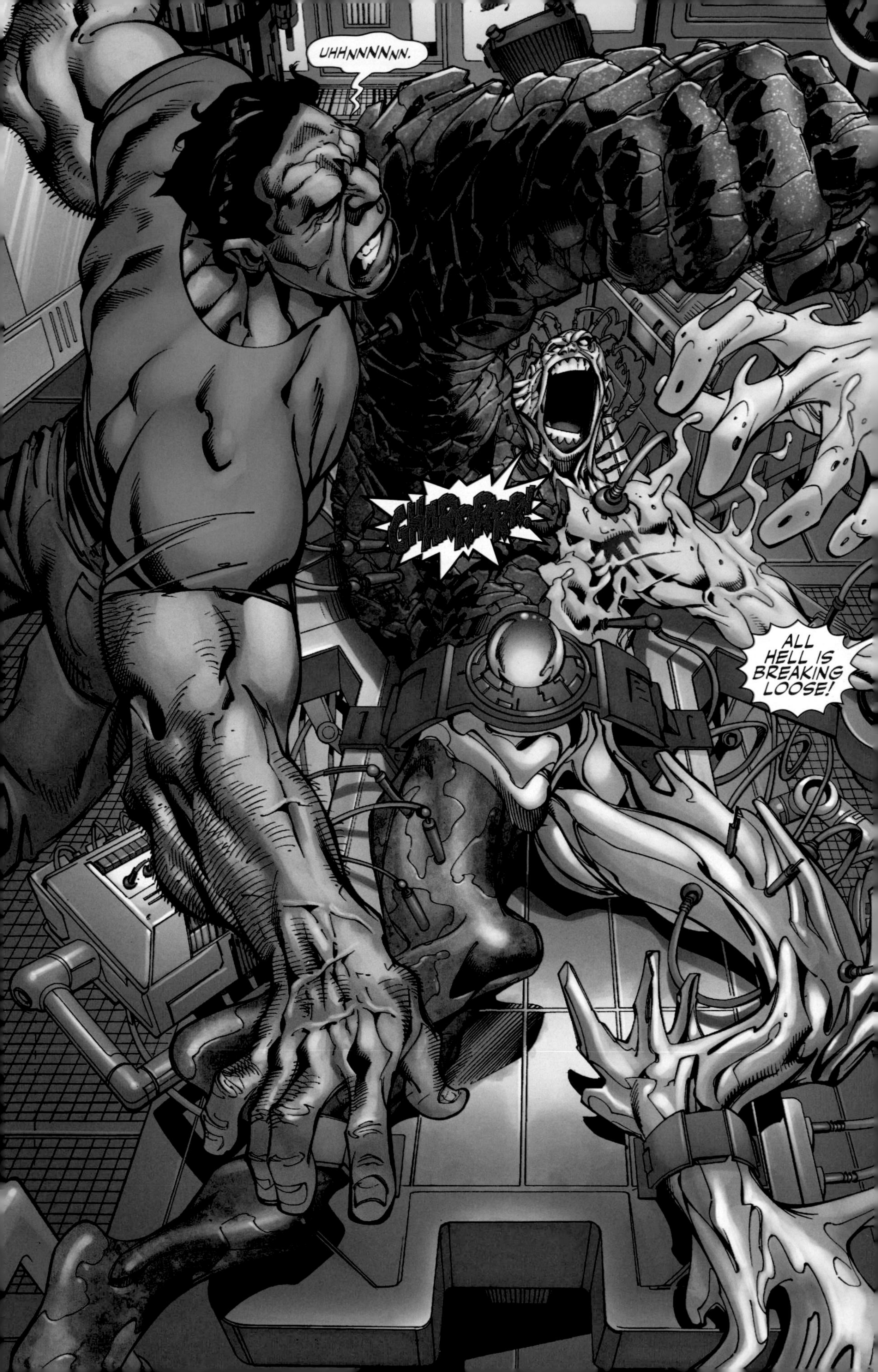
UHHNNNNNN.
GHHRRRRR!
ALL HELL IS BREAKING LOOSE!

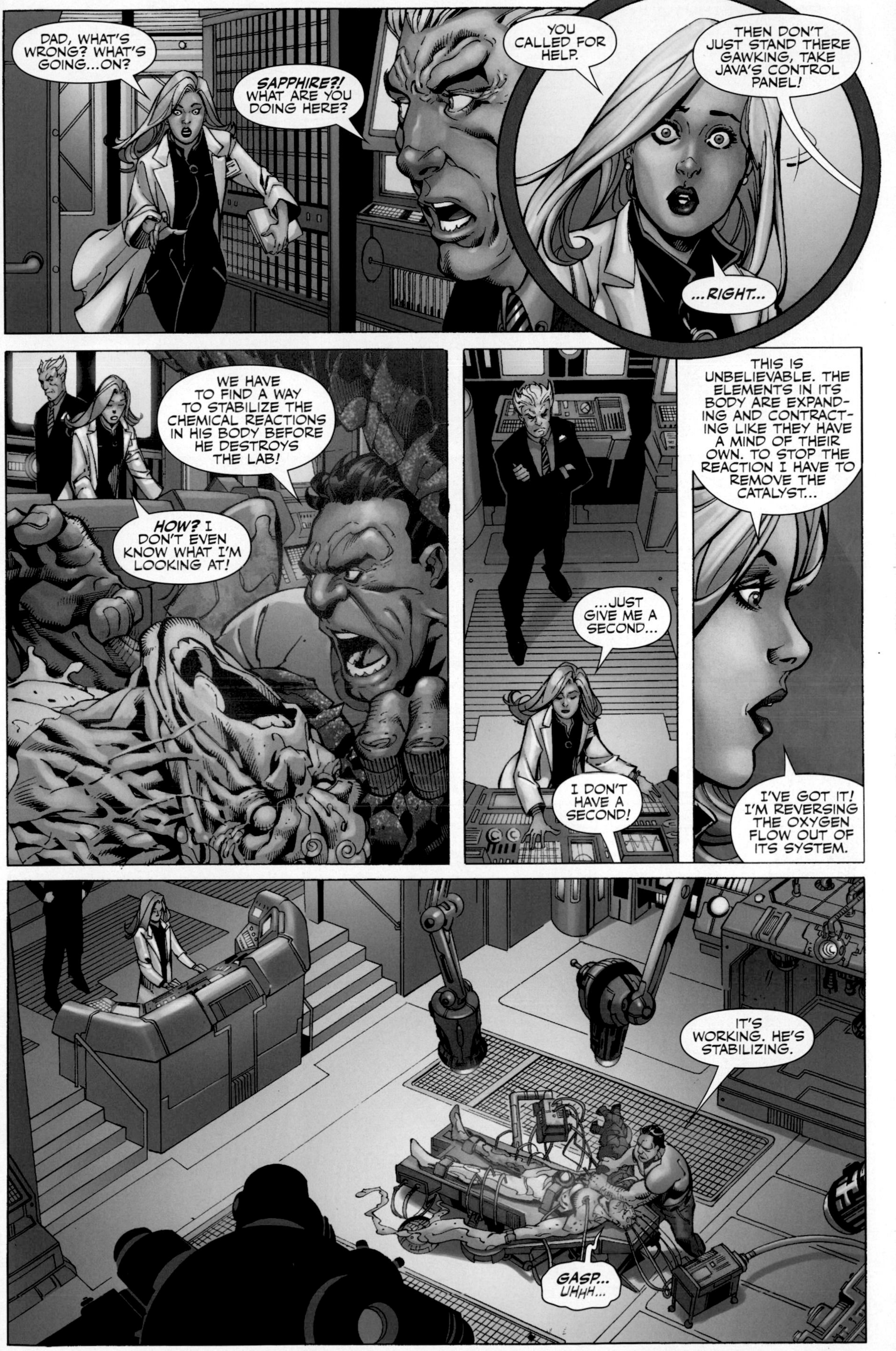
DAD, WHAT'S WRONG? WHAT'S GOING...ON?
SAPPHIRE?! WHAT ARE YOU DOING HERE?
YOU CALLED FOR HELP.
THEN DON'T JUST STAND THERE GAWKING, TAKE JAVA'S CONTROL PANEL!
...RIGHT...
WE HAVE TO FIND A WAY TO STABILIZE THE CHEMICAL REACTIONS IN HIS BODY BEFORE HE DESTROYS THE LAB!
HOW? I DON'T EVEN KNOW WHAT I'M LOOKING AT!
...JUST GIVE ME A SECOND...
I DON'T HAVE A SECOND!
THIS IS UNBELIEVABLE. THE ELEMENTS IN ITS BODY ARE EXPANDING AND CONTRACTING LIKE THEY HAVE A MIND OF THEIR OWN. TO STOP THE REACTION I HAVE TO REMOVE THE CATALYST...
I'VE GOT IT! I'M REVERSING THE OXYGEN FLOW OUT OF ITS SYSTEM.
IT'S WORKING. HE'S STABILIZING.
GASP... UHHH...

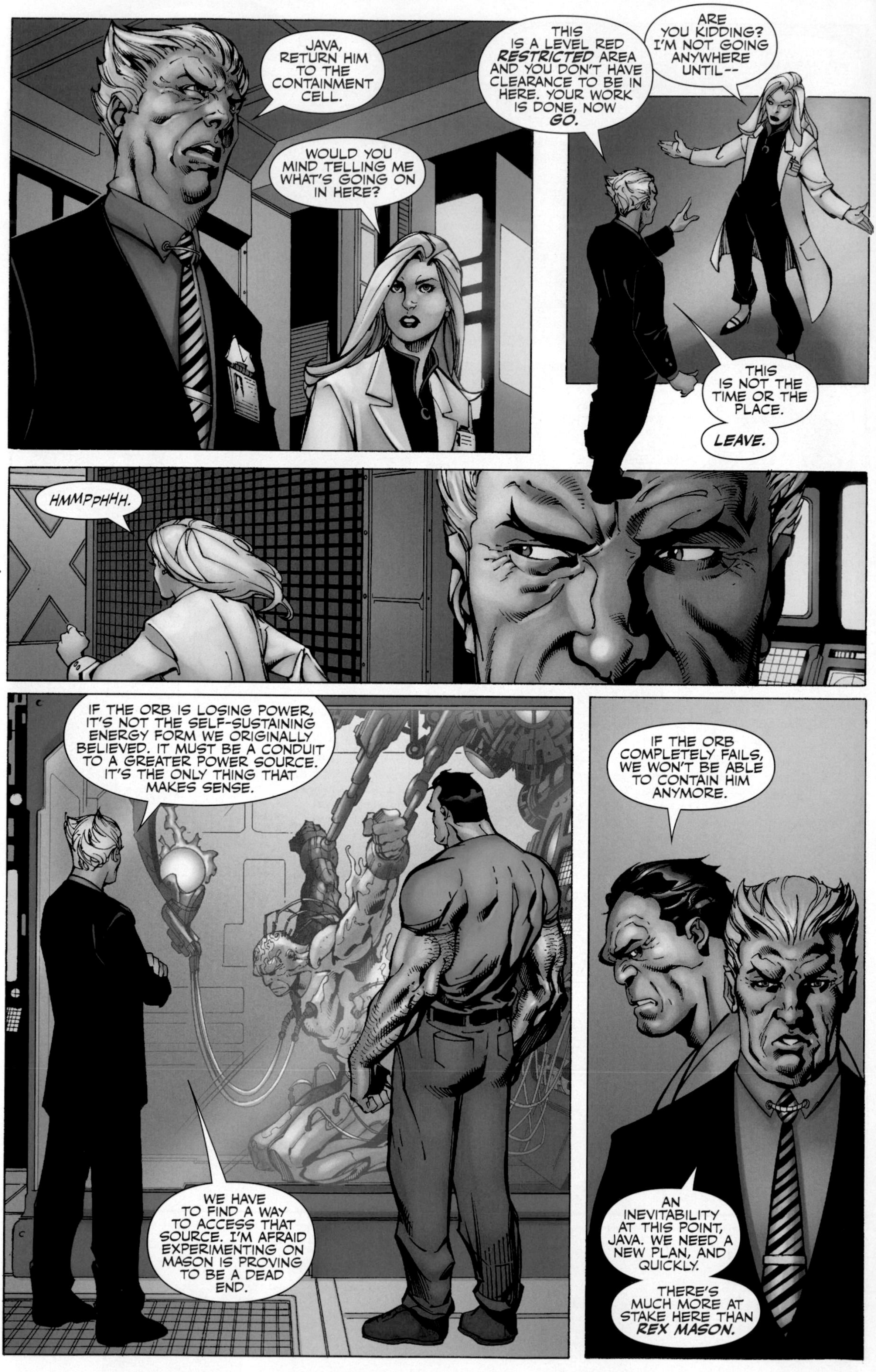
JAVA, RETURN HIM TO THE CONTAINMENT CELL.
WOULD YOU MIND TELLING ME WHAT'S GOING ON IN HERE?
THIS IS A LEVEL RED RESTRICTED AREA AND YOU DON'T HAVE CLEARANCE TO BE IN HERE. YOUR WORK IS DONE, NOW GO.
ARE YOU KIDDING? I'M NOT GOING ANYWHERE UNTIL--
THIS IS NOT THE TIME OR THE PLACE.
LEAVE.
HMMPpHHH.
IF THE ORB IS LOSING POWER, IT'S NOT THE SELF-SUSTAINING ENERGY FORM WE ORIGINALLY BELIEVED. IT MUST BE A CONDUIT TO A GREATER POWER SOURCE. IT'S THE ONLY THING THAT MAKES SENSE.
WE HAVE TO FIND A WAY TO ACCESS THAT SOURCE. I'M AFRAID EXPERIMENTING ON MASON IS PROVING TO BE A DEAD END.
IF THE ORB COMPLETELY FAILS, WE WON'T BE ABLE TO CONTAIN HIM ANYMORE.
AN INEVITABILITY AT THIS POINT, JAVA. WE NEED A NEW PLAN, AND QUICKLY.
THERE'S MUCH MORE AT STAKE HERE THAN REX MASON.

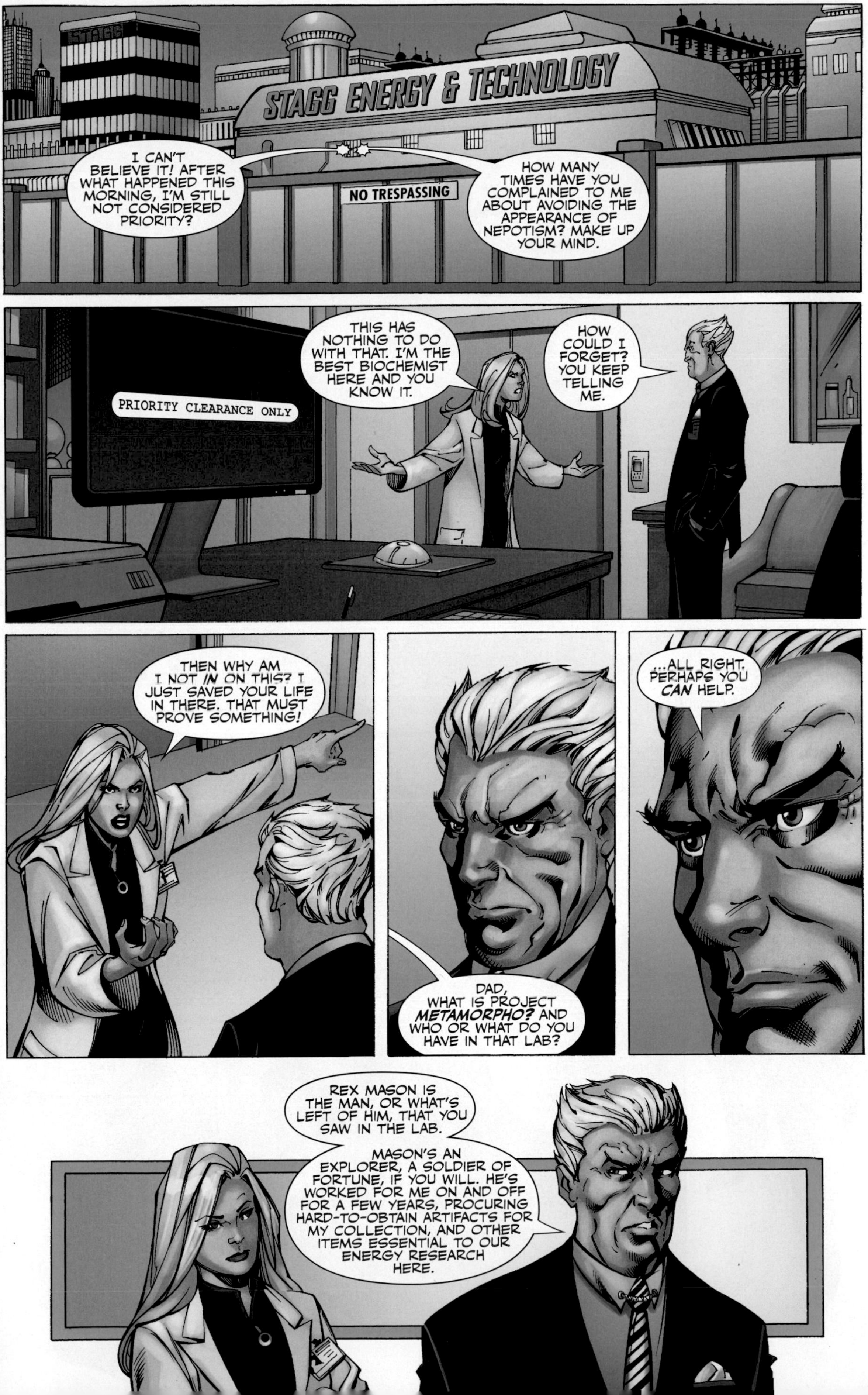
STAGG ENERGY & TECHNOLOGY
NO TRESPASSING
I CAN'T BELIEVE IT! AFTER WHAT HAPPENED THIS MORNING, I'M STILL NOT CONSIDERED PRIORITY?
HOW MANY TIMES HAVE YOU COMPLAINED TO ME ABOUT AVOIDING THE APPEARANCE OF NEPOTISM? MAKE UP YOUR MIND.
PRIORITY CLEARANCE ONLY
THIS HAS NOTHING TO DO WITH THAT. I'M THE BEST BIOCHEMIST HERE AND YOU KNOW IT.
HOW COULD I FORGET? YOU KEEP TELLING ME.
THEN WHY AM I NOT *IN* ON THIS? I JUST SAVED YOUR LIFE IN THERE. THAT MUST PROVE SOMETHING!
DAD, WHAT IS PROJECT ***METAMORPHO?*** AND WHO OR WHAT DO YOU HAVE IN THAT LAB?
...ALL RIGHT. PERHAPS YOU *CAN* HELP.
REX MASON IS THE MAN, OR WHAT'S LEFT OF HIM, THAT YOU SAW IN THE LAB.
MASON'S AN EXPLORER, A SOLDIER OF FORTUNE, IF YOU WILL. HE'S WORKED FOR ME ON AND OFF FOR A FEW YEARS, PROCURING HARD-TO-OBTAIN ARTIFACTS FOR MY COLLECTION, AND OTHER ITEMS ESSENTIAL TO OUR ENERGY RESEARCH HERE.

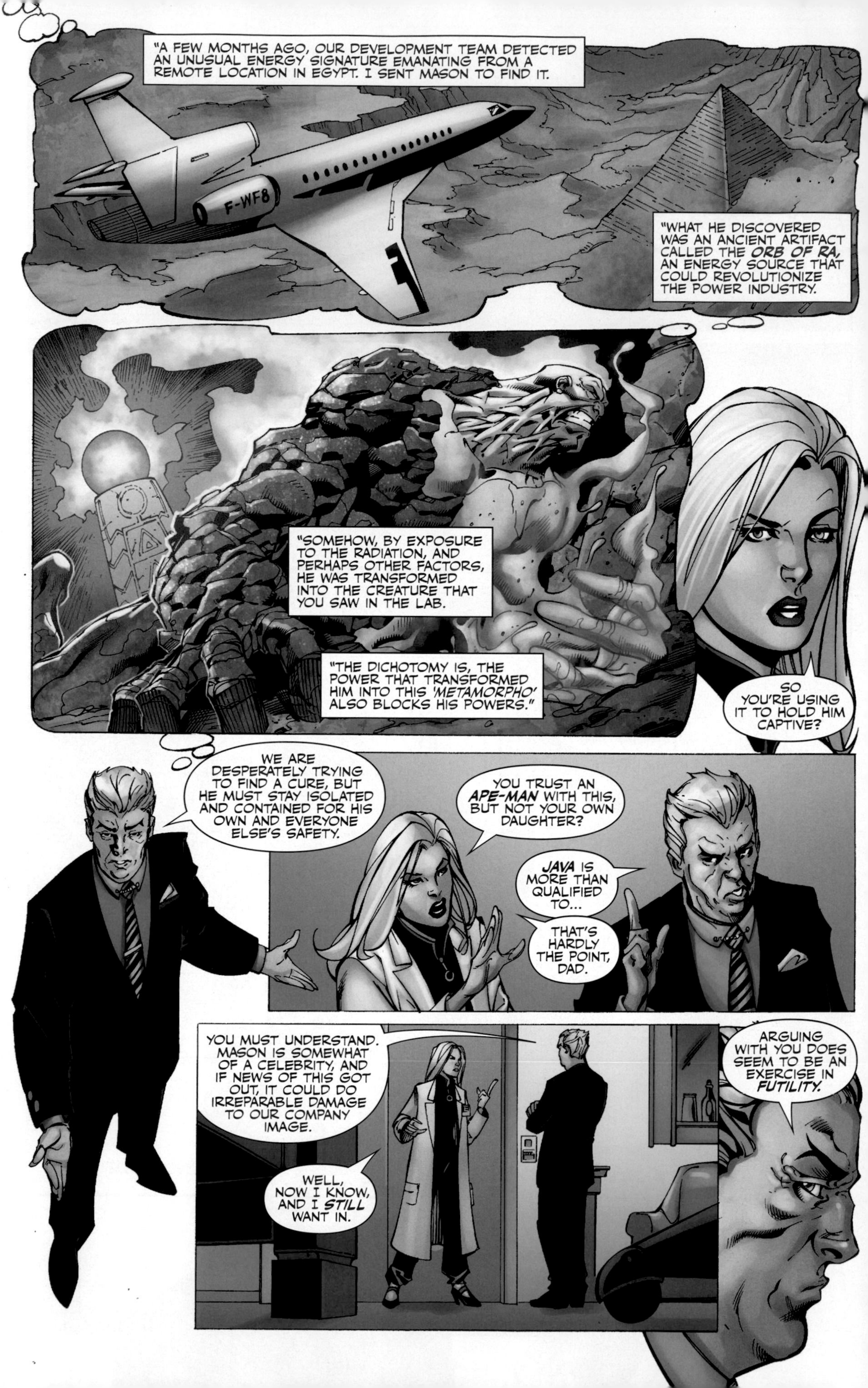
"A FEW MONTHS AGO, OUR DEVELOPMENT TEAM DETECTED AN UNUSUAL ENERGY SIGNATURE EMANATING FROM A REMOTE LOCATION IN EGYPT. I SENT MASON TO FIND IT.
F-WF8
"WHAT HE DISCOVERED WAS AN ANCIENT ARTIFACT CALLED THE *ORB OF RA,* AN ENERGY SOURCE THAT COULD REVOLUTIONIZE THE POWER INDUSTRY.
"SOMEHOW, BY EXPOSURE TO THE RADIATION, AND PERHAPS OTHER FACTORS, HE WAS TRANSFORMED INTO THE CREATURE THAT YOU SAW IN THE LAB.
"THE DICHOTOMY IS, THE POWER THAT TRANSFORMED HIM INTO THIS *'METAMORPHO'* ALSO BLOCKS HIS POWERS."
SO YOU'RE USING IT TO HOLD HIM CAPTIVE?
WE ARE DESPERATELY TRYING TO FIND A CURE, BUT HE MUST STAY ISOLATED AND CONTAINED FOR HIS OWN AND EVERYONE ELSE'S SAFETY.
YOU TRUST AN *APE-MAN* WITH THIS, BUT NOT YOUR OWN DAUGHTER?
JAVA IS MORE THAN QUALIFIED TO...
THAT'S HARDLY THE POINT, DAD.
YOU MUST UNDERSTAND. MASON IS SOMEWHAT OF A CELEBRITY, AND IF NEWS OF THIS GOT OUT, IT COULD DO IRREPARABLE DAMAGE TO OUR COMPANY IMAGE.
WELL, NOW I KNOW, AND I *STILL* WANT IN.
ARGUING WITH YOU DOES SEEM TO BE AN EXERCISE IN *FUTILITY.*

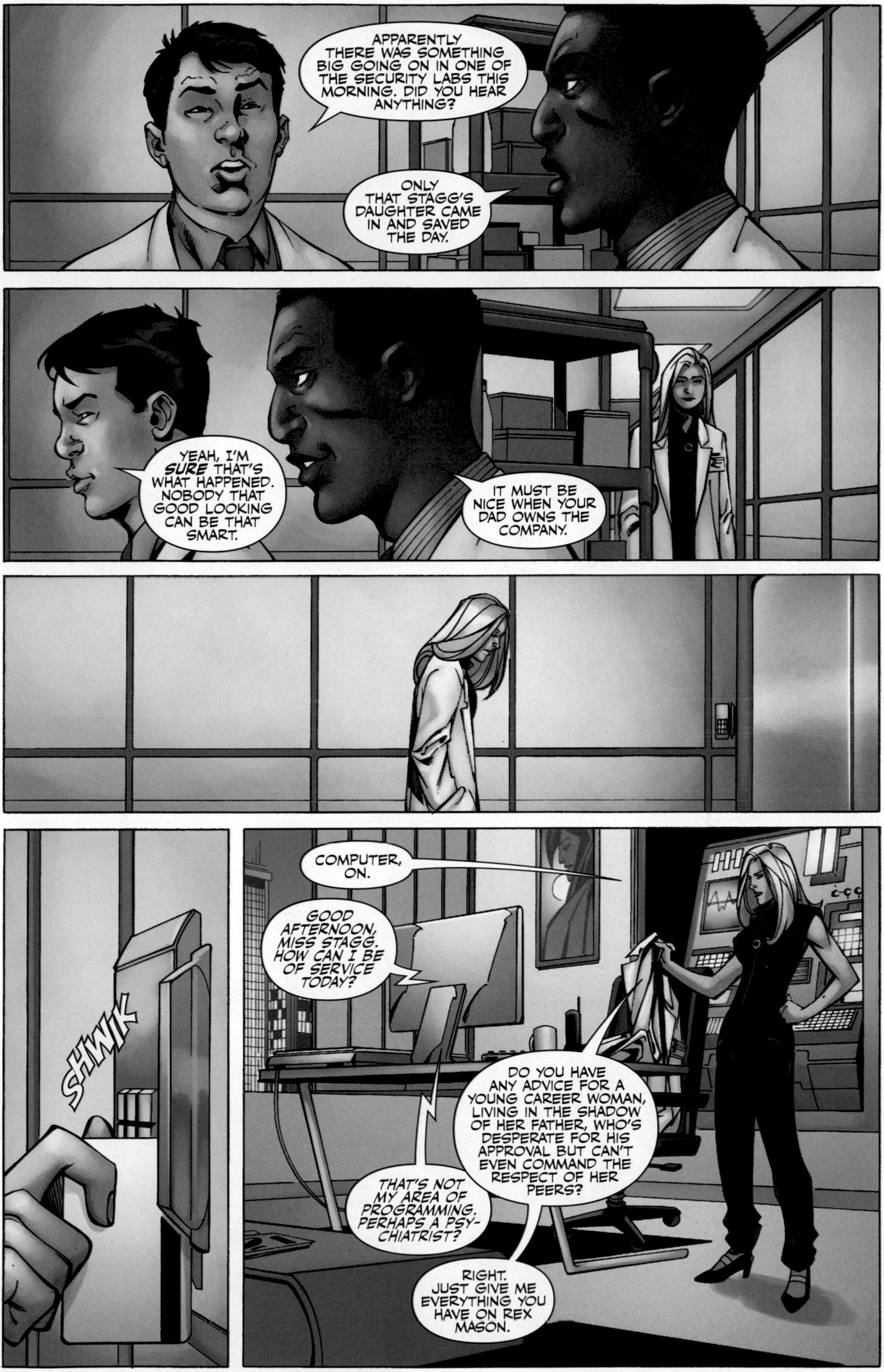
APPARENTLY THERE WAS SOMETHING BIG GOING ON IN ONE OF THE SECURITY LABS THIS MORNING. DID YOU HEAR ANYTHING?
ONLY THAT STAGG'S DAUGHTER CAME IN AND SAVED THE DAY.
YEAH, I'M *SURE* THAT'S WHAT HAPPENED. NOBODY THAT GOOD LOOKING CAN BE THAT SMART.
IT MUST BE NICE WHEN YOUR DAD OWNS THE COMPANY.
SHWIK
COMPUTER, ON.
GOOD AFTERNOON, MISS STAGG. HOW CAN I BE OF SERVICE TODAY?
DO YOU HAVE ANY ADVICE FOR A YOUNG CAREER WOMAN, LIVING IN THE SHADOW OF HER FATHER, WHO'S DESPERATE FOR HIS APPROVAL BUT CAN'T EVEN COMMAND THE RESPECT OF HER PEERS?
THAT'S NOT MY AREA OF PROGRAMMING. PERHAPS A PSYCHIATRIST?
RIGHT. JUST GIVE ME EVERYTHING YOU HAVE ON REX MASON.

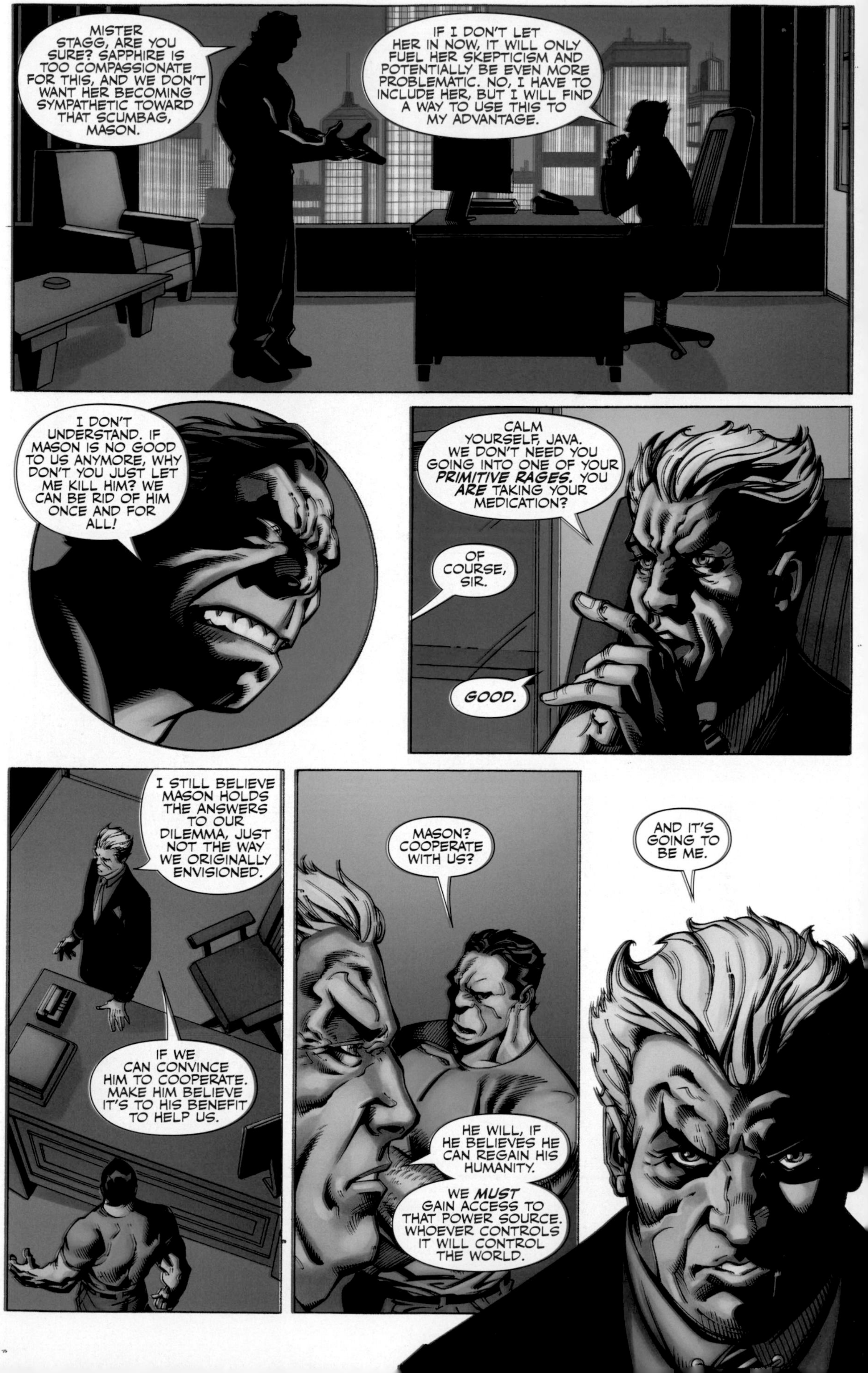
MISTER STAGG, ARE YOU SURE? SAPPHIRE IS TOO COMPASSIONATE FOR THIS, AND WE DON'T WANT HER BECOMING SYMPATHETIC TOWARD THAT SCUMBAG, MASON.
IF I DON'T LET HER IN NOW, IT WILL ONLY FUEL HER SKEPTICISM AND POTENTIALLY BE EVEN MORE PROBLEMATIC. NO, I HAVE TO INCLUDE HER, BUT I WILL FIND A WAY TO USE THIS TO MY ADVANTAGE.
I DON'T UNDERSTAND. IF MASON IS NO GOOD TO US ANYMORE, WHY DON'T YOU JUST LET ME KILL HIM? WE CAN BE RID OF HIM ONCE AND FOR ALL!
CALM YOURSELF, JAVA. WE DON'T NEED YOU GOING INTO ONE OF YOUR *PRIMITIVE RAGES.* YOU *ARE* TAKING YOUR MEDICATION?
OF COURSE, SIR.
GOOD.
I STILL BELIEVE MASON HOLDS THE ANSWERS TO OUR DILEMMA, JUST NOT THE WAY WE ORIGINALLY ENVISIONED.
IF WE CAN CONVINCE HIM TO COOPERATE. MAKE HIM BELIEVE IT'S TO HIS BENEFIT TO HELP US.
MASON? COOPERATE WITH US?
HE WILL, IF HE BELIEVES HE CAN REGAIN HIS HUMANITY.
WE *MUST* GAIN ACCESS TO THAT POWER SOURCE. WHOEVER CONTROLS IT WILL CONTROL THE WORLD.
AND IT'S GOING TO BE ME.

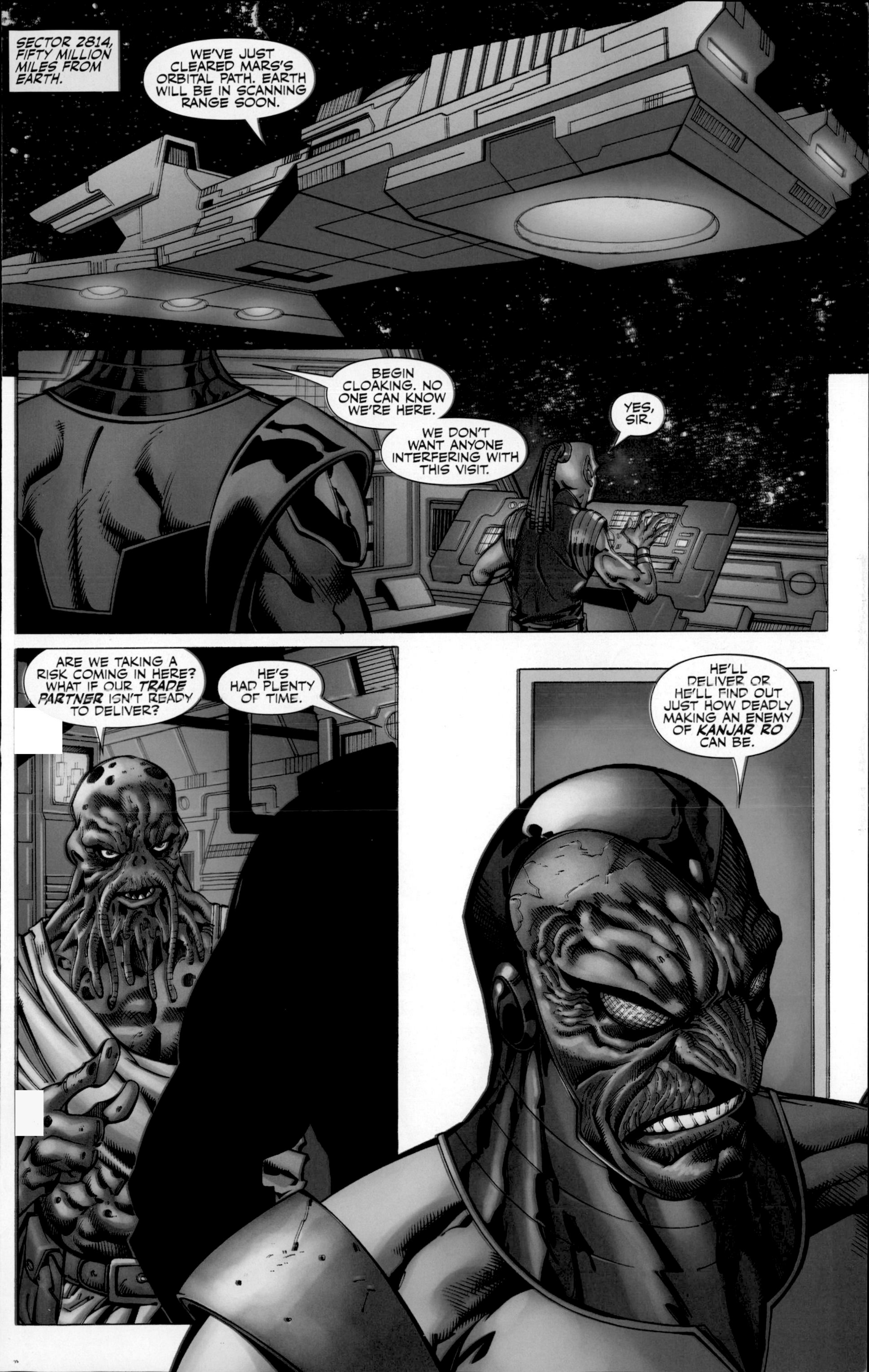
SECTOR 2814, FIFTY MILLION MILES FROM EARTH.
WE'VE JUST CLEARED MARS'S ORBITAL PATH. EARTH WILL BE IN SCANNING RANGE SOON.
BEGIN CLOAKING. NO ONE CAN KNOW WE'RE HERE.
WE DON'T WANT ANYONE INTERFERING WITH THIS VISIT.
YES, SIR.
ARE WE TAKING A RISK COMING IN HERE? WHAT IF OUR TRADE PARTNER ISN'T READY TO DELIVER?
HE'S HAD PLENTY OF TIME.
HE'LL DELIVER OR HE'LL FIND OUT JUST HOW DEADLY MAKING AN ENEMY OF KANJAR RO CAN BE.

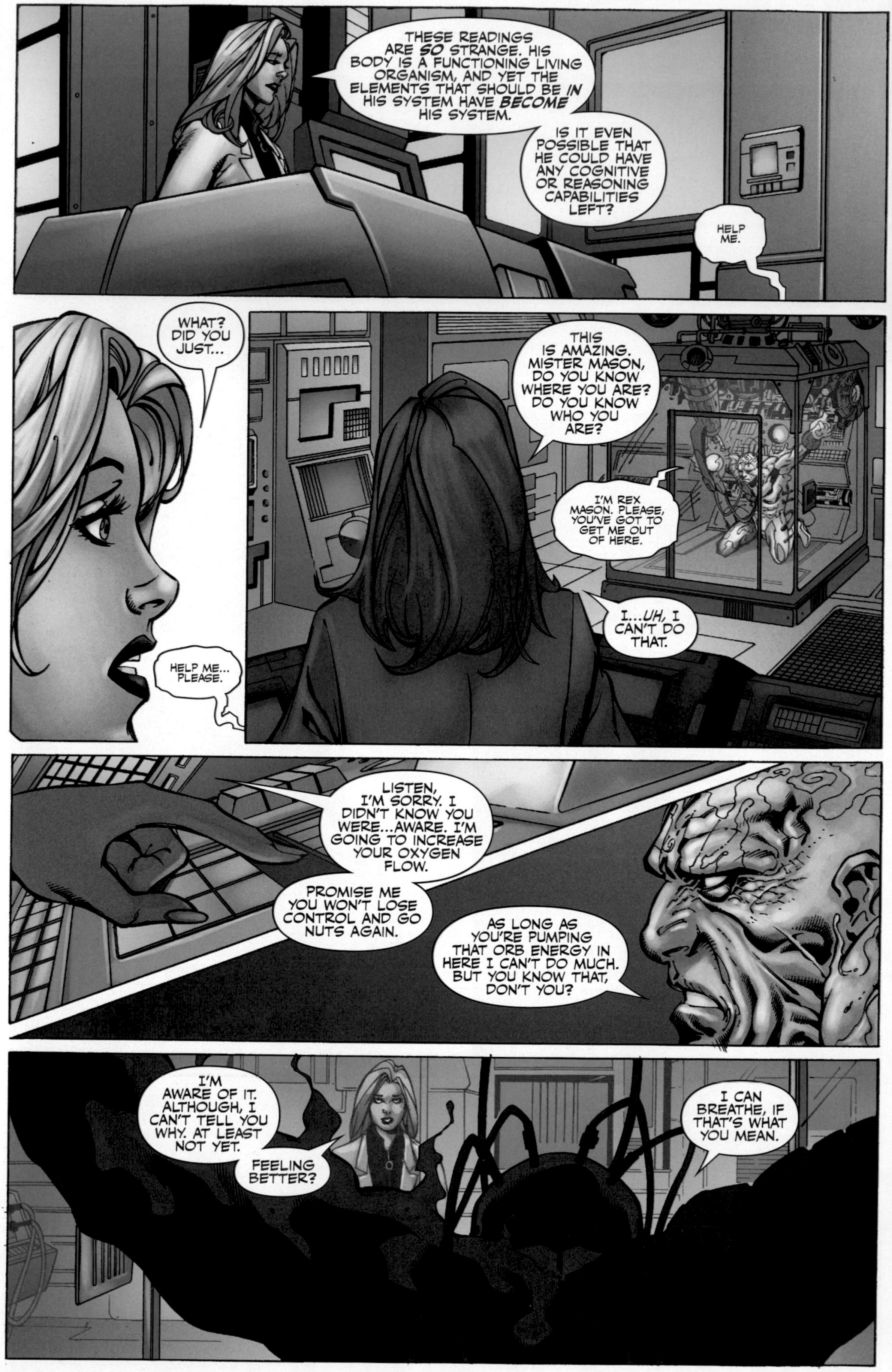
THESE READINGS ARE SO STRANGE. HIS BODY IS A FUNCTIONING LIVING ORGANISM, AND YET THE ELEMENTS THAT SHOULD BE IN HIS SYSTEM HAVE BECOME HIS SYSTEM.
IS IT EVEN POSSIBLE THAT HE COULD HAVE ANY COGNITIVE OR REASONING CAPABILITIES LEFT?
HELP ME.
WHAT? DID YOU JUST...
HELP ME... PLEASE.
THIS IS AMAZING. MISTER MASON, DO YOU KNOW WHERE YOU ARE? DO YOU KNOW WHO YOU ARE?
I'M REX MASON. PLEASE, YOU'VE GOT TO GET ME OUT OF HERE.
I...UH, I CAN'T DO THAT.
LISTEN, I'M SORRY. I DIDN'T KNOW YOU WERE...AWARE. I'M GOING TO INCREASE YOUR OXYGEN FLOW.
PROMISE ME YOU WON'T LOSE CONTROL AND GO NUTS AGAIN.
AS LONG AS YOU'RE PUMPING THAT ORB ENERGY IN HERE I CAN'T DO MUCH. BUT YOU KNOW THAT, DON'T YOU?
I'M AWARE OF IT. ALTHOUGH, I CAN'T TELL YOU WHY. AT LEAST NOT YET.
FEELING BETTER?
I CAN BREATHE, IF THAT'S WHAT YOU MEAN.

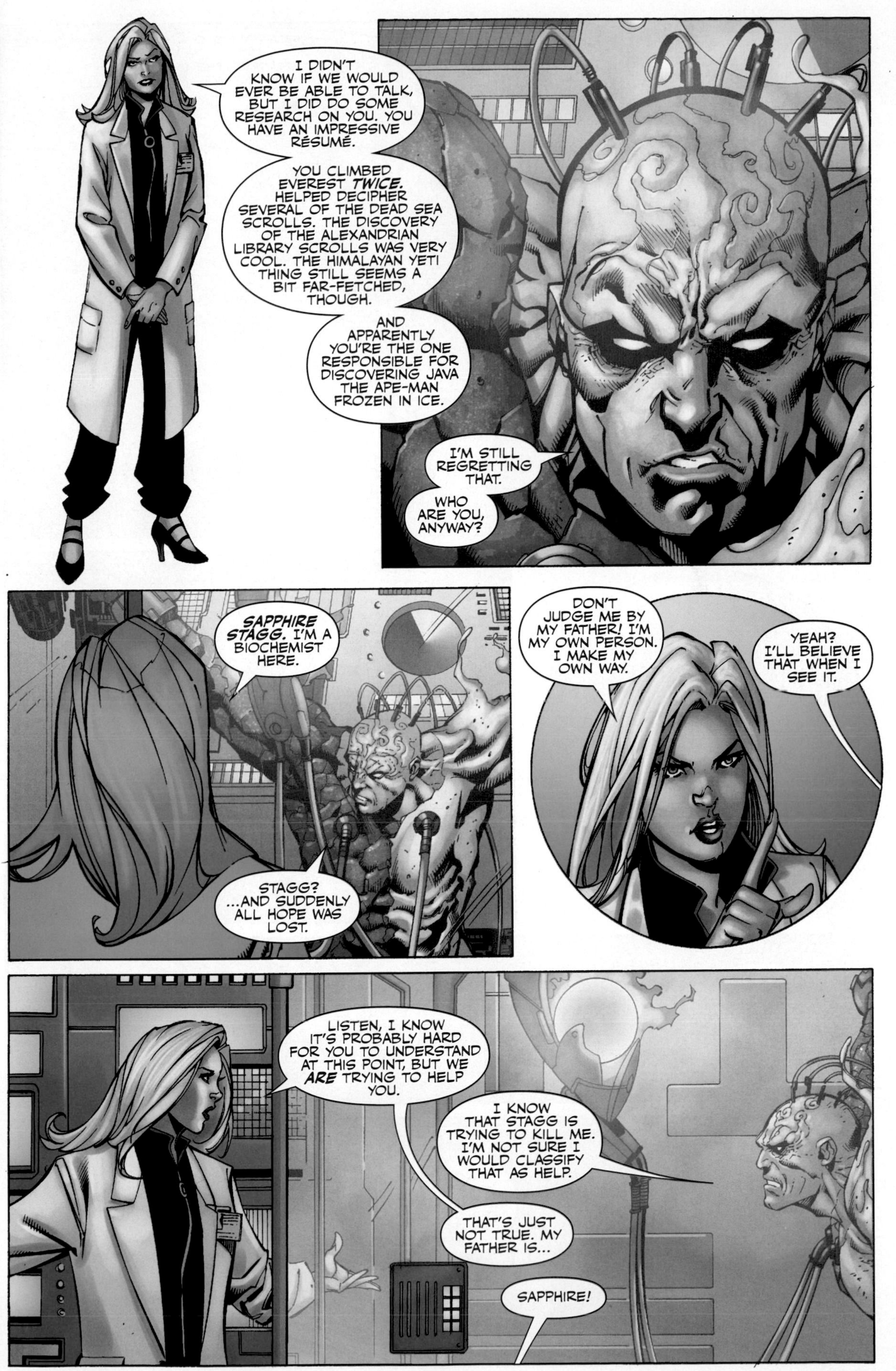
I DIDN'T KNOW IF WE WOULD EVER BE ABLE TO TALK, BUT I DID DO SOME RESEARCH ON YOU. YOU HAVE AN IMPRESSIVE RÉSUMÉ.
YOU CLIMBED EVEREST *TWICE.* HELPED DECIPHER SEVERAL OF THE DEAD SEA SCROLLS. THE DISCOVERY OF THE ALEXANDRIAN LIBRARY SCROLLS WAS VERY COOL. THE HIMALAYAN YETI THING STILL SEEMS A BIT FAR-FETCHED, THOUGH.
AND APPARENTLY YOU'RE THE ONE RESPONSIBLE FOR DISCOVERING JAVA THE APE-MAN FROZEN IN ICE.
I'M STILL REGRETTING THAT.
WHO ARE YOU, ANYWAY?
SAPPHIRE STAGG. I'M A BIOCHEMIST HERE.
STAGG? ...AND SUDDENLY ALL HOPE WAS LOST.
DON'T JUDGE ME BY MY FATHER! I'M MY OWN PERSON. I MAKE MY OWN WAY.
YEAH? I'LL BELIEVE THAT WHEN I SEE IT.
LISTEN, I KNOW IT'S PROBABLY HARD FOR YOU TO UNDERSTAND AT THIS POINT, BUT WE *ARE* TRYING TO HELP YOU.
I KNOW THAT STAGG IS TRYING TO KILL ME. I'M NOT SURE I WOULD CLASSIFY THAT AS HELP.
THAT'S JUST NOT TRUE. MY FATHER IS...
SAPPHIRE!

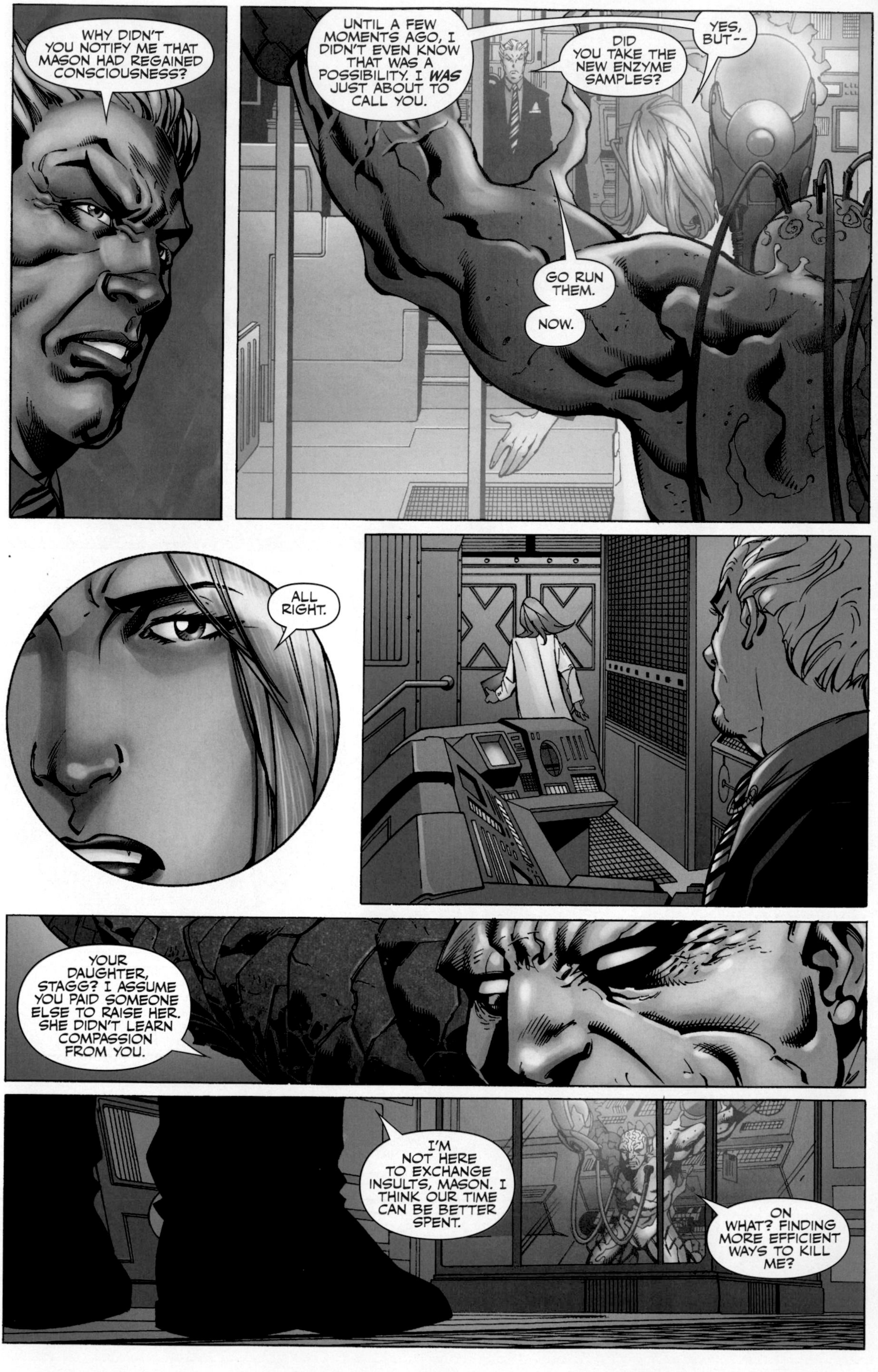
WHY DIDN'T YOU NOTIFY ME THAT MASON HAD REGAINED CONSCIOUSNESS?
UNTIL A FEW MOMENTS AGO, I DIDN'T EVEN KNOW THAT WAS A POSSIBILITY. I *WAS* JUST ABOUT TO CALL YOU.
DID YOU TAKE THE NEW ENZYME SAMPLES?
YES, BUT--
GO RUN THEM.
NOW.
ALL RIGHT.
YOUR DAUGHTER, STAGG? I ASSUME YOU PAID SOMEONE ELSE TO RAISE HER. SHE DIDN'T LEARN COMPASSION FROM YOU.
I'M NOT HERE TO EXCHANGE INSULTS, MASON. I THINK OUR TIME CAN BE BETTER SPENT.
ON WHAT? FINDING MORE EFFICIENT WAYS TO KILL ME?

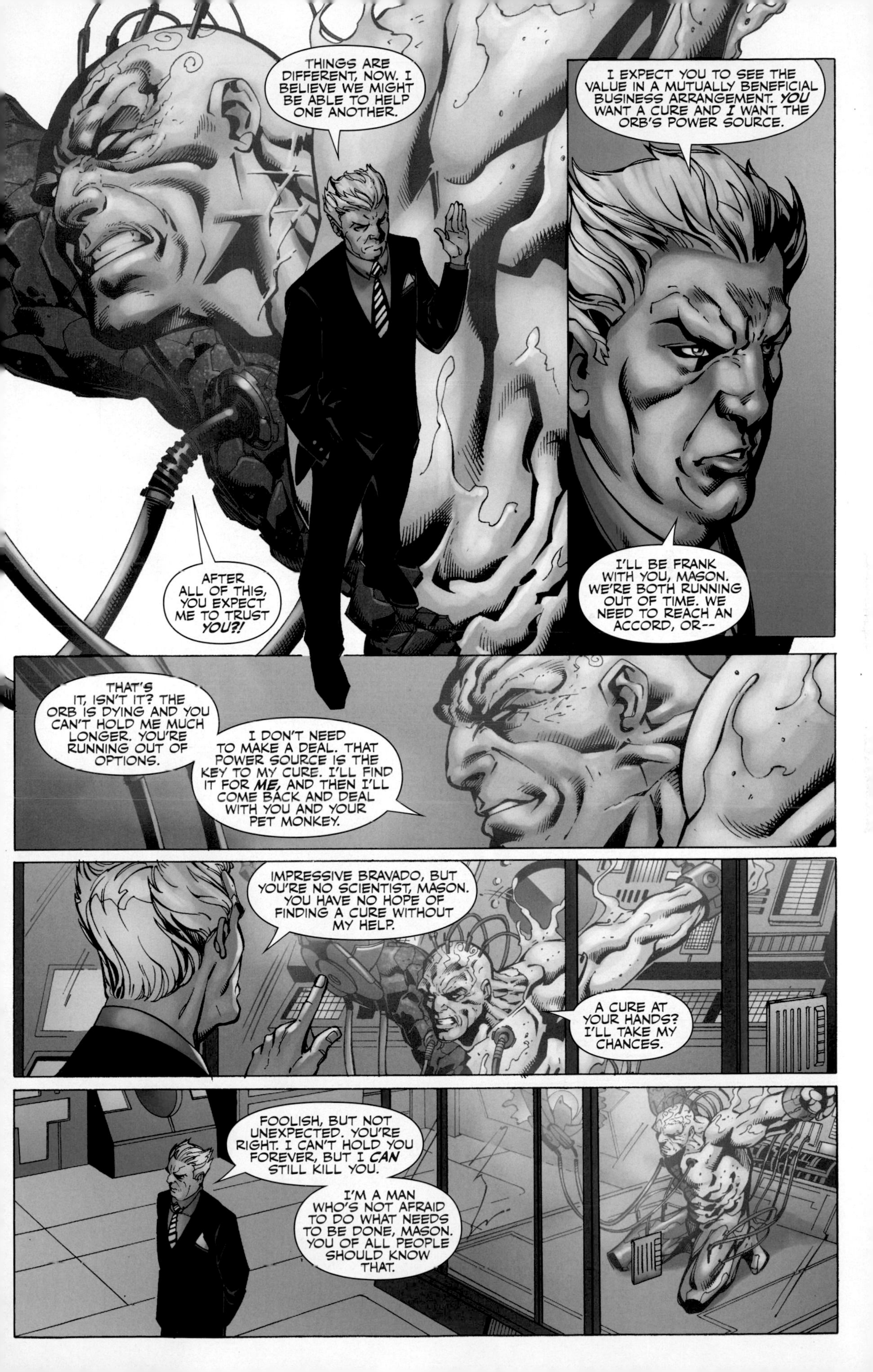
THINGS ARE DIFFERENT, NOW. I BELIEVE WE MIGHT BE ABLE TO HELP ONE ANOTHER.
I EXPECT YOU TO SEE THE VALUE IN A MUTUALLY BENEFICIAL BUSINESS ARRANGEMENT. YOU WANT A CURE AND I WANT THE ORB'S POWER SOURCE.
AFTER ALL OF THIS, YOU EXPECT ME TO TRUST YOU?!
I'LL BE FRANK WITH YOU, MASON. WE'RE BOTH RUNNING OUT OF TIME. WE NEED TO REACH AN ACCORD, OR--
THAT'S IT, ISN'T IT? THE ORB IS DYING AND YOU CAN'T HOLD ME MUCH LONGER. YOU'RE RUNNING OUT OF OPTIONS.
I DON'T NEED TO MAKE A DEAL. THAT POWER SOURCE IS THE KEY TO MY CURE. I'LL FIND IT FOR ME, AND THEN I'LL COME BACK AND DEAL WITH YOU AND YOUR PET MONKEY.
IMPRESSIVE BRAVADO, BUT YOU'RE NO SCIENTIST, MASON. YOU HAVE NO HOPE OF FINDING A CURE WITHOUT MY HELP.
A CURE AT YOUR HANDS? I'LL TAKE MY CHANCES.
FOOLISH, BUT NOT UNEXPECTED. YOU'RE RIGHT. I CAN'T HOLD YOU FOREVER, BUT I CAN STILL KILL YOU.
I'M A MAN WHO'S NOT AFRAID TO DO WHAT NEEDS TO BE DONE, MASON. YOU OF ALL PEOPLE SHOULD KNOW THAT.

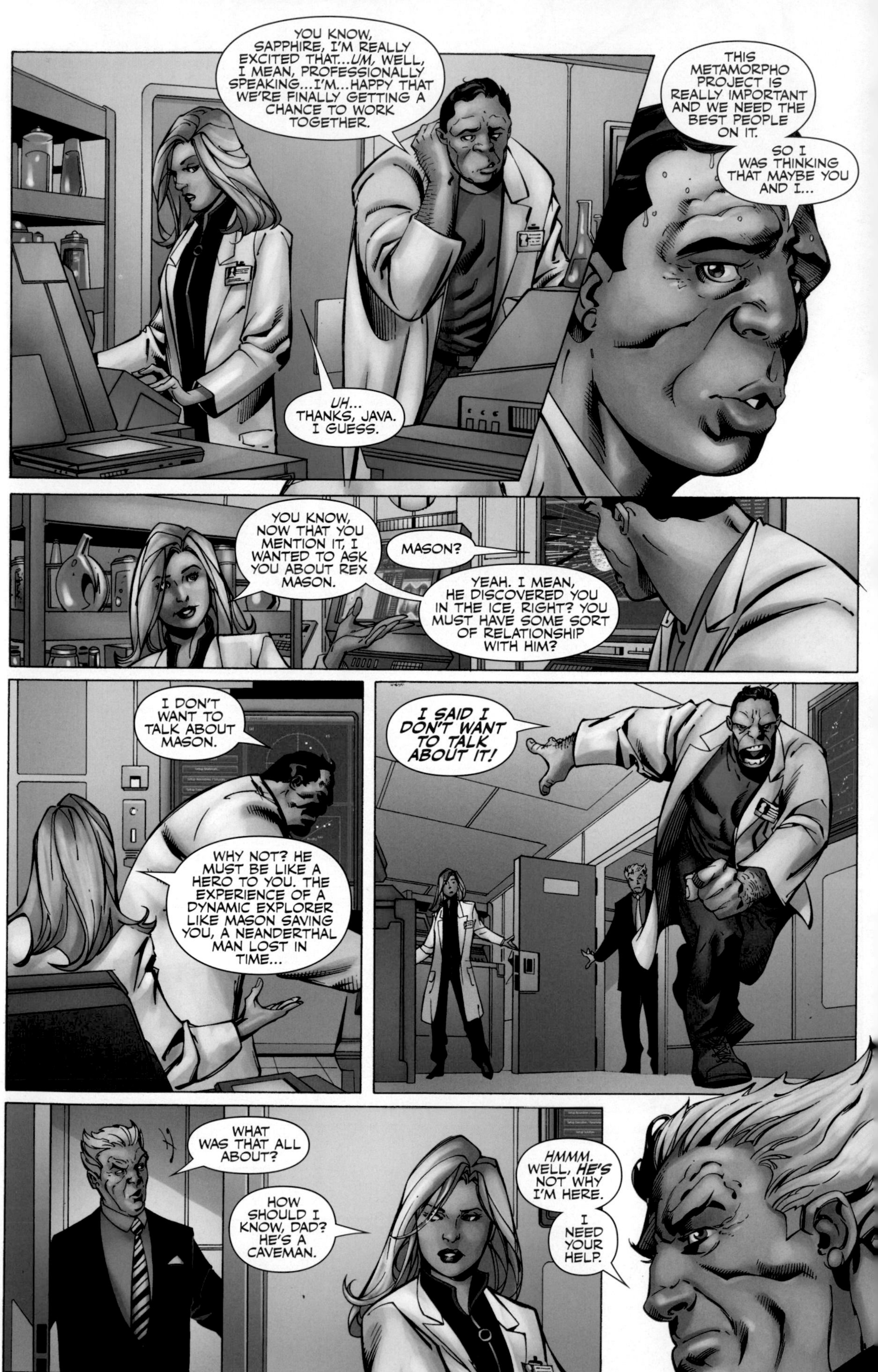
YOU KNOW, SAPPHIRE, I'M REALLY EXCITED THAT...UM, WELL, I MEAN, PROFESSIONALLY SPEAKING...I'M...HAPPY THAT WE'RE FINALLY GETTING A CHANCE TO WORK TOGETHER.
UH... THANKS, JAVA. I GUESS.
THIS METAMORPHO PROJECT IS REALLY IMPORTANT AND WE NEED THE BEST PEOPLE ON IT.
SO I WAS THINKING THAT MAYBE YOU AND I...
YOU KNOW, NOW THAT YOU MENTION IT, I WANTED TO ASK YOU ABOUT REX MASON.
MASON?
YEAH. I MEAN, HE DISCOVERED YOU IN THE ICE, RIGHT? YOU MUST HAVE SOME SORT OF RELATIONSHIP WITH HIM?
I DON'T WANT TO TALK ABOUT MASON.
WHY NOT? HE MUST BE LIKE A HERO TO YOU. THE EXPERIENCE OF A DYNAMIC EXPLORER LIKE MASON SAVING YOU, A NEANDERTHAL MAN LOST IN TIME...
I SAID I DON'T WANT TO TALK ABOUT IT!
WHAT WAS THAT ALL ABOUT?
HOW SHOULD I KNOW, DAD? HE'S A CAVEMAN.
HMMM. WELL, HE'S NOT WHY I'M HERE.
I NEED YOUR HELP.

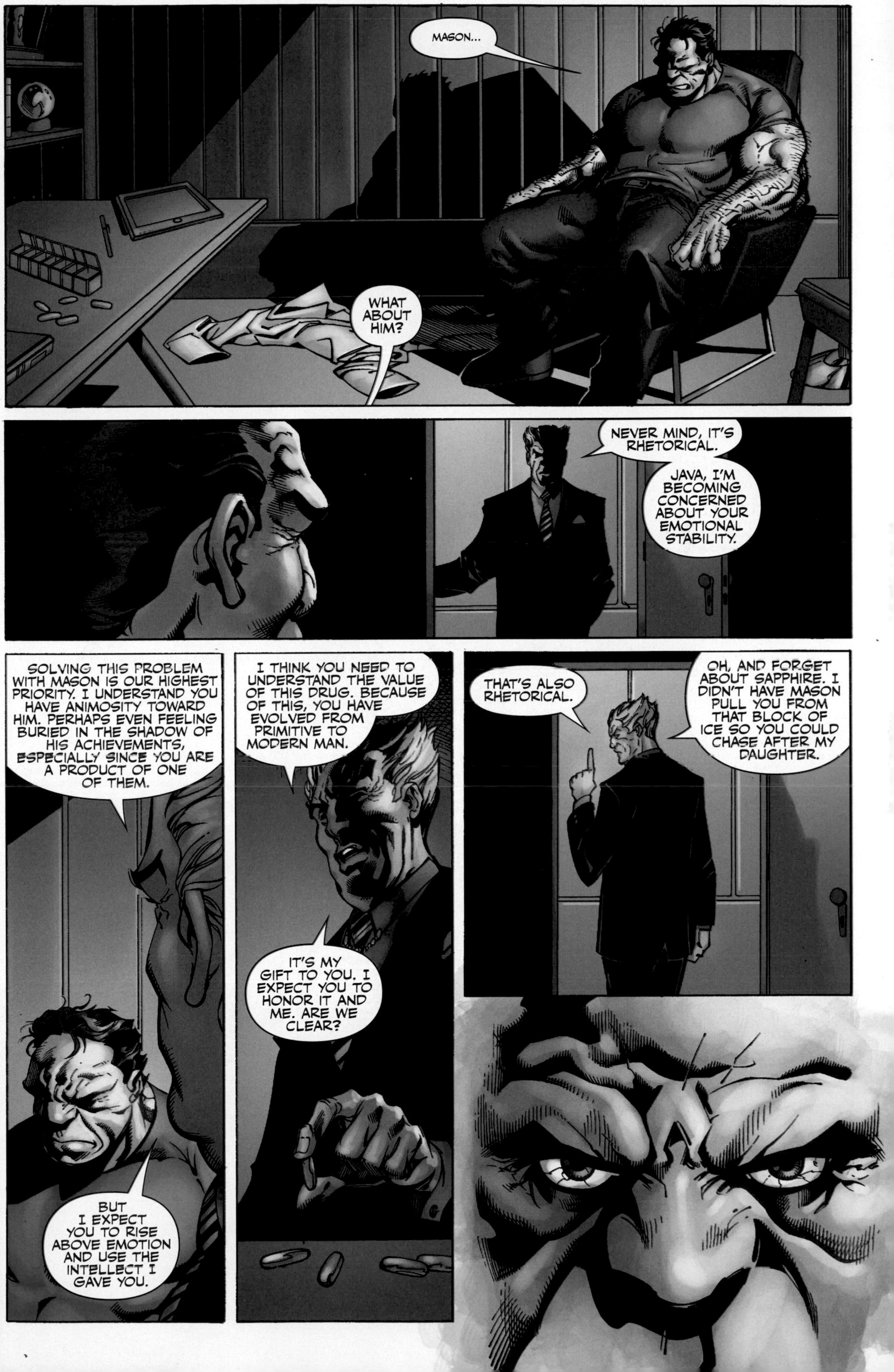
MASON...
WHAT ABOUT HIM?
NEVER MIND, IT'S RHETORICAL.
JAVA, I'M BECOMING CONCERNED ABOUT YOUR EMOTIONAL STABILITY.
SOLVING THIS PROBLEM WITH MASON IS OUR HIGHEST PRIORITY. I UNDERSTAND YOU HAVE ANIMOSITY TOWARD HIM. PERHAPS EVEN FEELING BURIED IN THE SHADOW OF HIS ACHIEVEMENTS, ESPECIALLY SINCE YOU ARE A PRODUCT OF ONE OF THEM.
BUT I EXPECT YOU TO RISE ABOVE EMOTION AND USE THE INTELLECT I GAVE YOU.
I THINK YOU NEED TO UNDERSTAND THE VALUE OF THIS DRUG. BECAUSE OF THIS, YOU HAVE EVOLVED FROM PRIMITIVE TO MODERN MAN.
IT'S MY GIFT TO YOU. I EXPECT YOU TO HONOR IT AND ME. ARE WE CLEAR?
THAT'S ALSO RHETORICAL.
OH, AND FORGET ABOUT SAPPHIRE. I DIDN'T HAVE MASON PULL YOU FROM THAT BLOCK OF ICE SO YOU COULD CHASE AFTER MY DAUGHTER.

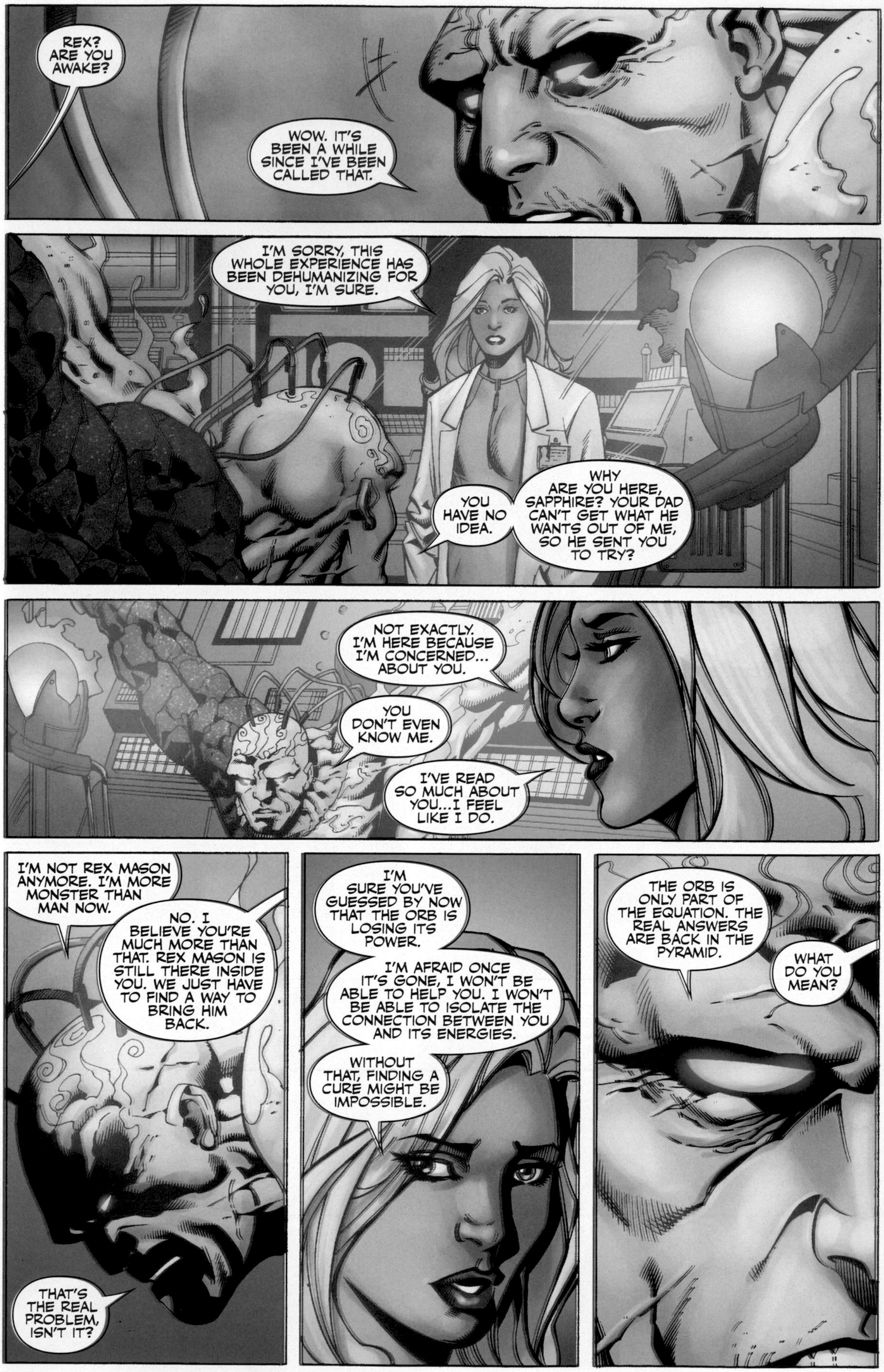
REX? ARE YOU AWAKE?
WOW. IT'S BEEN A WHILE SINCE I'VE BEEN CALLED THAT.
I'M SORRY, THIS WHOLE EXPERIENCE HAS BEEN DEHUMANIZING FOR YOU, I'M SURE.
YOU HAVE NO IDEA.
WHY ARE YOU HERE, SAPPHIRE? YOUR DAD CAN'T GET WHAT HE WANTS OUT OF ME, SO HE SENT YOU TO TRY?
NOT EXACTLY. I'M HERE BECAUSE I'M CONCERNED... ABOUT YOU.
YOU DON'T EVEN KNOW ME.
I'VE READ SO MUCH ABOUT YOU...I FEEL LIKE I DO.
I'M NOT REX MASON ANYMORE. I'M MORE MONSTER THAN MAN NOW.
NO. I BELIEVE YOU'RE MUCH MORE THAN THAT. REX MASON IS STILL THERE INSIDE YOU. WE JUST HAVE TO FIND A WAY TO BRING HIM BACK.
THAT'S THE REAL PROBLEM, ISN'T IT?
I'M SURE YOU'VE GUESSED BY NOW THAT THE ORB IS LOSING ITS POWER.
I'M AFRAID ONCE IT'S GONE, I WON'T BE ABLE TO HELP YOU. I WON'T BE ABLE TO ISOLATE THE CONNECTION BETWEEN YOU AND ITS ENERGIES.
WITHOUT THAT, FINDING A CURE MIGHT BE IMPOSSIBLE.
THE ORB IS ONLY PART OF THE EQUATION. THE REAL ANSWERS ARE BACK IN THE PYRAMID.
WHAT DO YOU MEAN?

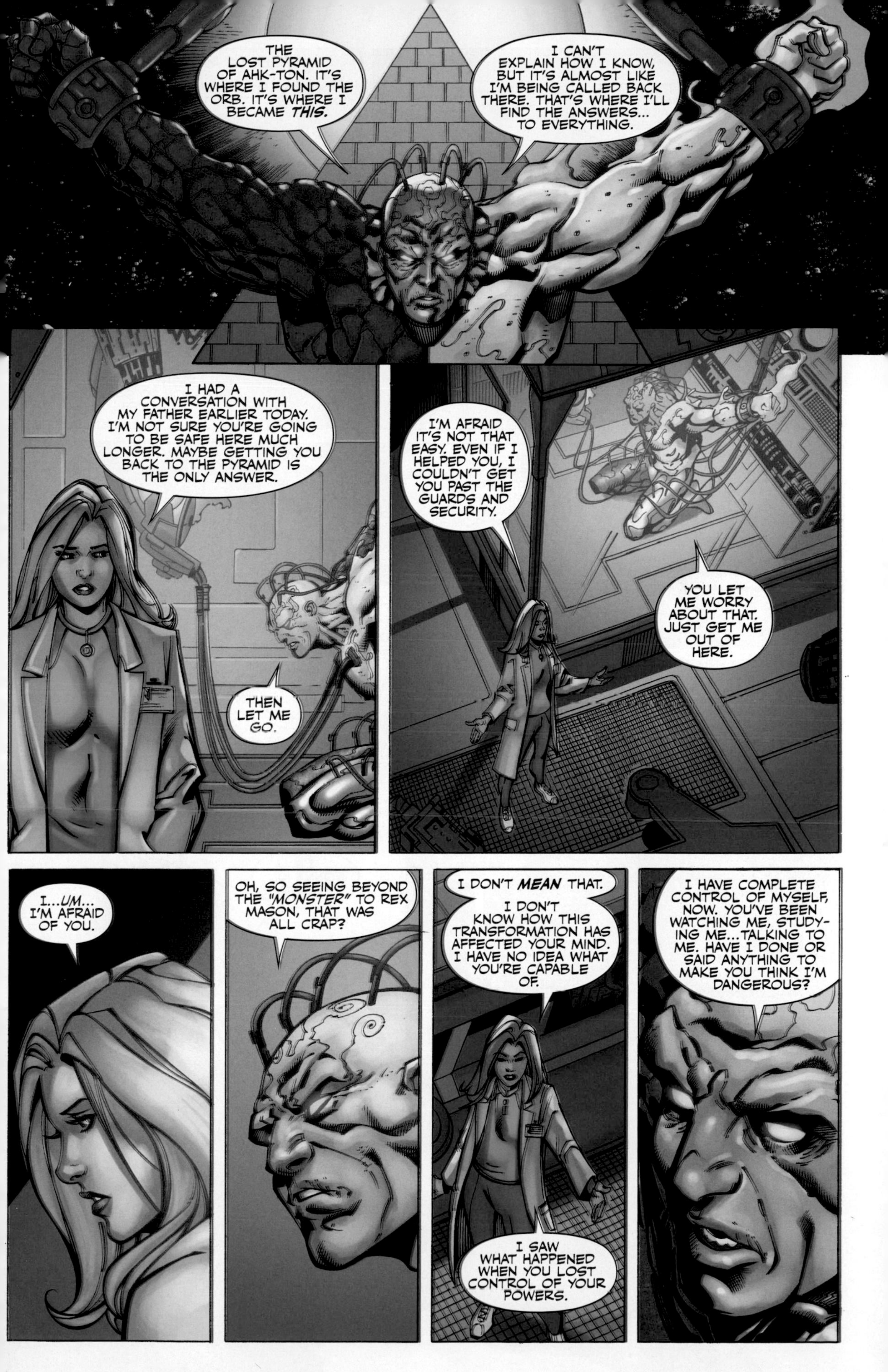
THE LOST PYRAMID OF AHK-TON. IT'S WHERE I FOUND THE ORB. IT'S WHERE I BECAME *THIS.*
I CAN'T EXPLAIN HOW I KNOW, BUT IT'S ALMOST LIKE I'M BEING CALLED BACK THERE. THAT'S WHERE I'LL FIND THE ANSWERS... TO EVERYTHING.
I HAD A CONVERSATION WITH MY FATHER EARLIER TODAY. I'M NOT SURE YOU'RE GOING TO BE SAFE HERE MUCH LONGER. MAYBE GETTING YOU BACK TO THE PYRAMID IS THE ONLY ANSWER.
THEN LET ME GO.
I'M AFRAID IT'S NOT THAT EASY. EVEN IF I HELPED YOU, I COULDN'T GET YOU PAST THE GUARDS AND SECURITY.
YOU LET ME WORRY ABOUT THAT. JUST GET ME OUT OF HERE.
I...*UM*... I'M AFRAID OF YOU.
OH, SO SEEING BEYOND THE *"MONSTER"* TO REX MASON, THAT WAS ALL CRAP?
I DON'T *MEAN* THAT.
I DON'T KNOW HOW THIS TRANSFORMATION HAS AFFECTED YOUR MIND. I HAVE NO IDEA WHAT YOU'RE CAPABLE OF.
I SAW WHAT HAPPENED WHEN YOU LOST CONTROL OF YOUR POWERS.
I HAVE COMPLETE CONTROL OF MYSELF, NOW. YOU'VE BEEN WATCHING ME, STUDYING ME...TALKING TO ME. HAVE I DONE OR SAID ANYTHING TO MAKE YOU THINK I'M DANGEROUS?

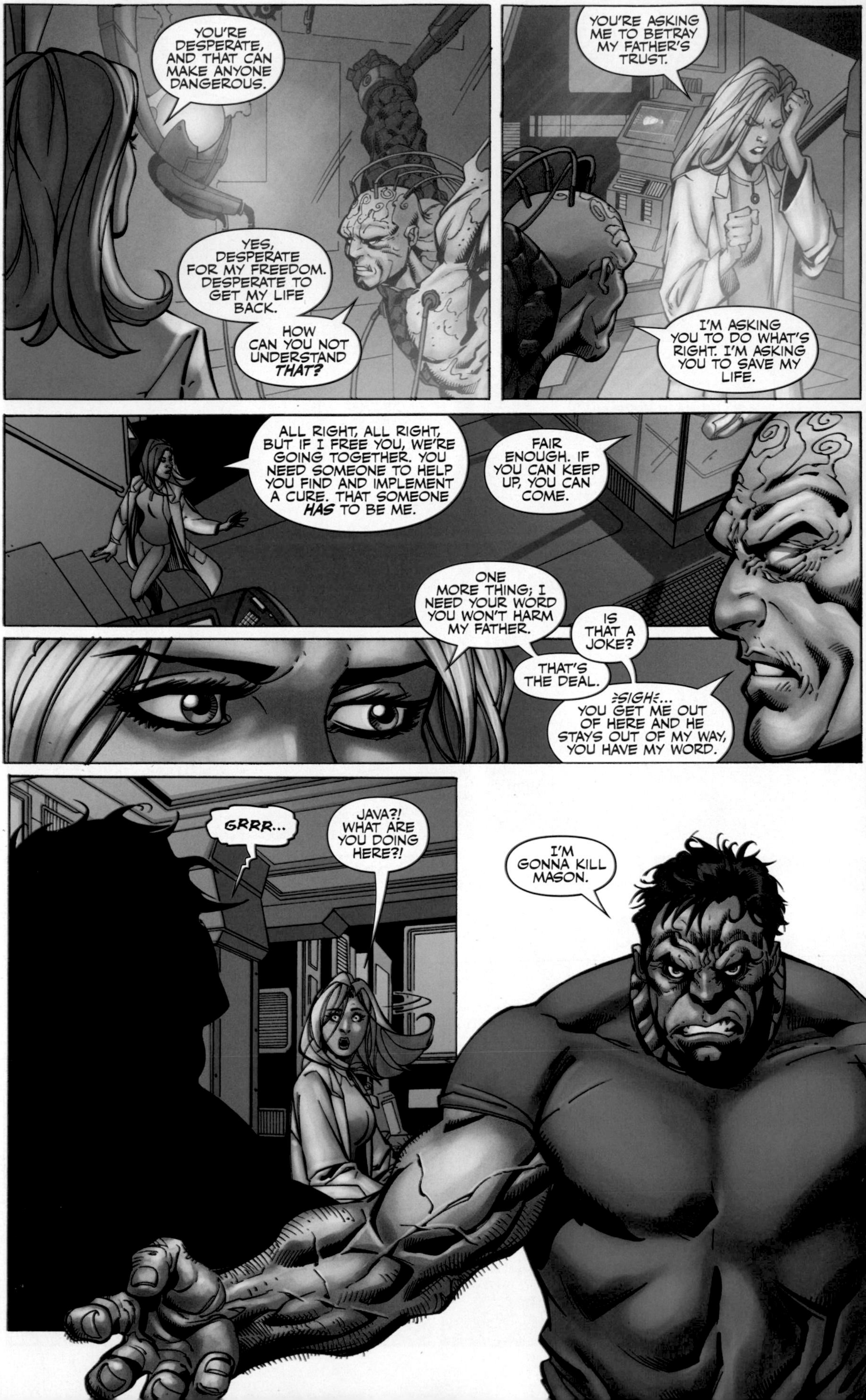
YOU'RE DESPERATE, AND THAT CAN MAKE ANYONE DANGEROUS.
YES, DESPERATE FOR MY FREEDOM. DESPERATE TO GET MY LIFE BACK.
HOW CAN YOU NOT UNDERSTAND THAT?
YOU'RE ASKING ME TO BETRAY MY FATHER'S TRUST.
I'M ASKING YOU TO DO WHAT'S RIGHT. I'M ASKING YOU TO SAVE MY LIFE.
ALL RIGHT, ALL RIGHT, BUT IF I FREE YOU, WE'RE GOING TOGETHER. YOU NEED SOMEONE TO HELP YOU FIND AND IMPLEMENT A CURE. THAT SOMEONE HAS TO BE ME.
FAIR ENOUGH. IF YOU CAN KEEP UP, YOU CAN COME.
ONE MORE THING; I NEED YOUR WORD YOU WON'T HARM MY FATHER.
IS THAT A JOKE?
THAT'S THE DEAL.
SIGH... YOU GET ME OUT OF HERE AND HE STAYS OUT OF MY WAY, YOU HAVE MY WORD.
GRRR...
JAVA?! WHAT ARE YOU DOING HERE?!
I'M GONNA KILL MASON.

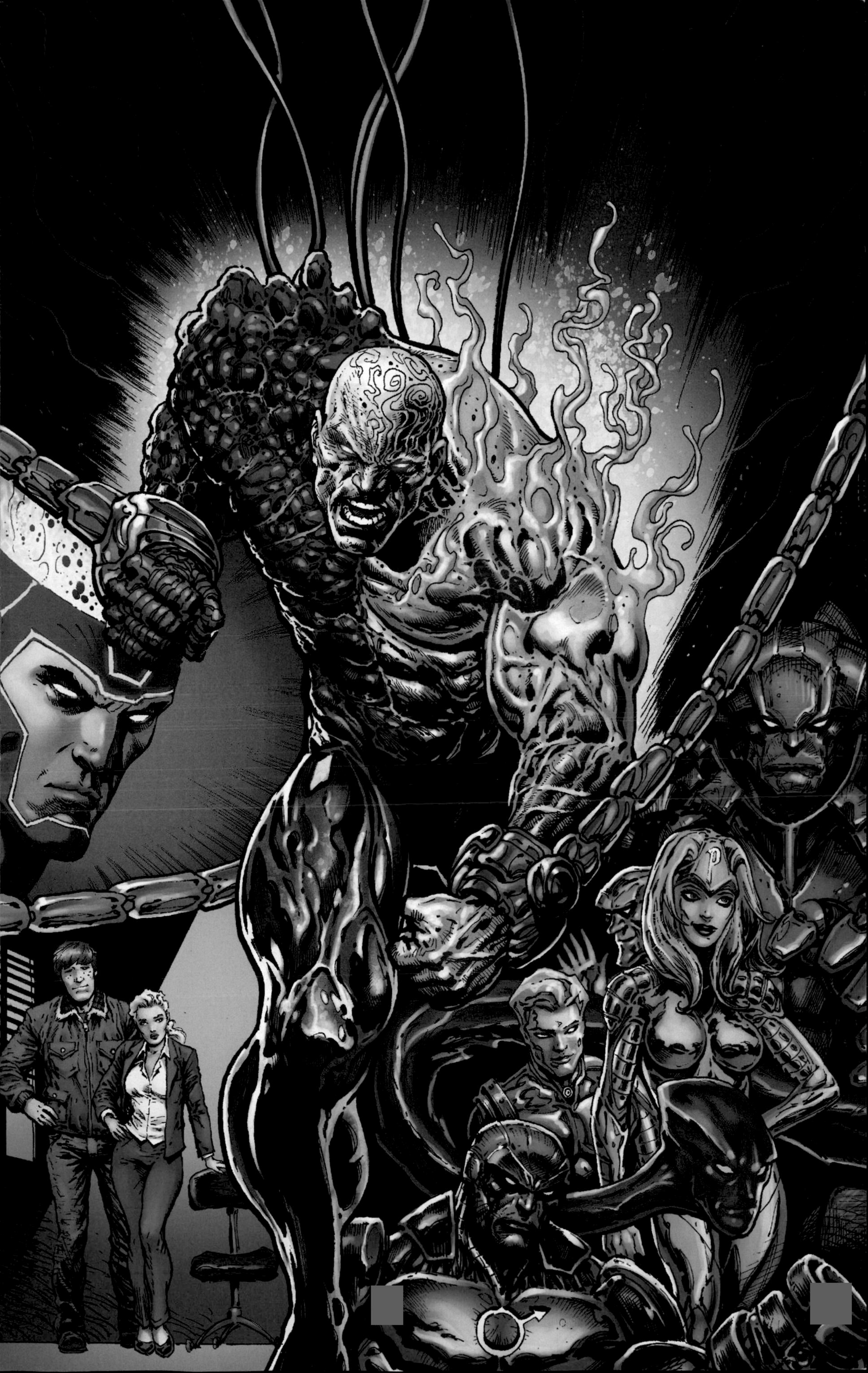

ESCAPE PLAN

AARON LOPRESTI writer/penciller MATT BANNING inker CHRIS SOTOMAYOR colorist MICHAEL HEISLER letterer
LIAM SHARP with CHRIS SOTOMAYOR cover

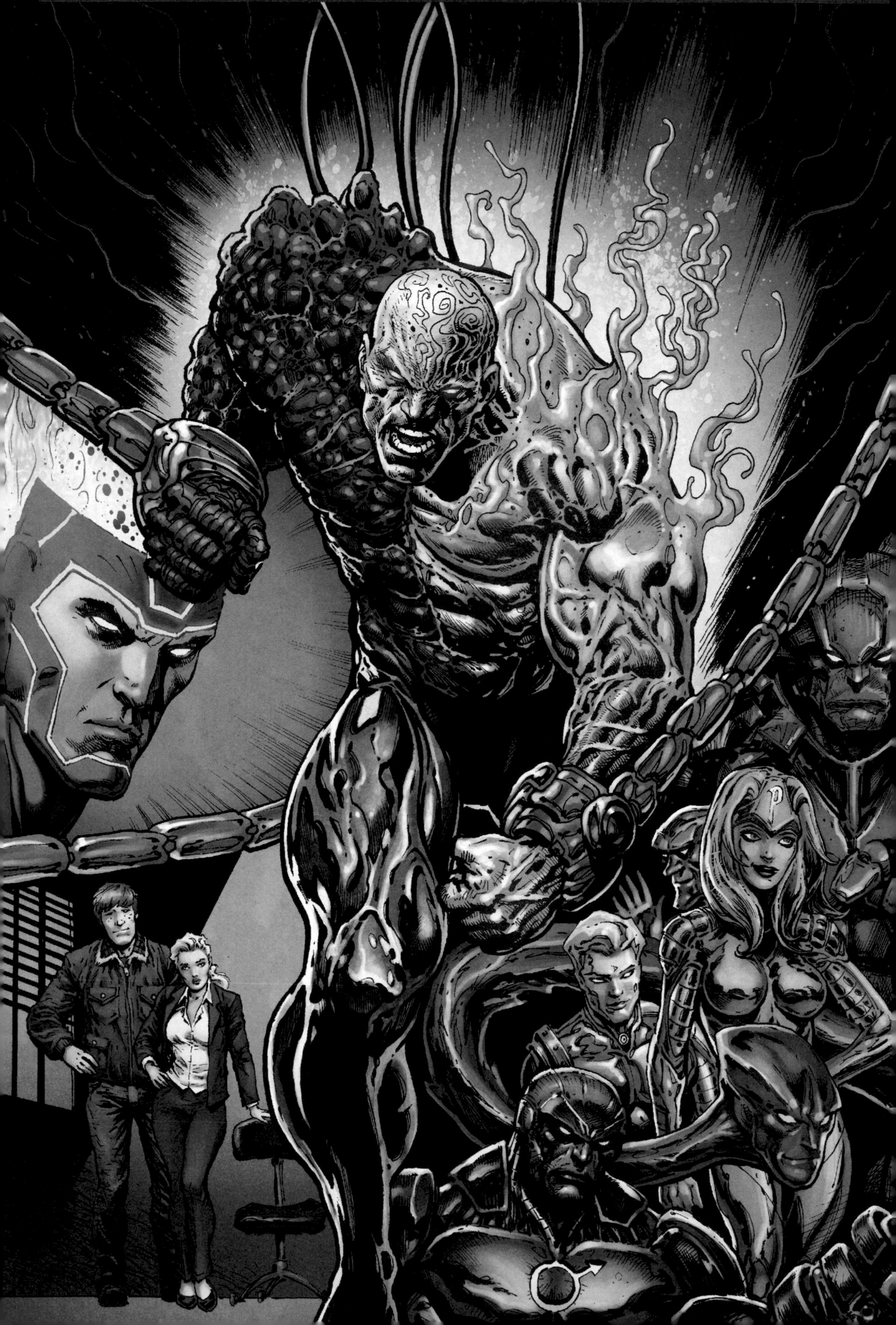

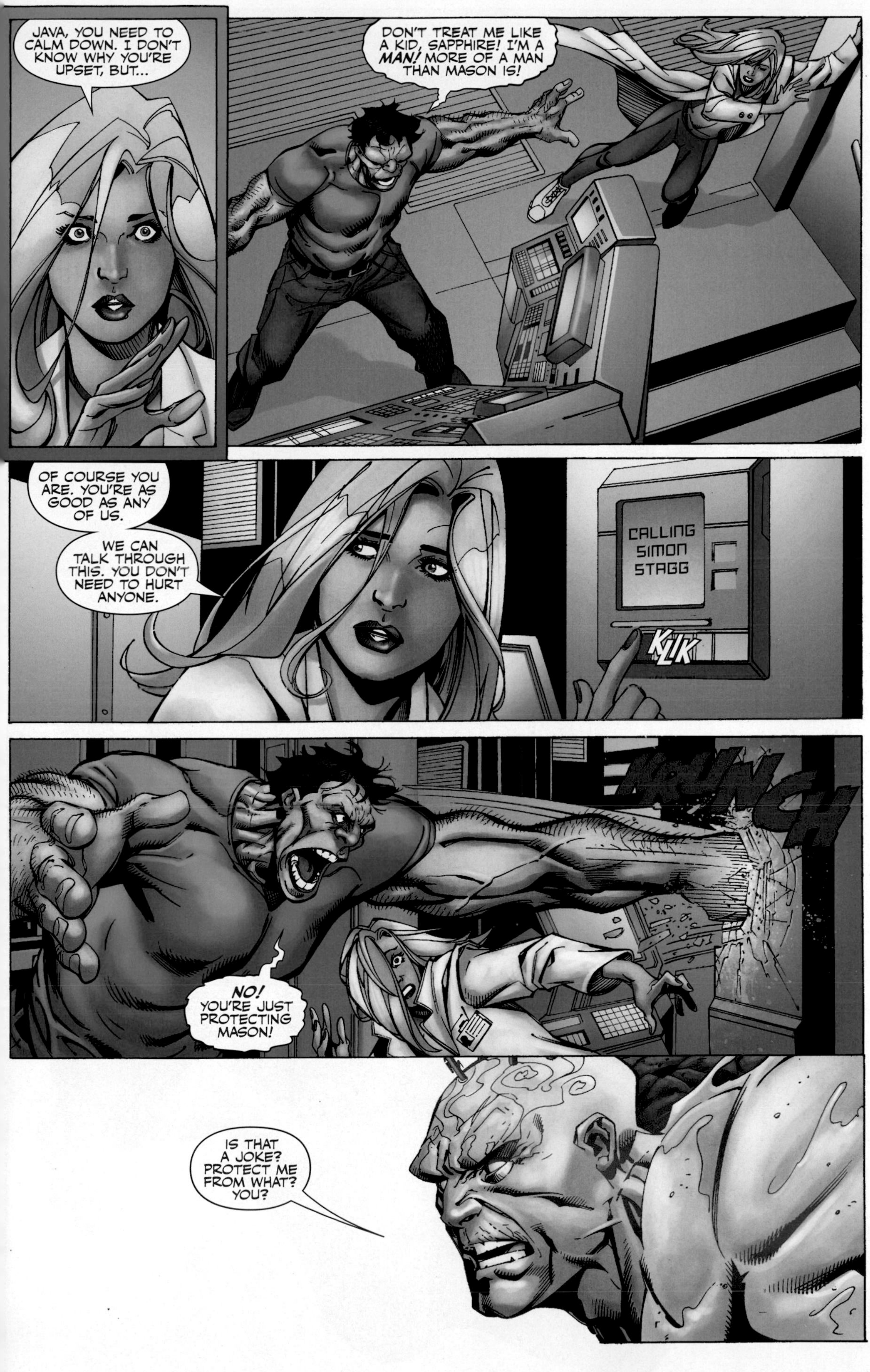
JAVA, YOU NEED TO CALM DOWN. I DON'T KNOW WHY YOU'RE UPSET, BUT...
DON'T TREAT ME LIKE A KID, SAPPHIRE! I'M A MAN! MORE OF A MAN THAN MASON IS!
OF COURSE YOU ARE. YOU'RE AS GOOD AS ANY OF US.
WE CAN TALK THROUGH THIS. YOU DON'T NEED TO HURT ANYONE.
CALLING SIMON STAGG
KLIK
KRUNCH
NO! YOU'RE JUST PROTECTING MASON!
IS THAT A JOKE? PROTECT ME FROM WHAT? YOU?

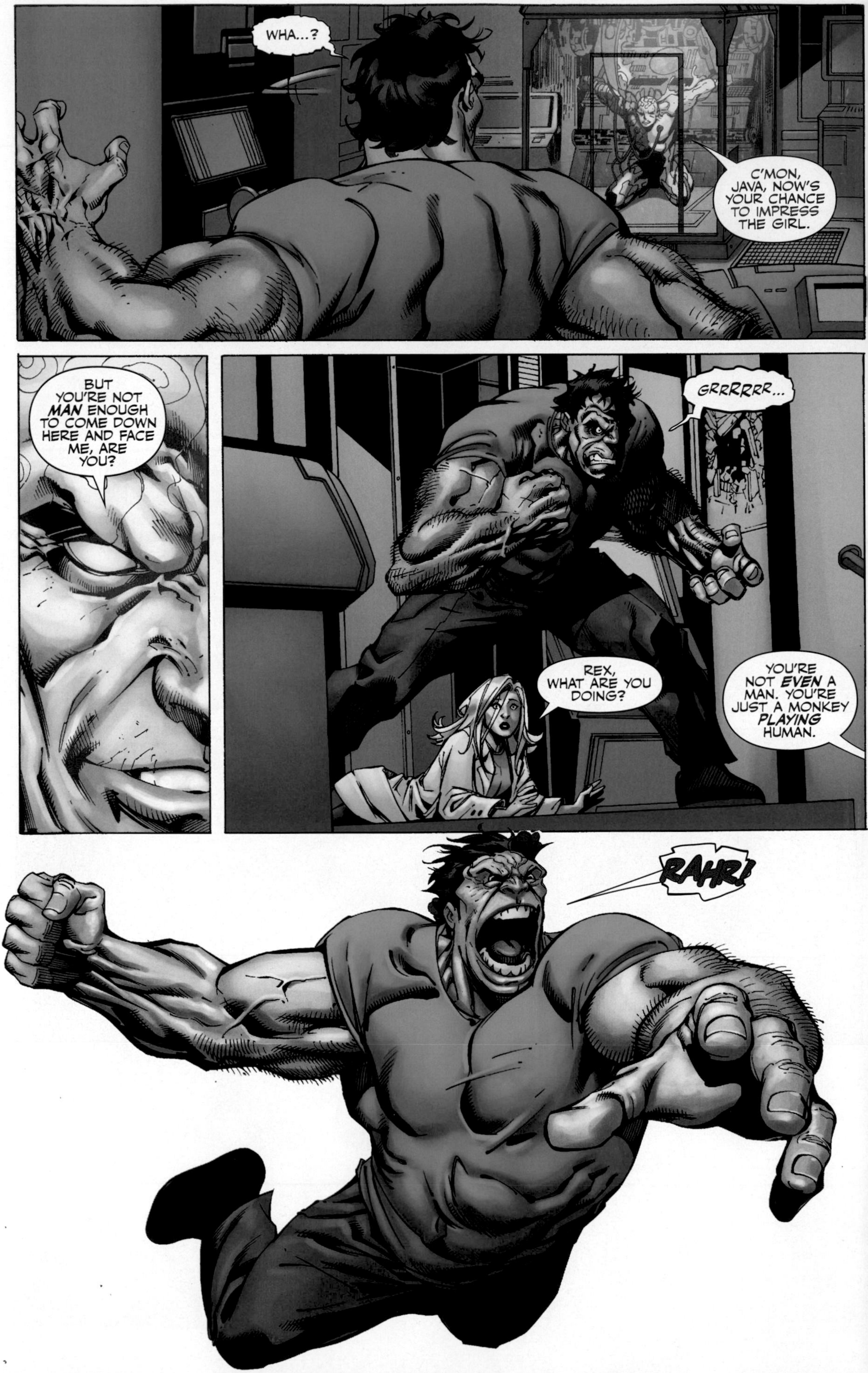
WHA...?
C'MON, JAVA, NOW'S YOUR CHANCE TO IMPRESS THE GIRL.
BUT YOU'RE NOT MAN ENOUGH TO COME DOWN HERE AND FACE ME, ARE YOU?
GRRRRRR...
REX, WHAT ARE YOU DOING?
YOU'RE NOT EVEN A MAN. YOU'RE JUST A MONKEY PLAYING HUMAN.
RAHR!

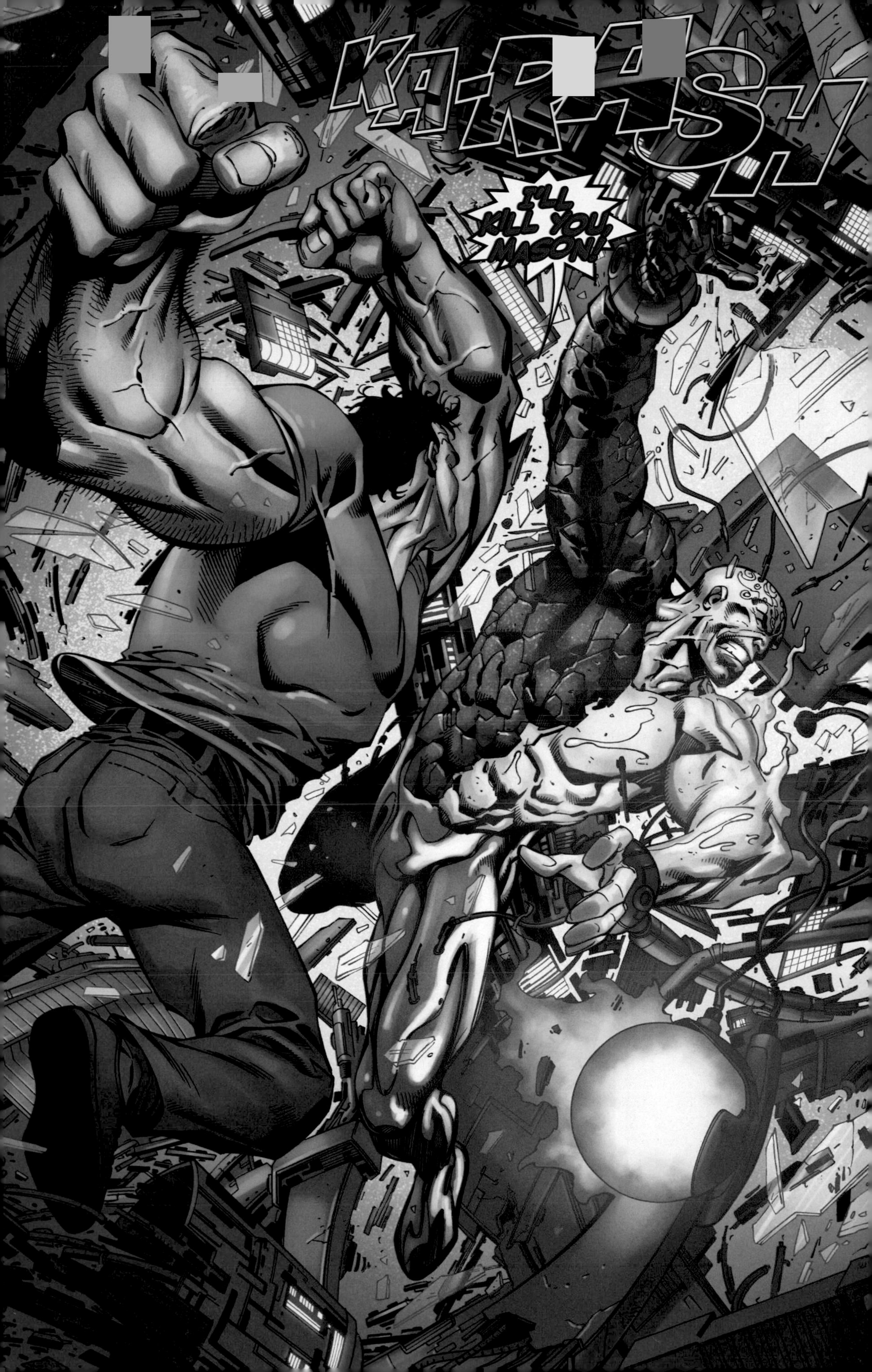
I'LL KILL YOU, MASON!

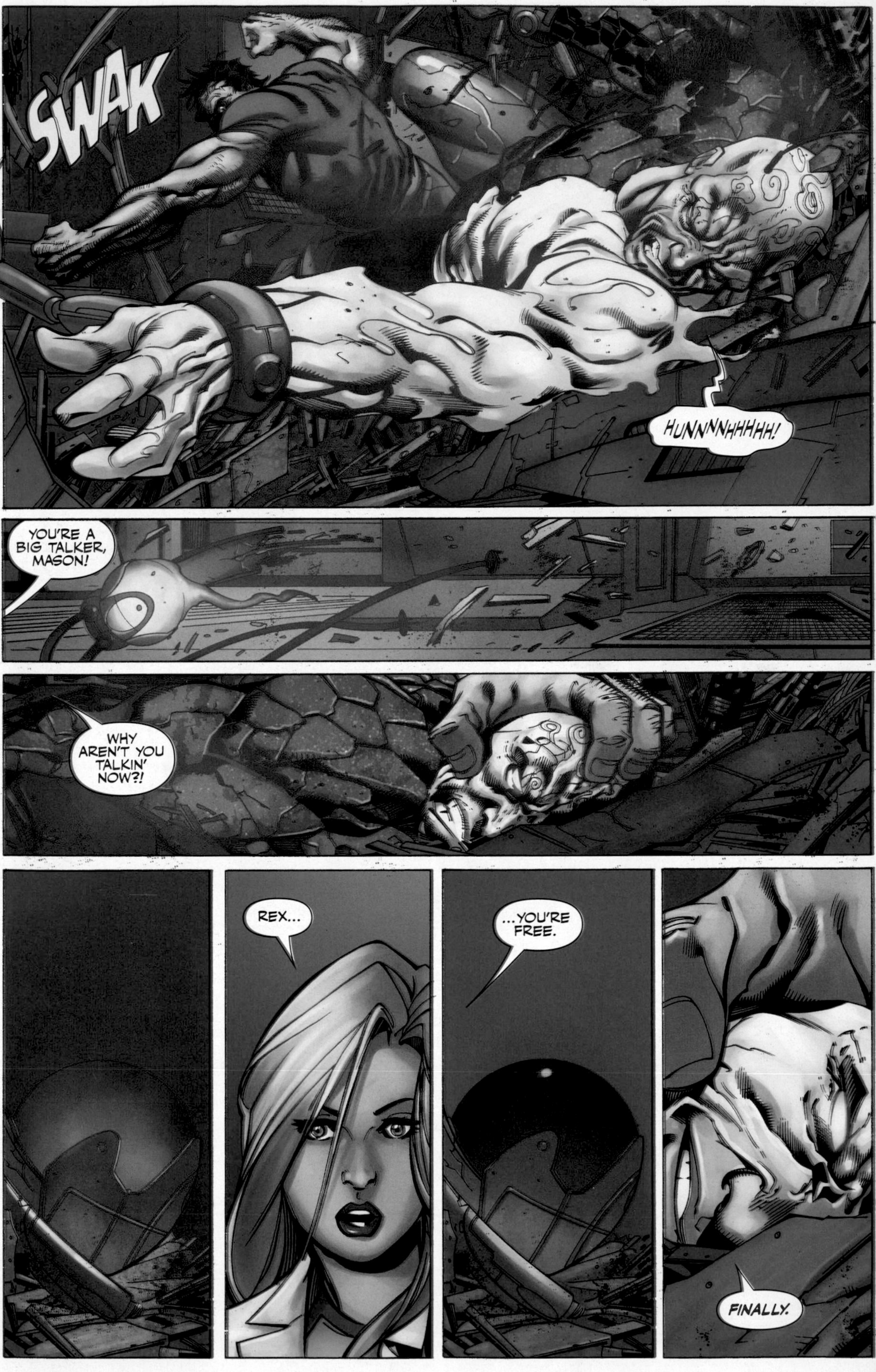
SWAK
HUNNNHHHHH!
YOU'RE A BIG TALKER, MASON!
WHY AREN'T YOU TALKIN' NOW?!
REX...
...YOU'RE FREE.
FINALLY.

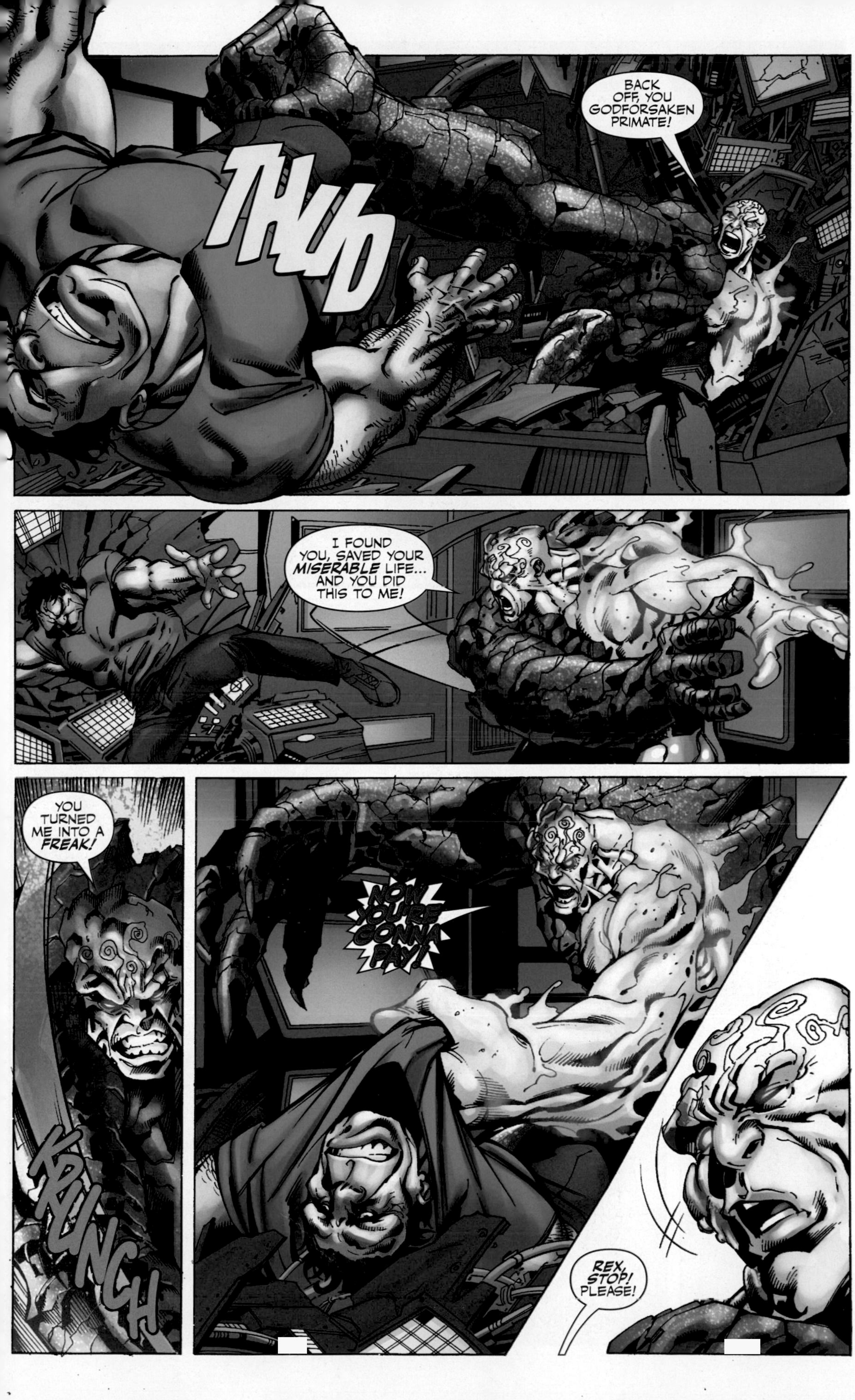
THUD
BACK OFF, YOU GODFORSAKEN PRIMATE!
I FOUND YOU, SAVED YOUR MISERABLE LIFE... AND YOU DID THIS TO ME!
YOU TURNED ME INTO A FREAK!
KRUNCH
NOW YOU'RE GONNA PAY!
REX, STOP! PLEASE!

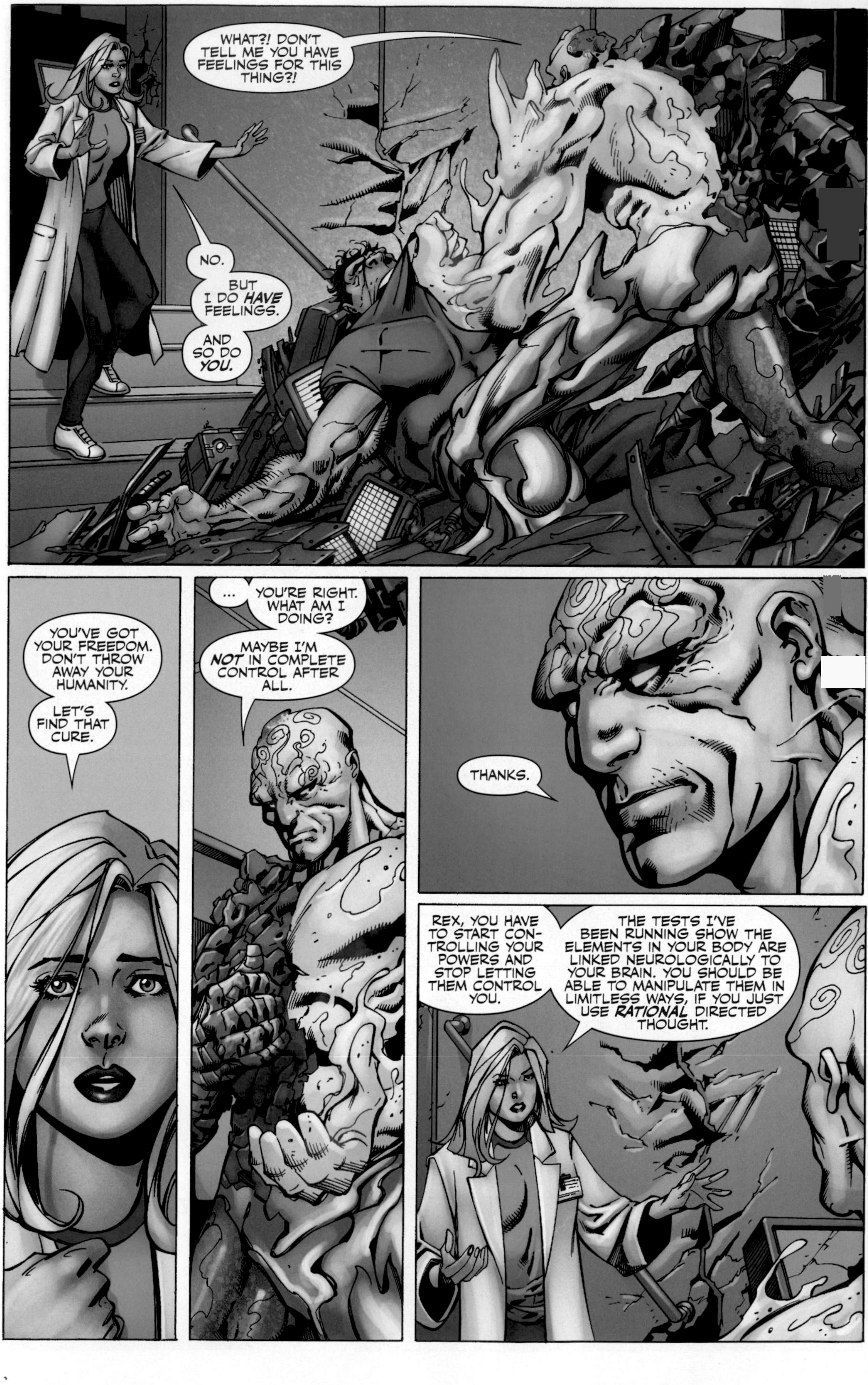
WHAT?! DON'T TELL ME YOU HAVE FEELINGS FOR THIS THING?!
NO.
BUT I DO *HAVE* FEELINGS.
AND SO DO *YOU.*
YOU'VE GOT YOUR FREEDOM. DON'T THROW AWAY YOUR HUMANITY.
LET'S FIND THAT CURE.
...
YOU'RE RIGHT. WHAT AM I DOING?
MAYBE I'M *NOT* IN COMPLETE CONTROL AFTER ALL.
THANKS.
REX, YOU HAVE TO START CONTROLLING YOUR POWERS AND STOP LETTING THEM CONTROL YOU.
THE TESTS I'VE BEEN RUNNING SHOW THE ELEMENTS IN YOUR BODY ARE LINKED NEUROLOGICALLY TO YOUR BRAIN. YOU SHOULD BE ABLE TO MANIPULATE THEM IN LIMITLESS WAYS, IF YOU JUST USE *RATIONAL* DIRECTED THOUGHT.

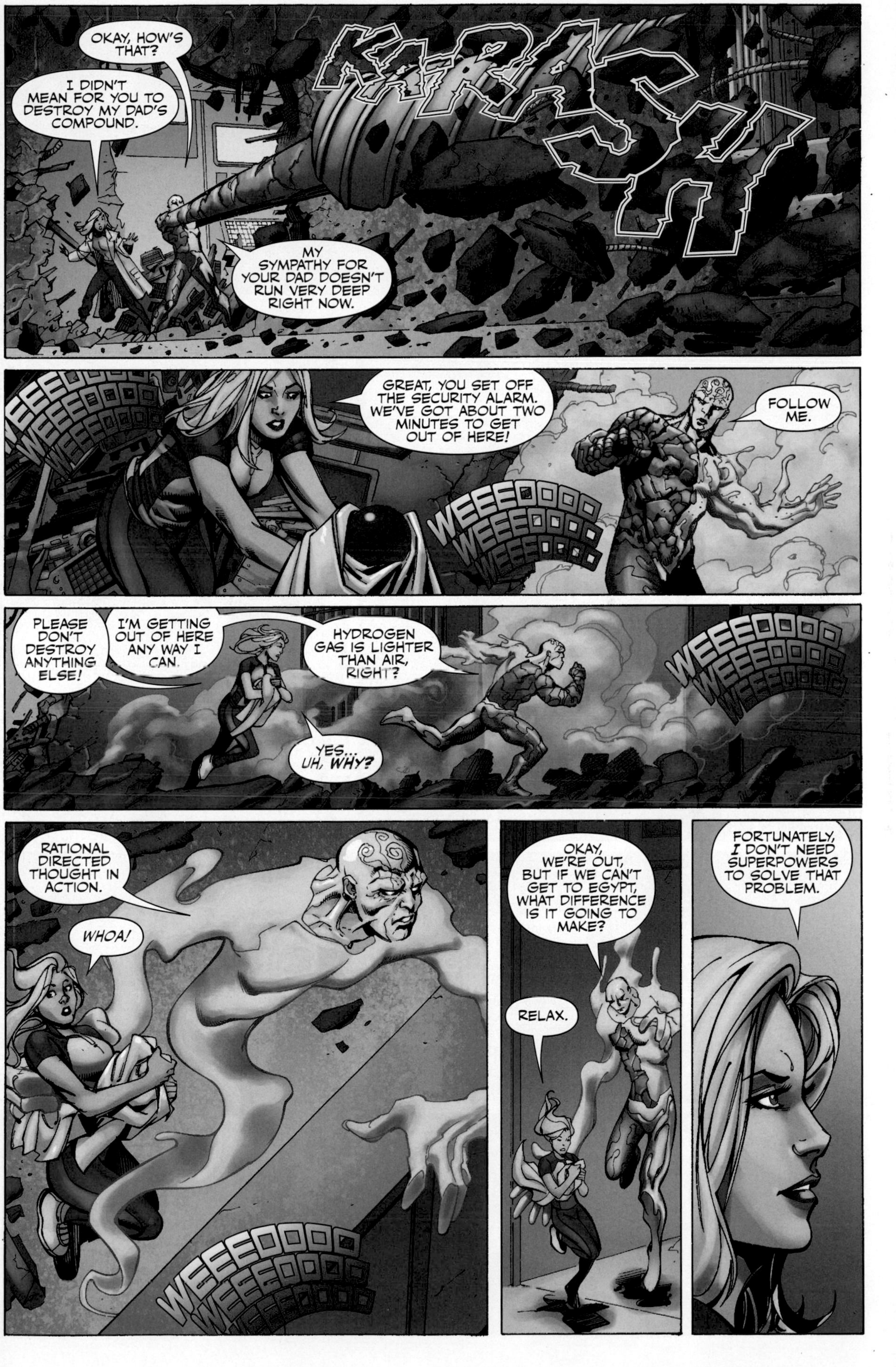
KA-BA-SH
OKAY, HOW'S THAT?
I DIDN'T MEAN FOR YOU TO DESTROY MY DAD'S COMPOUND.
MY SYMPATHY FOR YOUR DAD DOESN'T RUN VERY DEEP RIGHT NOW.
WEEEOOOO WEEEOOOO WEEEOOOO
GREAT, YOU SET OFF THE SECURITY ALARM. WE'VE GOT ABOUT TWO MINUTES TO GET OUT OF HERE!
FOLLOW ME.
WEEEOOOO WEEEOOOO WEEEOOOO
PLEASE DON'T DESTROY ANYTHING ELSE!
I'M GETTING OUT OF HERE ANY WAY I CAN.
HYDROGEN GAS IS LIGHTER THAN AIR, RIGHT?
YES... UH, WHY?
WEEEOOOO WEEEOOOO WEEEOOOO
RATIONAL DIRECTED THOUGHT IN ACTION.
WHOA!
WEEEOOOO WEEEOOOO WEEEOOOO
OKAY, WE'RE OUT, BUT IF WE CAN'T GET TO EGYPT, WHAT DIFFERENCE IS IT GOING TO MAKE?
RELAX.
FORTUNATELY, I DON'T NEED SUPERPOWERS TO SOLVE THAT PROBLEM.

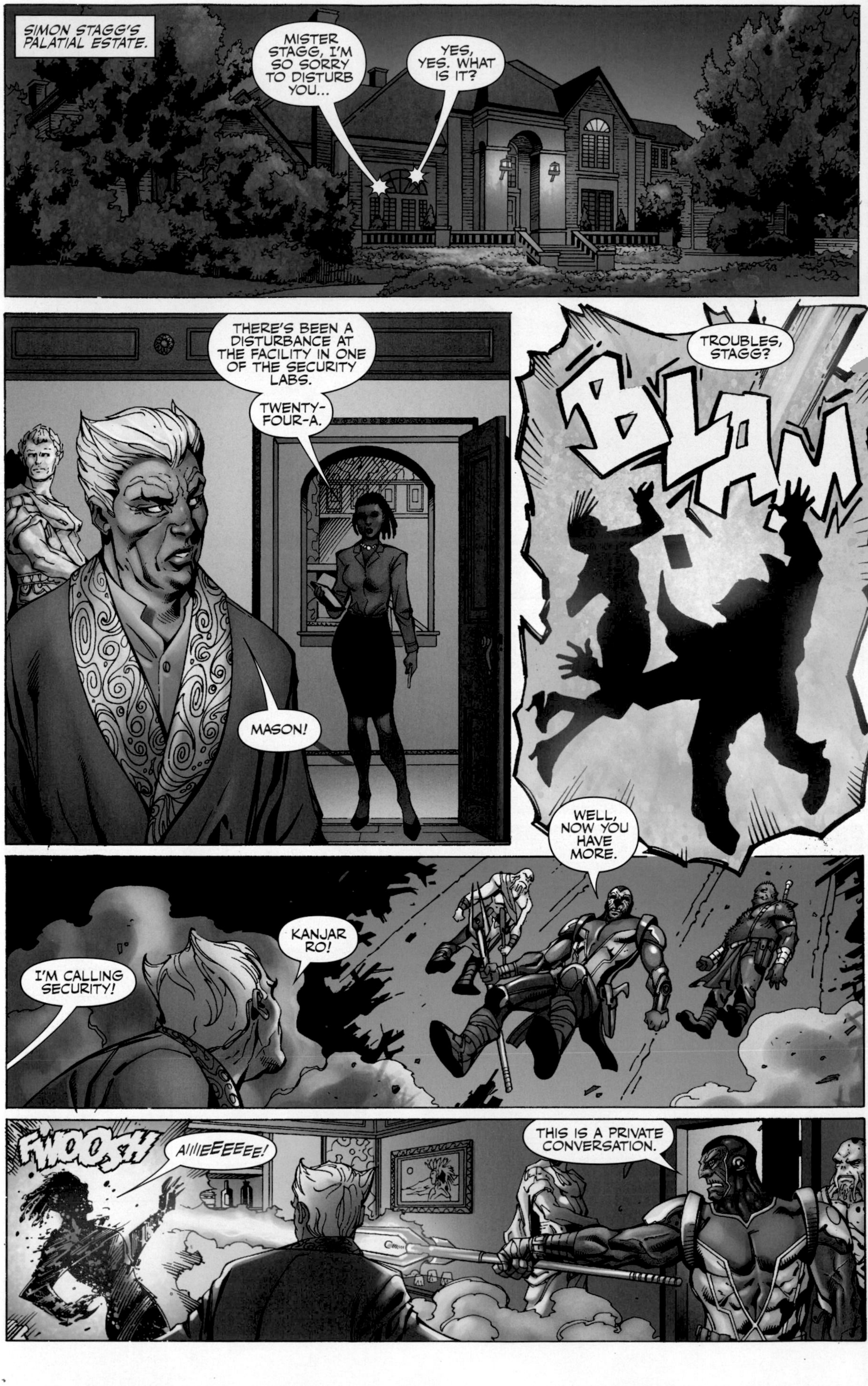
SIMON STAGG'S PALATIAL ESTATE.
MISTER STAGG, I'M SO SORRY TO DISTURB YOU...
YES, YES. WHAT IS IT?
THERE'S BEEN A DISTURBANCE AT THE FACILITY IN ONE OF THE SECURITY LABS.
TWENTY-FOUR-A.
MASON!
TROUBLES, STAGG?
BLAM
WELL, NOW YOU HAVE MORE.
KANJAR RO!
I'M CALLING SECURITY!
FWOOSH
AIIIEEEEEE!
THIS IS A PRIVATE CONVERSATION.

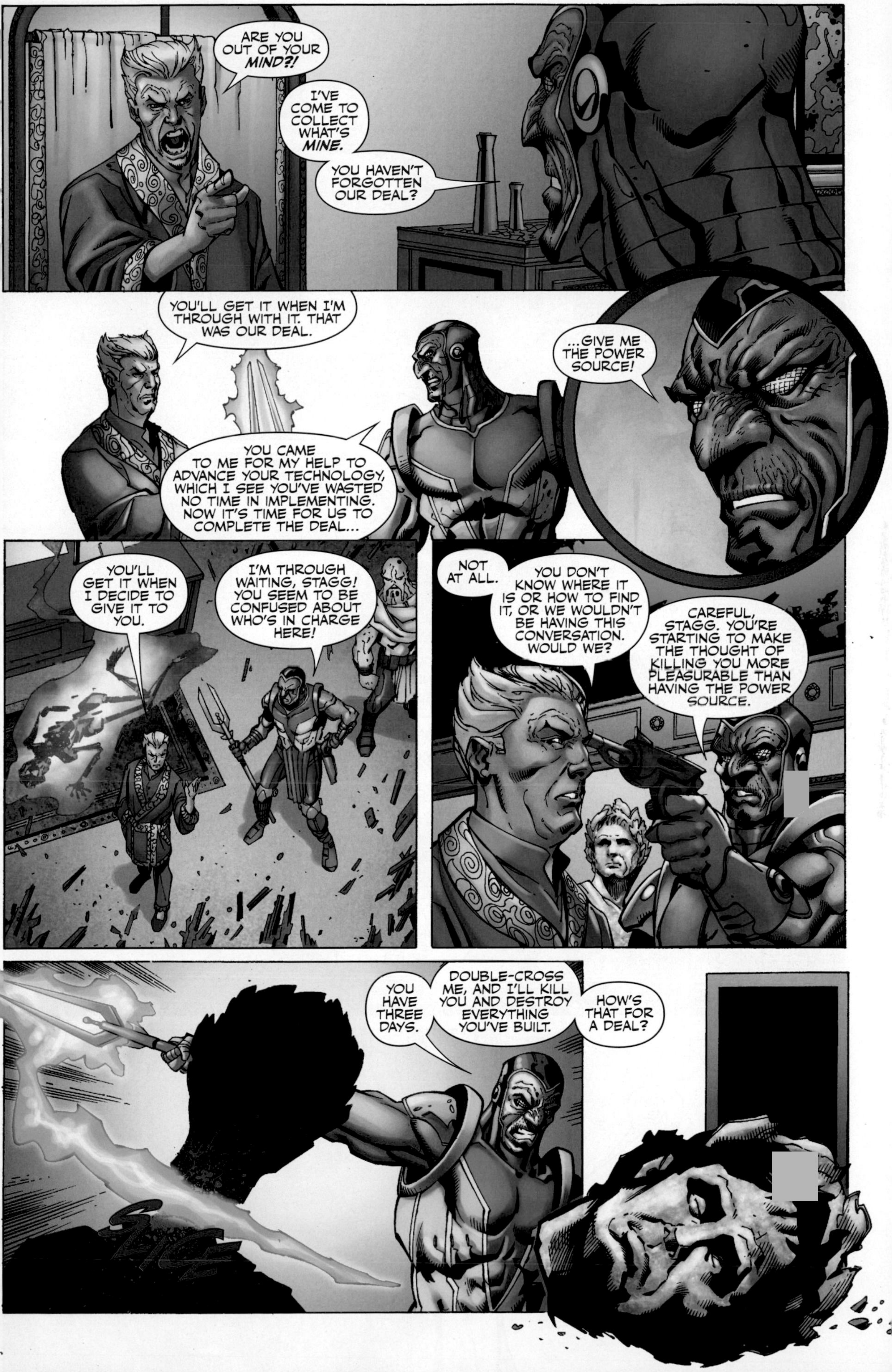
ARE YOU OUT OF YOUR *MIND?!*
I'VE COME TO COLLECT WHAT'S *MINE.*
YOU HAVEN'T FORGOTTEN OUR DEAL?
YOU'LL GET IT WHEN I'M THROUGH WITH IT. THAT WAS OUR DEAL.
YOU CAME TO ME FOR MY HELP TO ADVANCE YOUR TECHNOLOGY, WHICH I SEE YOU'VE WASTED NO TIME IN IMPLEMENTING. NOW IT'S TIME FOR US TO COMPLETE THE DEAL...
...GIVE ME THE POWER SOURCE!
YOU'LL GET IT WHEN I DECIDE TO GIVE IT TO YOU.
I'M THROUGH WAITING, STAGG! YOU SEEM TO BE CONFUSED ABOUT WHO'S IN CHARGE HERE!
NOT AT ALL.
YOU DON'T KNOW WHERE IT IS OR HOW TO FIND IT, OR WE WOULDN'T BE HAVING THIS CONVERSATION. WOULD WE?
CAREFUL, STAGG. YOU'RE STARTING TO MAKE THE THOUGHT OF KILLING YOU MORE PLEASURABLE THAN HAVING THE POWER SOURCE.
YOU HAVE THREE DAYS.
DOUBLE-CROSS ME, AND I'LL KILL YOU AND DESTROY EVERYTHING YOU'VE BUILT.
HOW'S THAT FOR A DEAL?

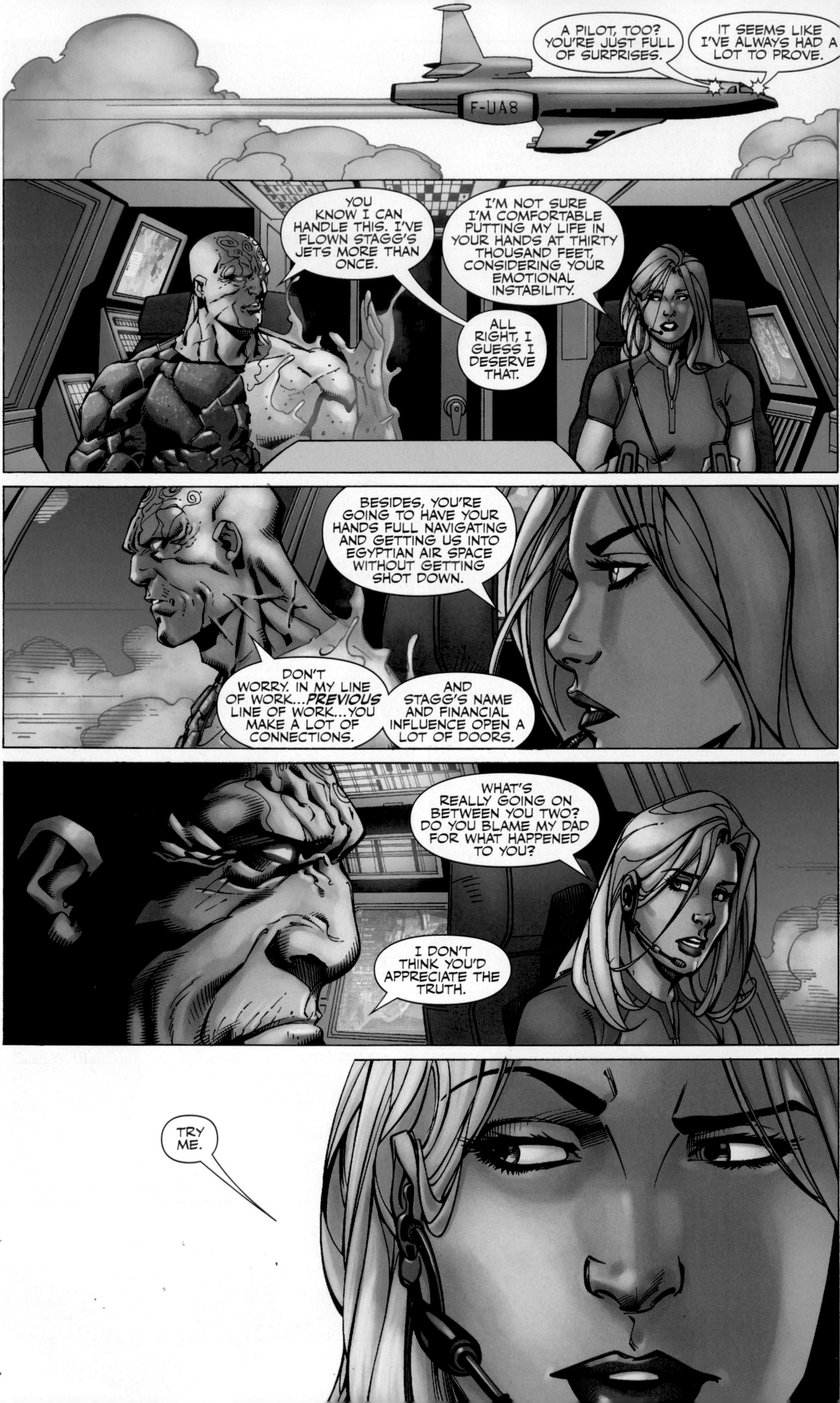

F-UA8
A PILOT, TOO? YOU'RE JUST FULL OF SURPRISES.
IT SEEMS LIKE I'VE ALWAYS HAD A LOT TO PROVE.
I'M NOT SURE I'M COMFORTABLE PUTTING MY LIFE IN YOUR HANDS AT THIRTY THOUSAND FEET, CONSIDERING YOUR EMOTIONAL INSTABILITY.
YOU KNOW I CAN HANDLE THIS. I'VE FLOWN STAGG'S JETS MORE THAN ONCE.
ALL RIGHT, I GUESS I DESERVE THAT.
BESIDES, YOU'RE GOING TO HAVE YOUR HANDS FULL NAVIGATING AND GETTING US INTO EGYPTIAN AIR SPACE WITHOUT GETTING SHOT DOWN.
DON'T WORRY. IN MY LINE OF WORK...*PREVIOUS* LINE OF WORK...YOU MAKE A LOT OF CONNECTIONS.
AND STAGG'S NAME AND FINANCIAL INFLUENCE OPEN A LOT OF DOORS.
WHAT'S REALLY GOING ON BETWEEN YOU TWO? DO YOU BLAME MY DAD FOR WHAT HAPPENED TO YOU?
I DON'T THINK YOU'D APPRECIATE THE TRUTH.
TRY ME.

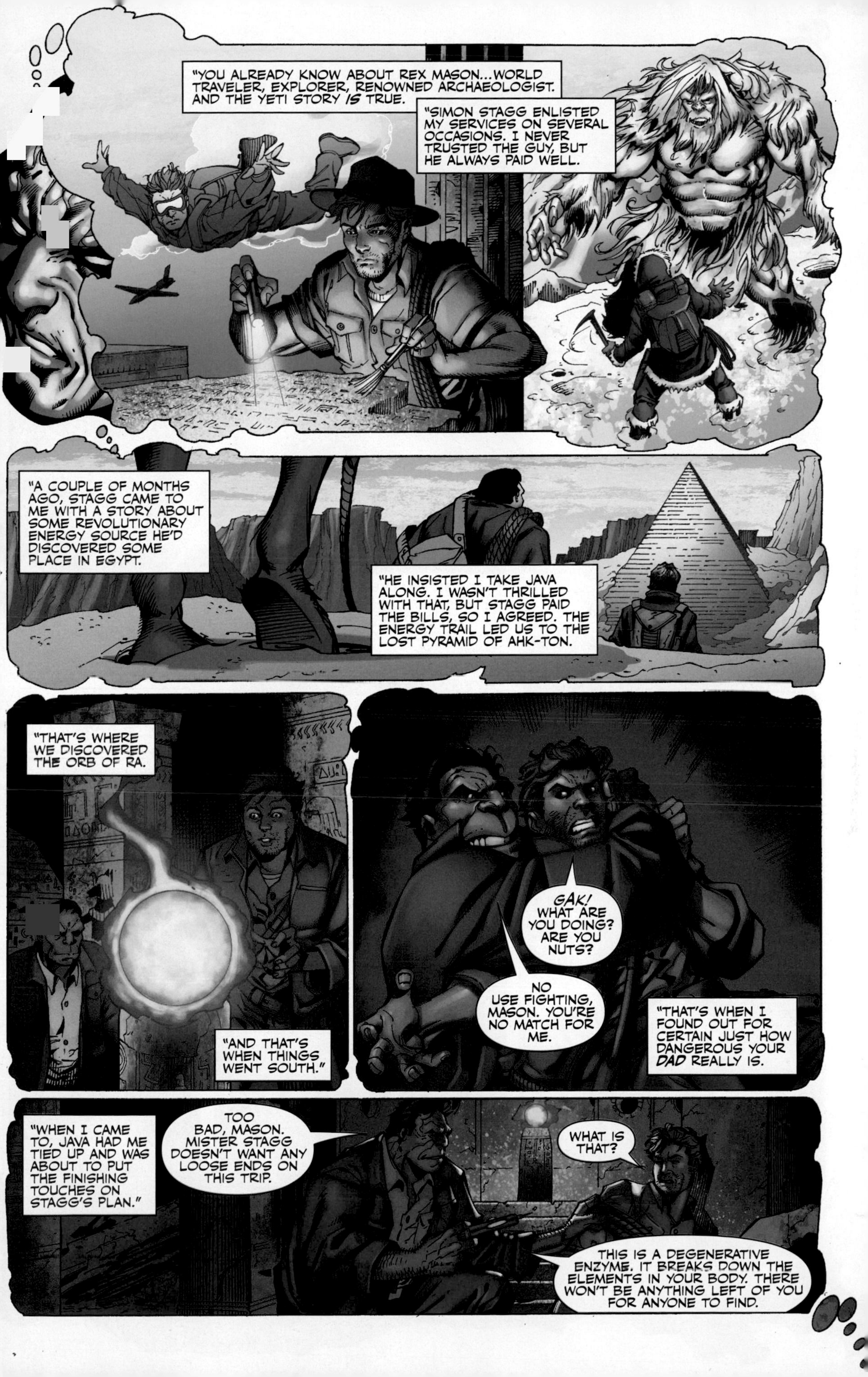
"YOU ALREADY KNOW ABOUT REX MASON...WORLD TRAVELER, EXPLORER, RENOWNED ARCHAEOLOGIST. AND THE YETI STORY *IS* TRUE.
"SIMON STAGG ENLISTED MY SERVICES ON SEVERAL OCCASIONS. I NEVER TRUSTED THE GUY, BUT HE ALWAYS PAID WELL.
"A COUPLE OF MONTHS AGO, STAGG CAME TO ME WITH A STORY ABOUT SOME REVOLUTIONARY ENERGY SOURCE HE'D DISCOVERED SOME PLACE IN EGYPT.
"HE INSISTED I TAKE JAVA ALONG. I WASN'T THRILLED WITH THAT, BUT STAGG PAID THE BILLS, SO I AGREED. THE ENERGY TRAIL LED US TO THE LOST PYRAMID OF AHK-TON.
"THAT'S WHERE WE DISCOVERED THE ORB OF RA.
"AND THAT'S WHEN THINGS WENT SOUTH."
GAK! WHAT ARE YOU DOING? ARE YOU NUTS?
NO USE FIGHTING, MASON. YOU'RE NO MATCH FOR ME.
"THAT'S WHEN I FOUND OUT FOR CERTAIN JUST HOW DANGEROUS YOUR *DAD* REALLY IS.
"WHEN I CAME TO, JAVA HAD ME TIED UP AND WAS ABOUT TO PUT THE FINISHING TOUCHES ON STAGG'S PLAN."
TOO BAD, MASON. MISTER STAGG DOESN'T WANT ANY LOOSE ENDS ON THIS TRIP.
WHAT IS THAT?
THIS IS A DEGENERATIVE ENZYME. IT BREAKS DOWN THE ELEMENTS IN YOUR BODY. THERE WON'T BE ANYTHING LEFT OF YOU FOR ANYONE TO FIND.

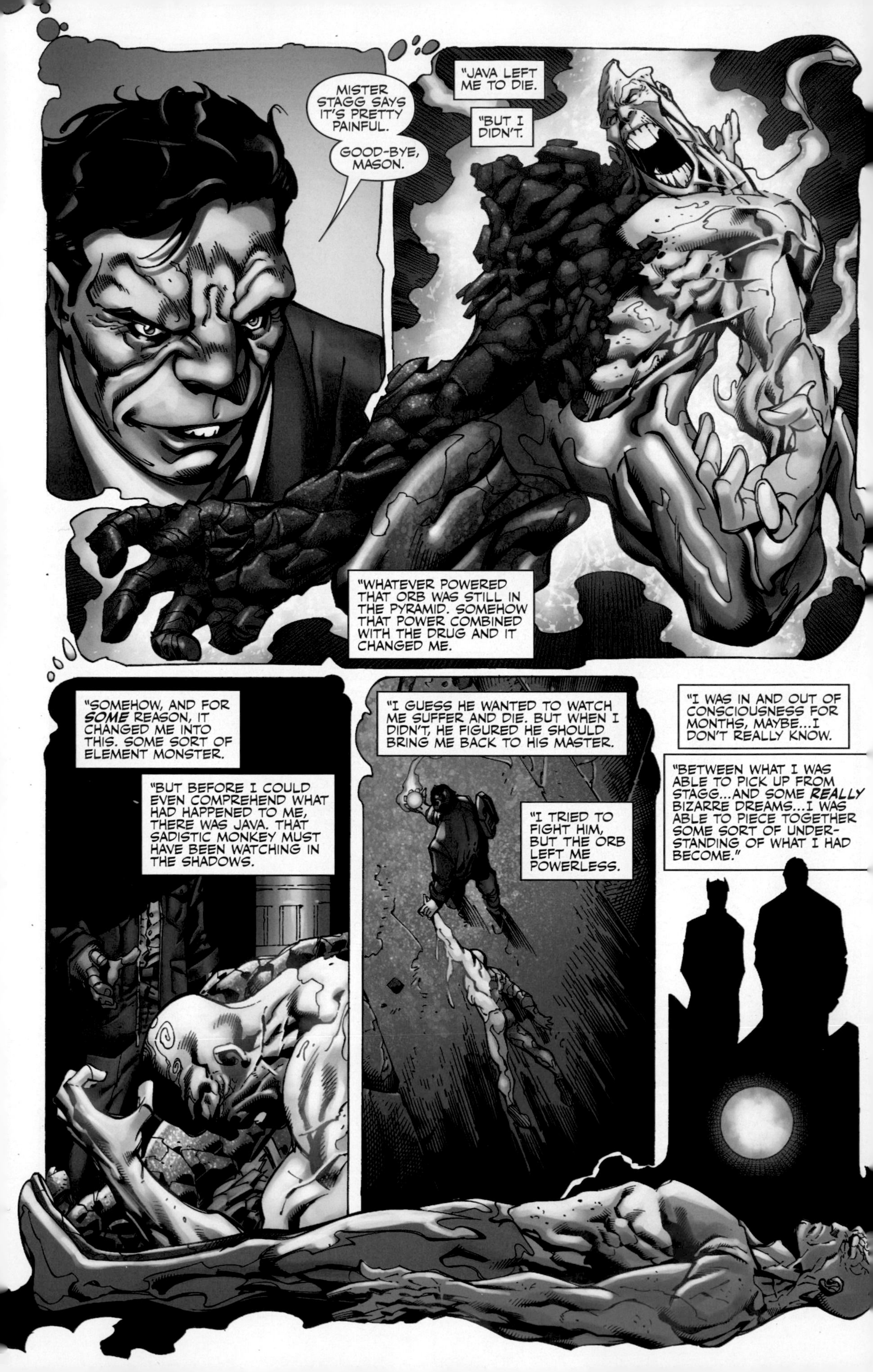
MISTER STAGG SAYS IT'S PRETTY PAINFUL.
GOOD-BYE, MASON.
"JAVA LEFT ME TO DIE.
"BUT I DIDN'T.
"WHATEVER POWERED THAT ORB WAS STILL IN THE PYRAMID. SOMEHOW THAT POWER COMBINED WITH THE DRUG AND IT CHANGED ME.
"SOMEHOW, AND FOR SOME REASON, IT CHANGED ME INTO THIS. SOME SORT OF ELEMENT MONSTER.
"BUT BEFORE I COULD EVEN COMPREHEND WHAT HAD HAPPENED TO ME, THERE WAS JAVA. THAT SADISTIC MONKEY MUST HAVE BEEN WATCHING IN THE SHADOWS.
"I GUESS HE WANTED TO WATCH ME SUFFER AND DIE. BUT WHEN I DIDN'T, HE FIGURED HE SHOULD BRING ME BACK TO HIS MASTER.
"I TRIED TO FIGHT HIM, BUT THE ORB LEFT ME POWERLESS.
"I WAS IN AND OUT OF CONSCIOUSNESS FOR MONTHS, MAYBE...I DON'T REALLY KNOW.
"BETWEEN WHAT I WAS ABLE TO PICK UP FROM STAGG...AND SOME REALLY BIZARRE DREAMS...I WAS ABLE TO PIECE TOGETHER SOME SORT OF UNDER-STANDING OF WHAT I HAD BECOME."

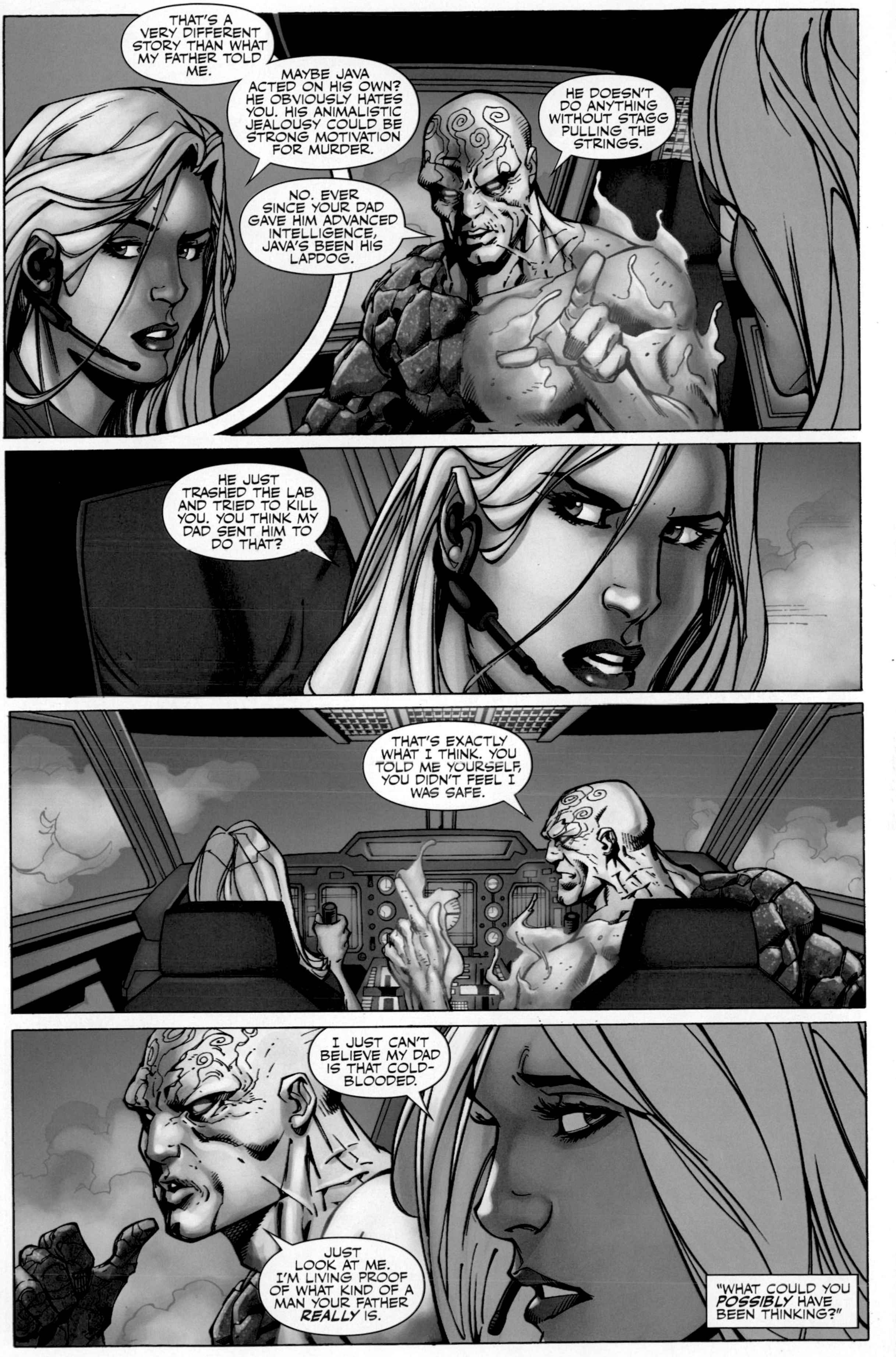
THAT'S A VERY DIFFERENT STORY THAN WHAT MY FATHER TOLD ME.
MAYBE JAVA ACTED ON HIS OWN? HE OBVIOUSLY HATES YOU. HIS ANIMALISTIC JEALOUSY COULD BE STRONG MOTIVATION FOR MURDER.
HE DOESN'T DO ANYTHING WITHOUT STAGG PULLING THE STRINGS.
NO. EVER SINCE YOUR DAD GAVE HIM ADVANCED INTELLIGENCE, JAVA'S BEEN HIS LAPDOG.
HE JUST TRASHED THE LAB AND TRIED TO KILL YOU. YOU THINK MY DAD SENT HIM TO DO THAT?
THAT'S EXACTLY WHAT I THINK. YOU TOLD ME YOURSELF, YOU DIDN'T FEEL I WAS SAFE.
I JUST CAN'T BELIEVE MY DAD IS THAT COLD-BLOODED.
JUST LOOK AT ME. I'M LIVING PROOF OF WHAT KIND OF A MAN YOUR FATHER *REALLY* IS.
"WHAT COULD YOU *POSSIBLY* HAVE BEEN THINKING?"

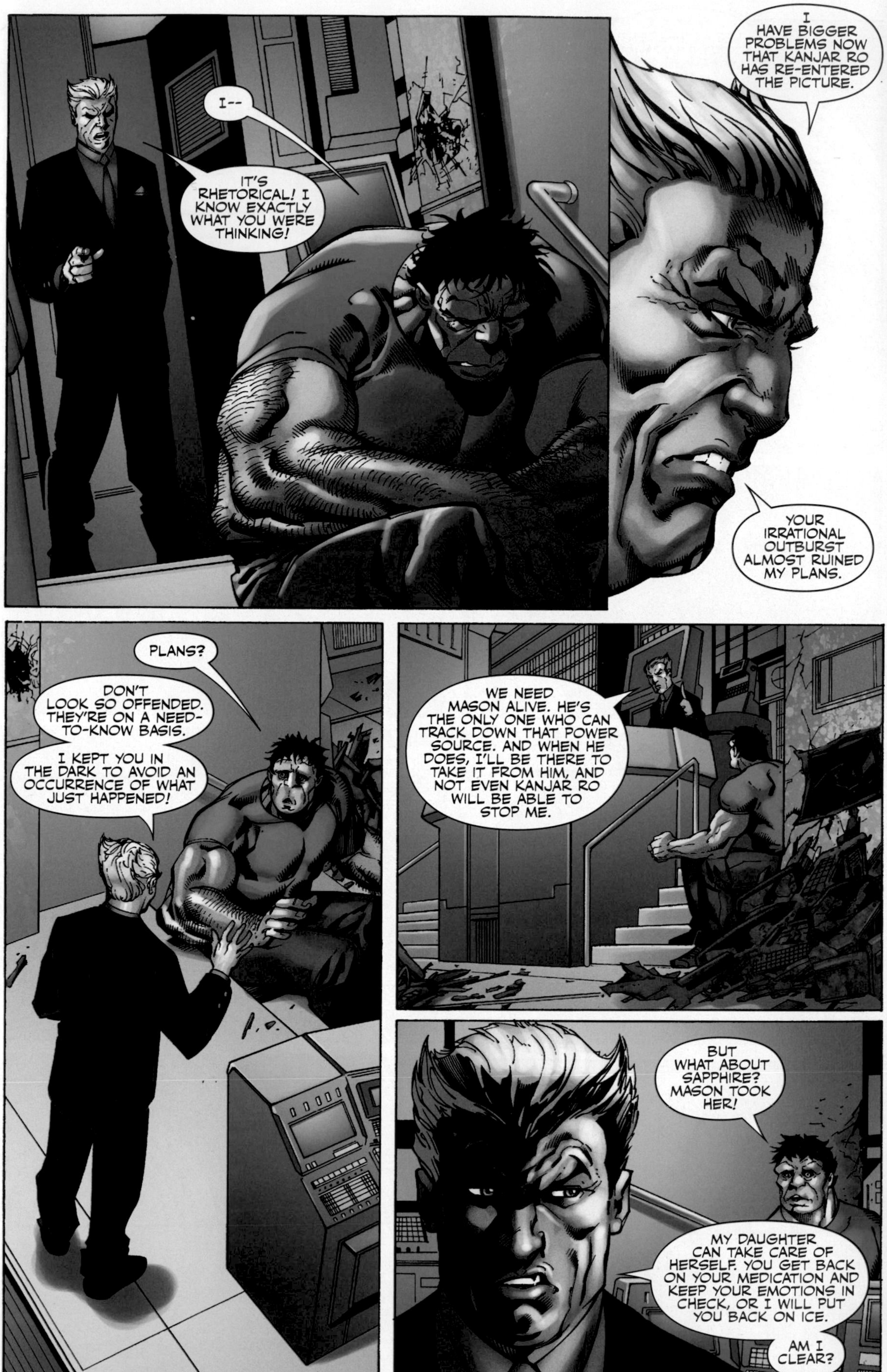
I--
IT'S RHETORICAL! I KNOW EXACTLY WHAT YOU WERE THINKING!
I HAVE BIGGER PROBLEMS NOW THAT KANJAR RO HAS RE-ENTERED THE PICTURE.
YOUR IRRATIONAL OUTBURST ALMOST RUINED MY PLANS.
PLANS?
DON'T LOOK SO OFFENDED. THEY'RE ON A NEED-TO-KNOW BASIS.
I KEPT YOU IN THE DARK TO AVOID AN OCCURRENCE OF WHAT JUST HAPPENED!
WE NEED MASON ALIVE. HE'S THE ONLY ONE WHO CAN TRACK DOWN THAT POWER SOURCE. AND WHEN HE DOES, I'LL BE THERE TO TAKE IT FROM HIM, AND NOT EVEN KANJAR RO WILL BE ABLE TO STOP ME.
BUT WHAT ABOUT SAPPHIRE? MASON TOOK HER!
MY DAUGHTER CAN TAKE CARE OF HERSELF. YOU GET BACK ON YOUR MEDICATION AND KEEP YOUR EMOTIONS IN CHECK, OR I WILL PUT YOU BACK ON ICE.
AM I CLEAR?

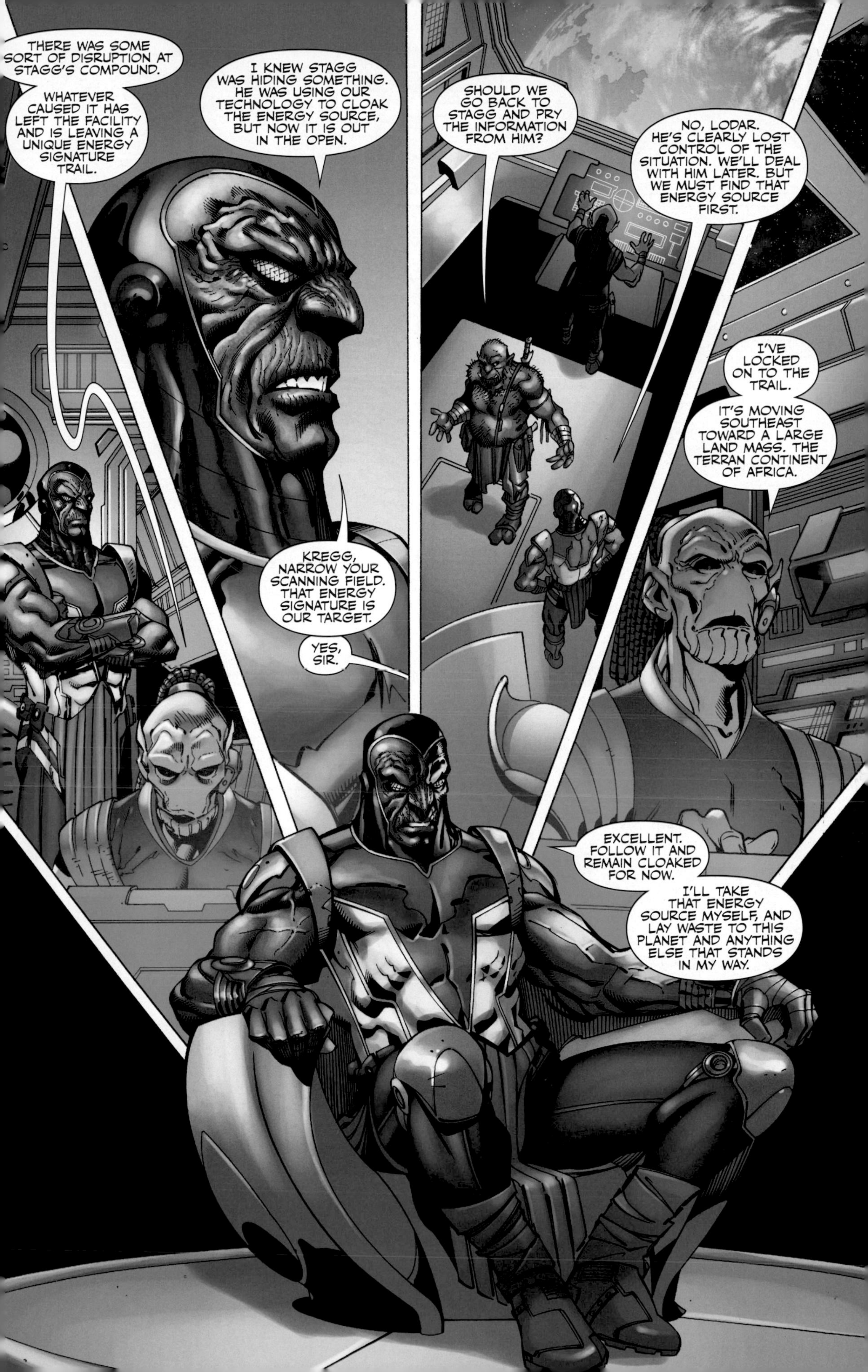
THERE WAS SOME SORT OF DISRUPTION AT STAGG'S COMPOUND.
WHATEVER CAUSED IT HAS LEFT THE FACILITY AND IS LEAVING A UNIQUE ENERGY SIGNATURE TRAIL.
I KNEW STAGG WAS HIDING SOMETHING. HE WAS USING OUR TECHNOLOGY TO CLOAK THE ENERGY SOURCE, BUT NOW IT IS OUT IN THE OPEN.
KREGG, NARROW YOUR SCANNING FIELD. THAT ENERGY SIGNATURE IS OUR TARGET.
YES, SIR.
SHOULD WE GO BACK TO STAGG AND PRY THE INFORMATION FROM HIM?
NO, LODAR. HE'S CLEARLY LOST CONTROL OF THE SITUATION. WE'LL DEAL WITH HIM LATER. BUT WE MUST FIND THAT ENERGY SOURCE FIRST.
I'VE LOCKED ON TO THE TRAIL.
IT'S MOVING SOUTHEAST TOWARD A LARGE LAND MASS. THE TERRAN CONTINENT OF AFRICA.
EXCELLENT. FOLLOW IT AND REMAIN CLOAKED FOR NOW.
I'LL TAKE THAT ENERGY SOURCE MYSELF, AND LAY WASTE TO THIS PLANET AND ANYTHING ELSE THAT STANDS IN MY WAY.

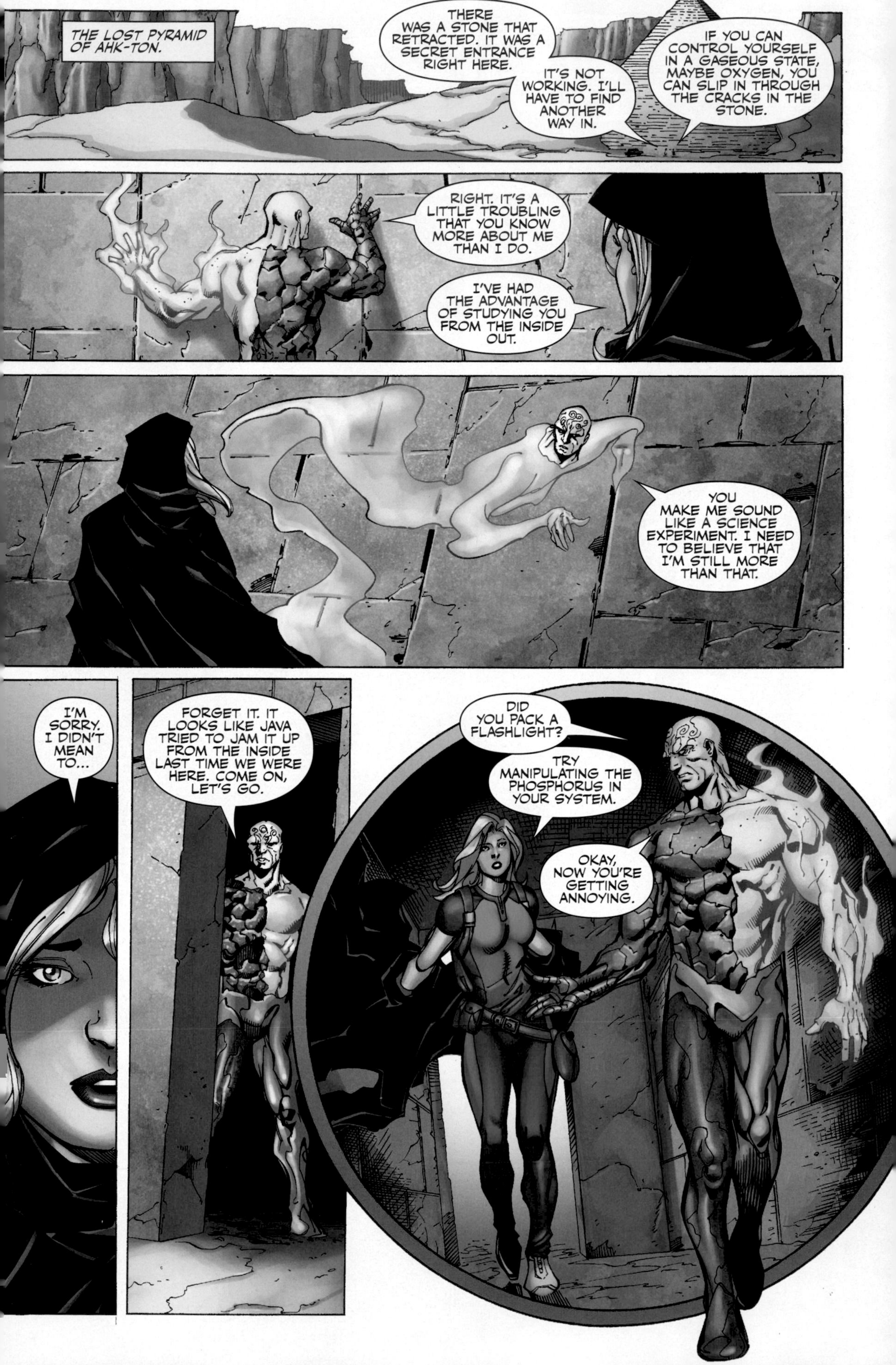
THE LOST PYRAMID OF AHK-TON.
THERE WAS A STONE THAT RETRACTED. IT WAS A SECRET ENTRANCE RIGHT HERE.
IT'S NOT WORKING. I'LL HAVE TO FIND ANOTHER WAY IN.
IF YOU CAN CONTROL YOURSELF IN A GASEOUS STATE, MAYBE OXYGEN, YOU CAN SLIP IN THROUGH THE CRACKS IN THE STONE.
RIGHT. IT'S A LITTLE TROUBLING THAT YOU KNOW MORE ABOUT ME THAN I DO.
I'VE HAD THE ADVANTAGE OF STUDYING YOU FROM THE INSIDE OUT.
YOU MAKE ME SOUND LIKE A SCIENCE EXPERIMENT. I NEED TO BELIEVE THAT I'M STILL MORE THAN THAT.
I'M SORRY. I DIDN'T MEAN TO...
FORGET IT. IT LOOKS LIKE JAVA TRIED TO JAM IT UP FROM THE INSIDE LAST TIME WE WERE HERE. COME ON, LET'S GO.
DID YOU PACK A FLASHLIGHT?
TRY MANIPULATING THE PHOSPHORUS IN YOUR SYSTEM.
OKAY, NOW YOU'RE GETTING ANNOYING.

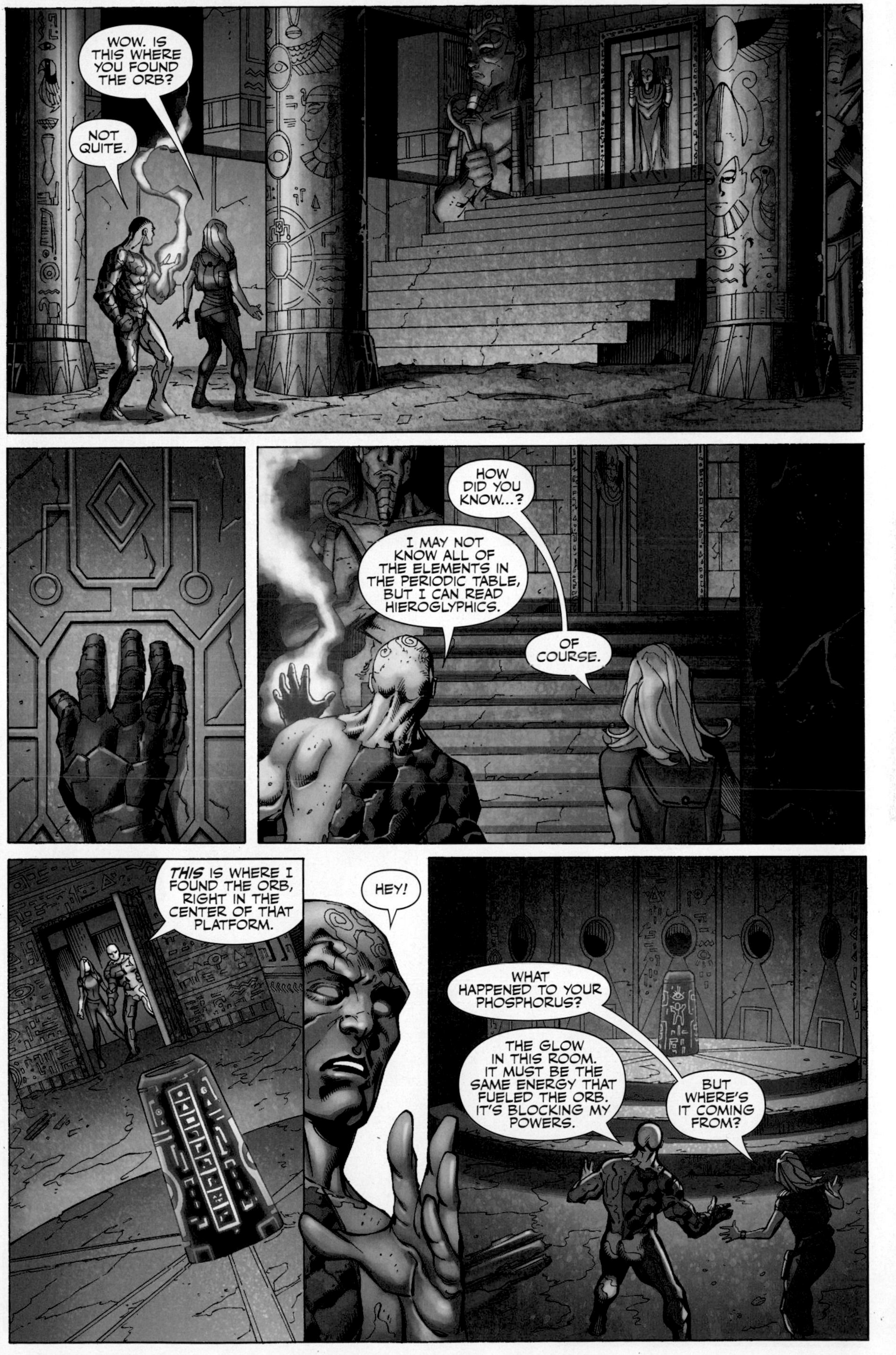
WOW. IS THIS WHERE YOU FOUND THE ORB?
NOT QUITE.
HOW DID YOU KNOW...?
I MAY NOT KNOW ALL OF THE ELEMENTS IN THE PERIODIC TABLE, BUT I CAN READ HIEROGLYPHICS.
OF COURSE.
THIS IS WHERE I FOUND THE ORB, RIGHT IN THE CENTER OF THAT PLATFORM.
HEY!
WHAT HAPPENED TO YOUR PHOSPHORUS?
THE GLOW IN THIS ROOM. IT MUST BE THE SAME ENERGY THAT FUELED THE ORB. IT'S BLOCKING MY POWERS.
BUT WHERE'S IT COMING FROM?

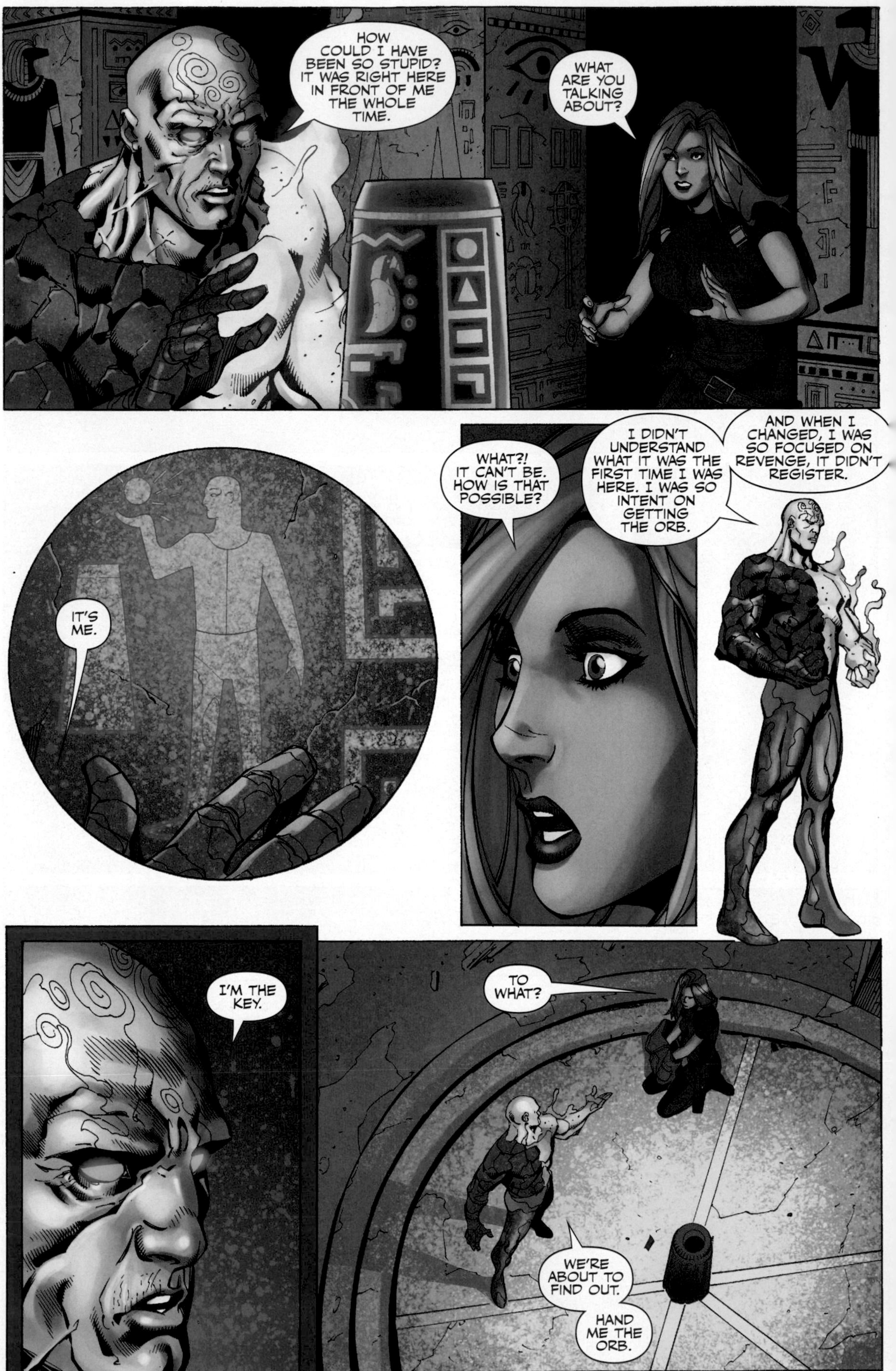
HOW COULD I HAVE BEEN SO STUPID? IT WAS RIGHT HERE IN FRONT OF ME THE WHOLE TIME.
WHAT ARE YOU TALKING ABOUT?
IT'S ME.
WHAT?! IT CAN'T BE. HOW IS THAT POSSIBLE?
I DIDN'T UNDERSTAND WHAT IT WAS THE FIRST TIME I WAS HERE. I WAS SO INTENT ON GETTING THE ORB.
AND WHEN I CHANGED, I WAS SO FOCUSED ON REVENGE, IT DIDN'T REGISTER.
I'M THE KEY.
TO WHAT?
WE'RE ABOUT TO FIND OUT.
HAND ME THE ORB.

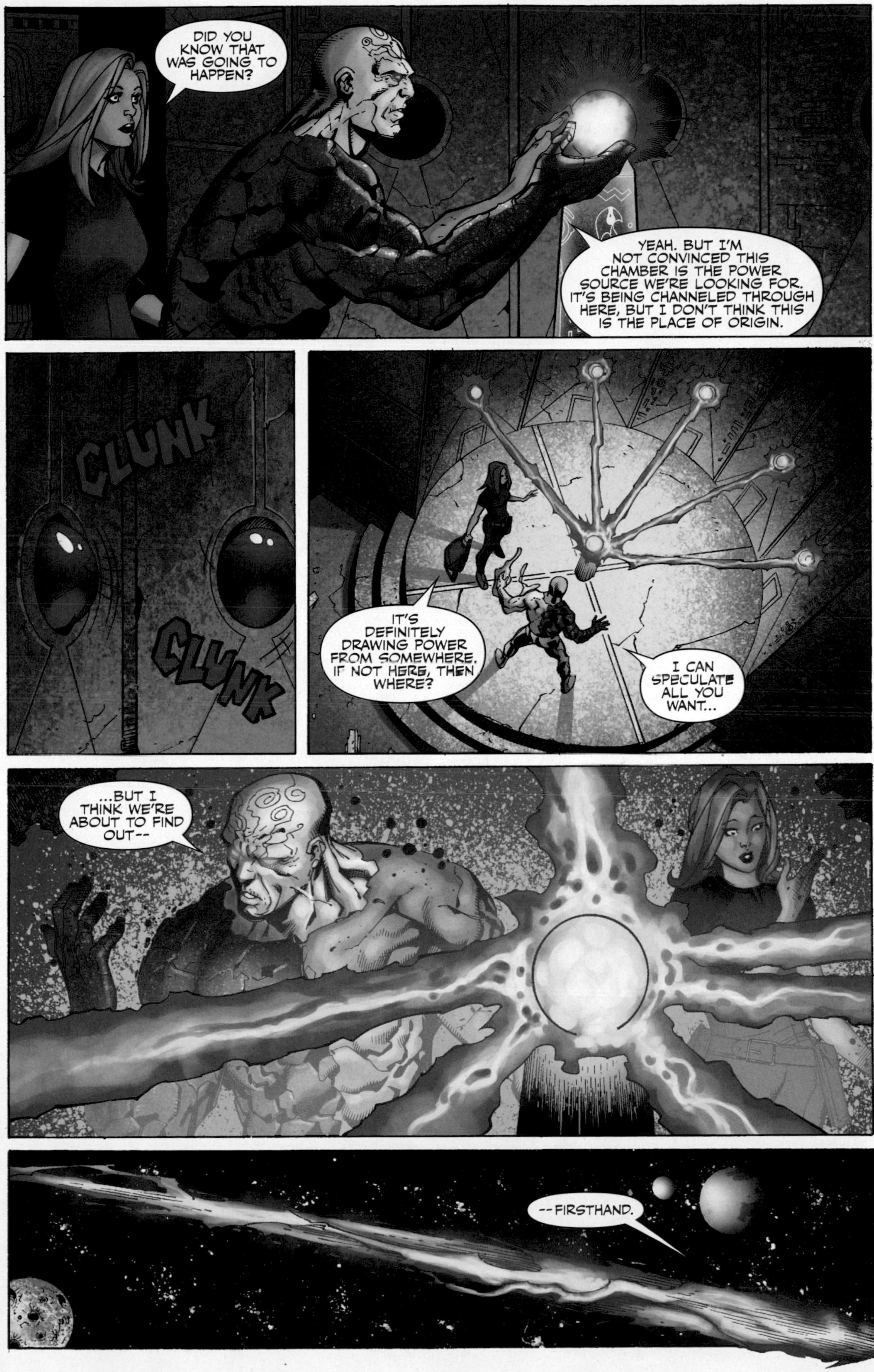
DID YOU KNOW THAT WAS GOING TO HAPPEN?
YEAH. BUT I'M NOT CONVINCED THIS CHAMBER IS THE POWER SOURCE WE'RE LOOKING FOR. IT'S BEING CHANNELED THROUGH HERE, BUT I DON'T THINK THIS IS THE PLACE OF ORIGIN.
CLUNK
CLUNK
IT'S DEFINITELY DRAWING POWER FROM SOMEWHERE. IF NOT HERE, THEN WHERE?
I CAN SPECULATE ALL YOU WANT...
...BUT I THINK WE'RE ABOUT TO FIND OUT--
--FIRSTHAND.

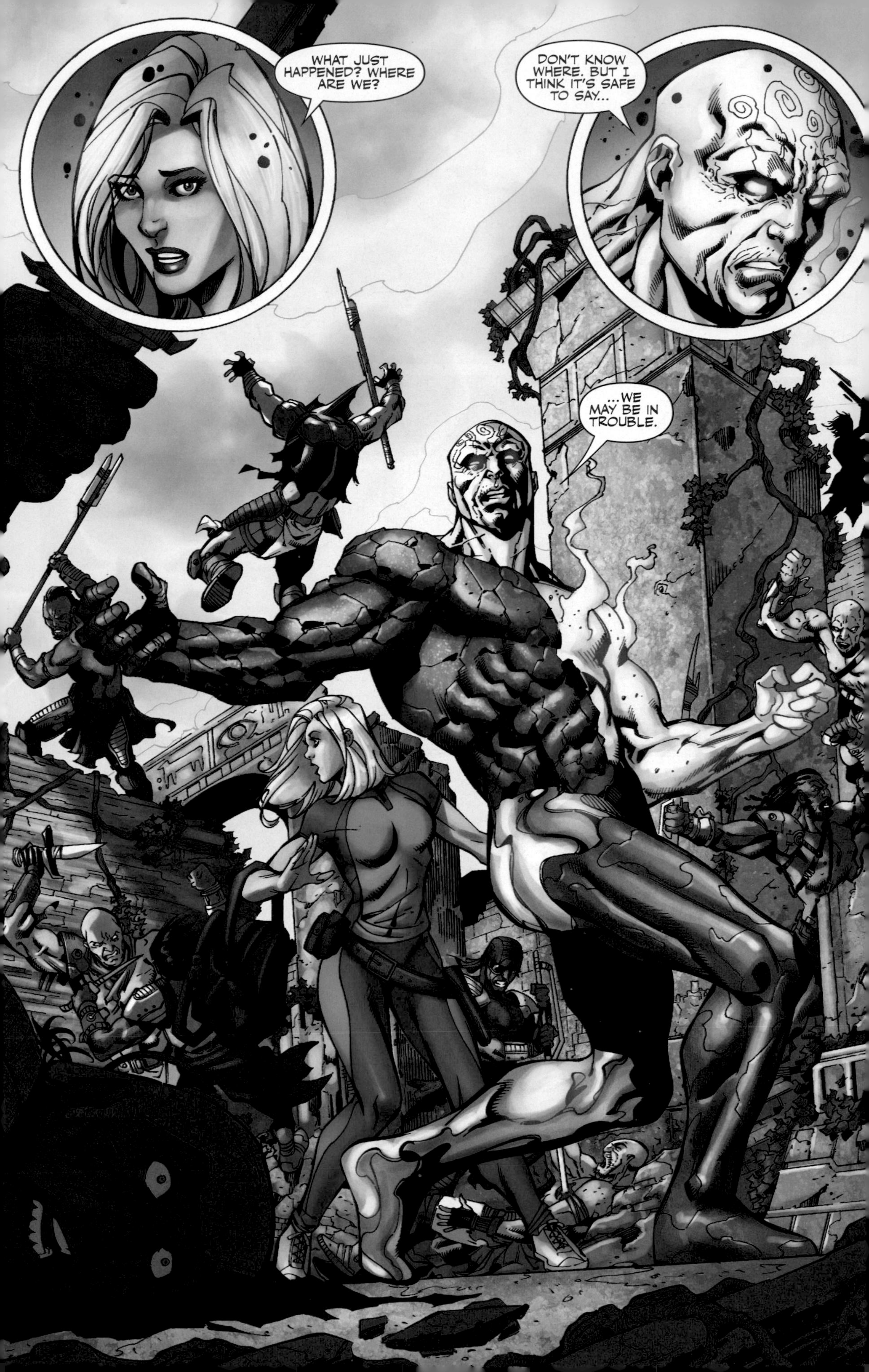
WHAT JUST HAPPENED? WHERE ARE WE?
DON'T KNOW WHERE. BUT I THINK IT'S SAFE TO SAY...
...WE MAY BE IN TROUBLE.

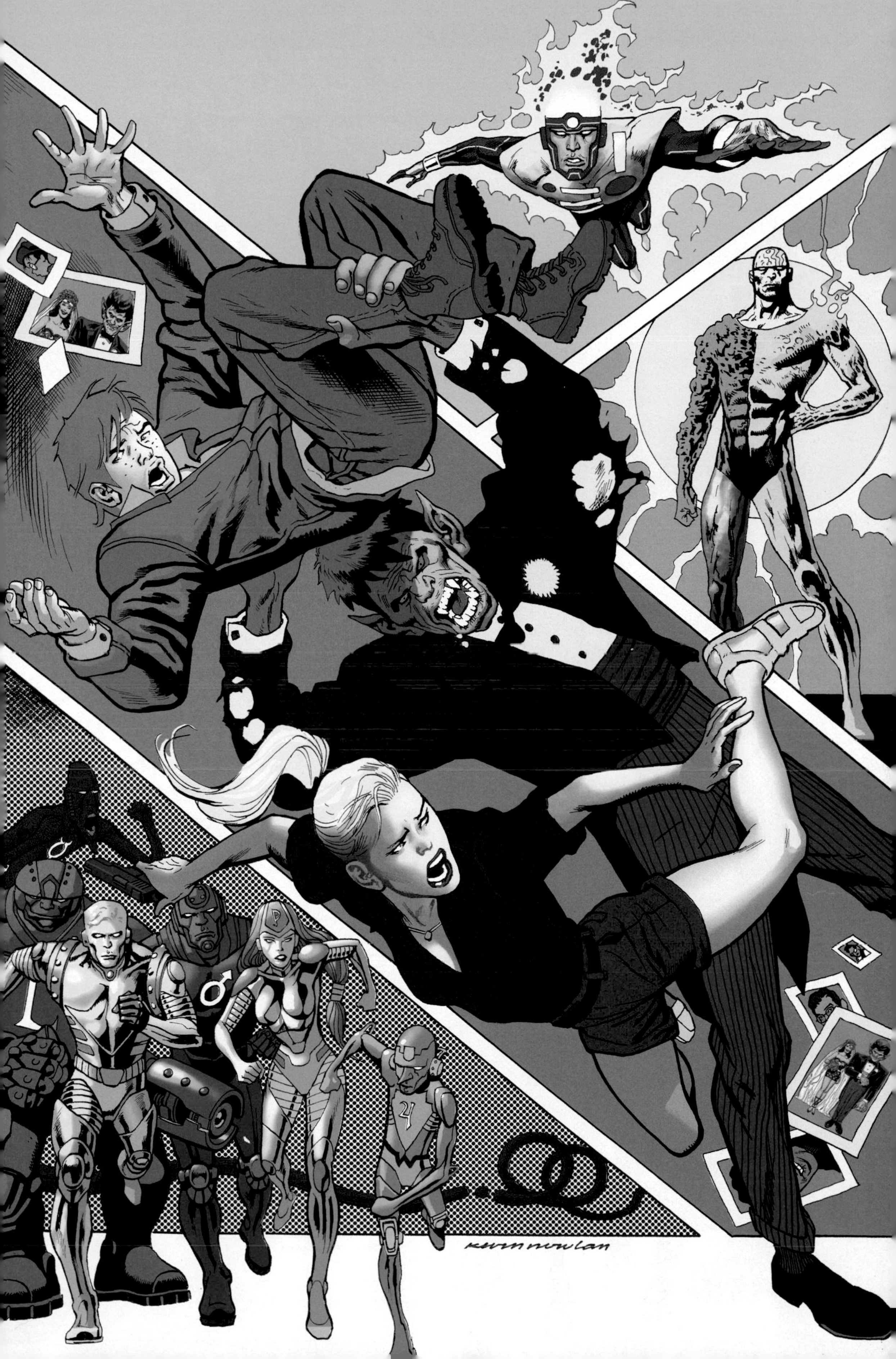
kevin nowlan

BRAVE NEW WORLD

AARON LOPRESTI writer/penciller JONATHAN GLAPION inker CHRIS SOTOMAYOR colorist MICHAEL HEISLER letterer
KEVIN NOWLAN cover

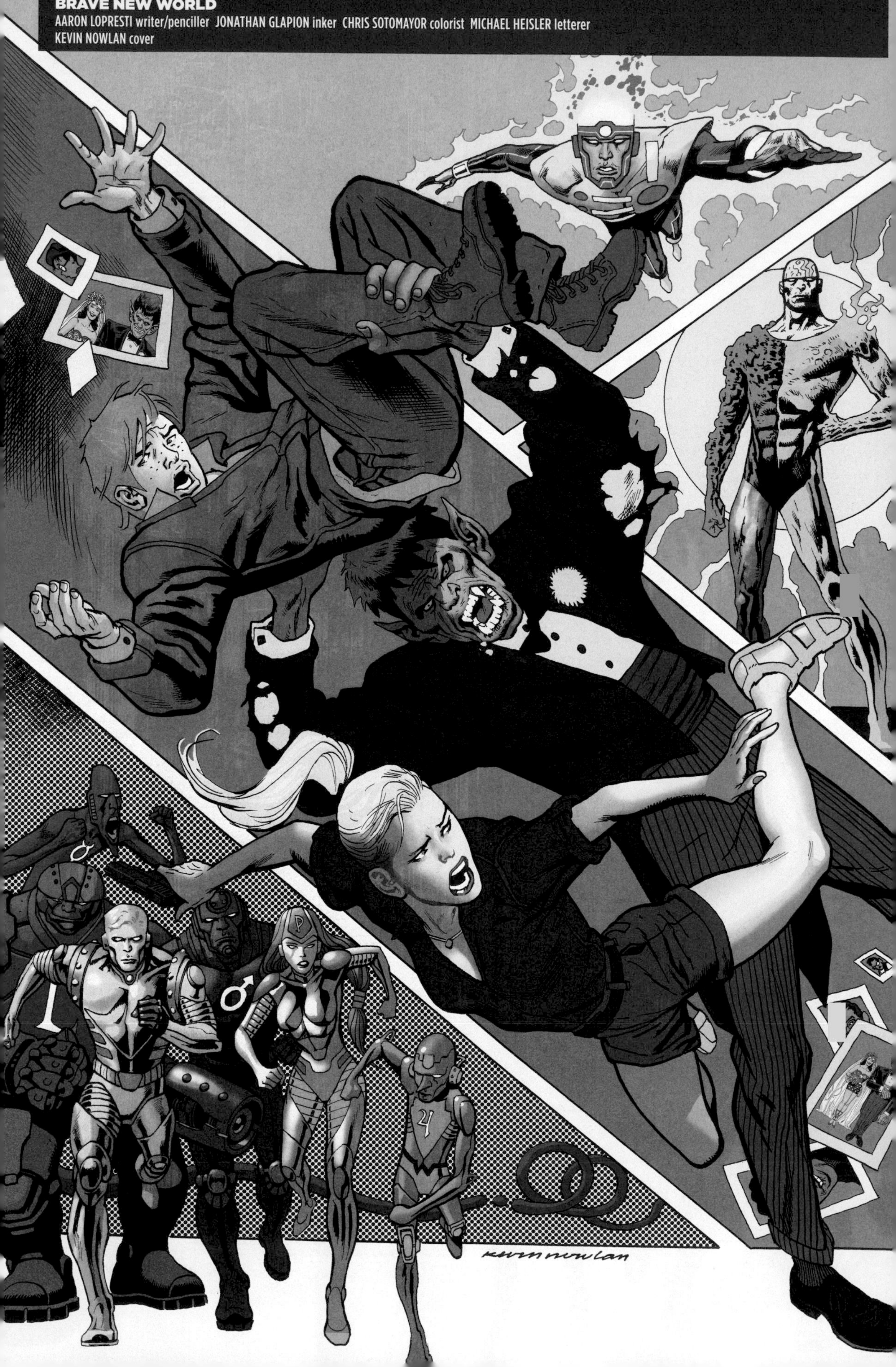
kevin nowlan

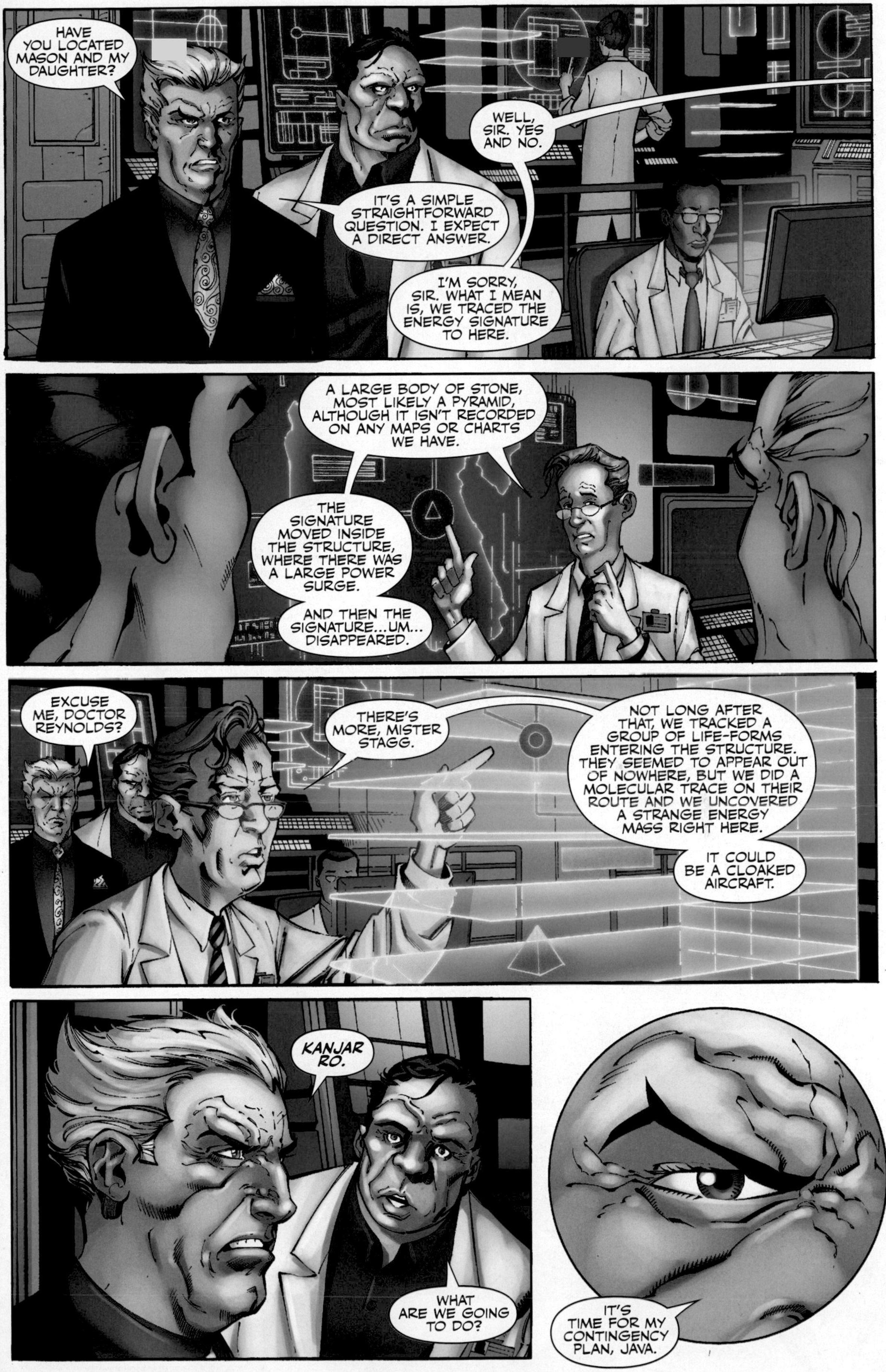
HAVE YOU LOCATED MASON AND MY DAUGHTER?
WELL, SIR. YES AND NO.
IT'S A SIMPLE STRAIGHTFORWARD QUESTION. I EXPECT A DIRECT ANSWER.
I'M SORRY, SIR. WHAT I MEAN IS, WE TRACED THE ENERGY SIGNATURE TO HERE.
A LARGE BODY OF STONE, MOST LIKELY A PYRAMID, ALTHOUGH IT ISN'T RECORDED ON ANY MAPS OR CHARTS WE HAVE.
THE SIGNATURE MOVED INSIDE THE STRUCTURE, WHERE THERE WAS A LARGE POWER SURGE.
AND THEN THE SIGNATURE...UM... DISAPPEARED.
EXCUSE ME, DOCTOR REYNOLDS?
THERE'S MORE, MISTER STAGG.
NOT LONG AFTER THAT, WE TRACKED A GROUP OF LIFE-FORMS ENTERING THE STRUCTURE. THEY SEEMED TO APPEAR OUT OF NOWHERE, BUT WE DID A MOLECULAR TRACE ON THEIR ROUTE AND WE UNCOVERED A STRANGE ENERGY MASS RIGHT HERE.
IT COULD BE A CLOAKED AIRCRAFT.
KANJAR RO.
WHAT ARE WE GOING TO DO?
IT'S TIME FOR MY CONTINGENCY PLAN, JAVA.

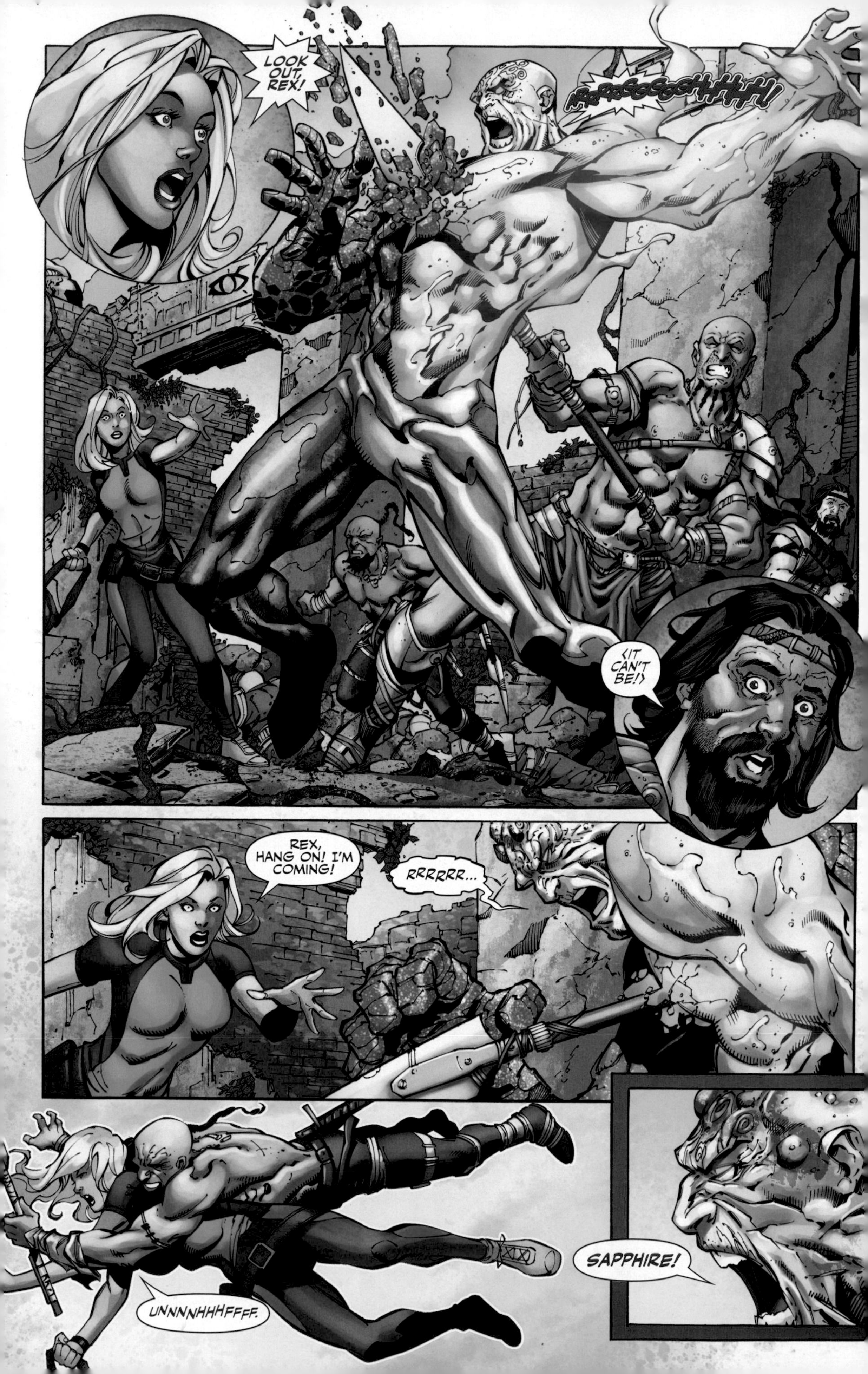
LOOK OUT, REX!
AAARRGGGGGHHHHH!
<IT CAN'T BE!>
REX, HANG ON! I'M COMING!
RRRRRR...
UNNNNHHHFFFF.
SAPPHIRE!

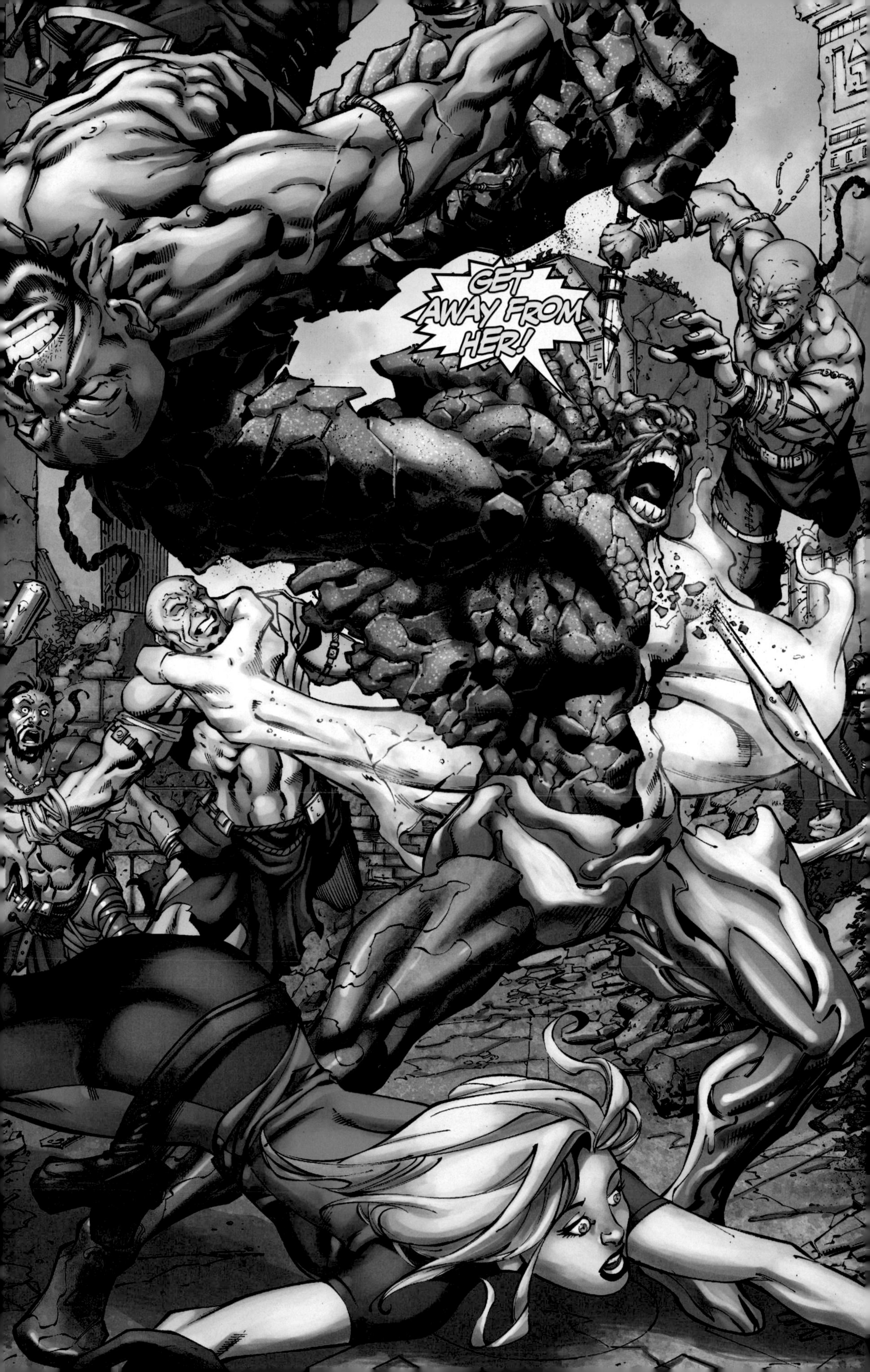
GET AWAY FROM HER!

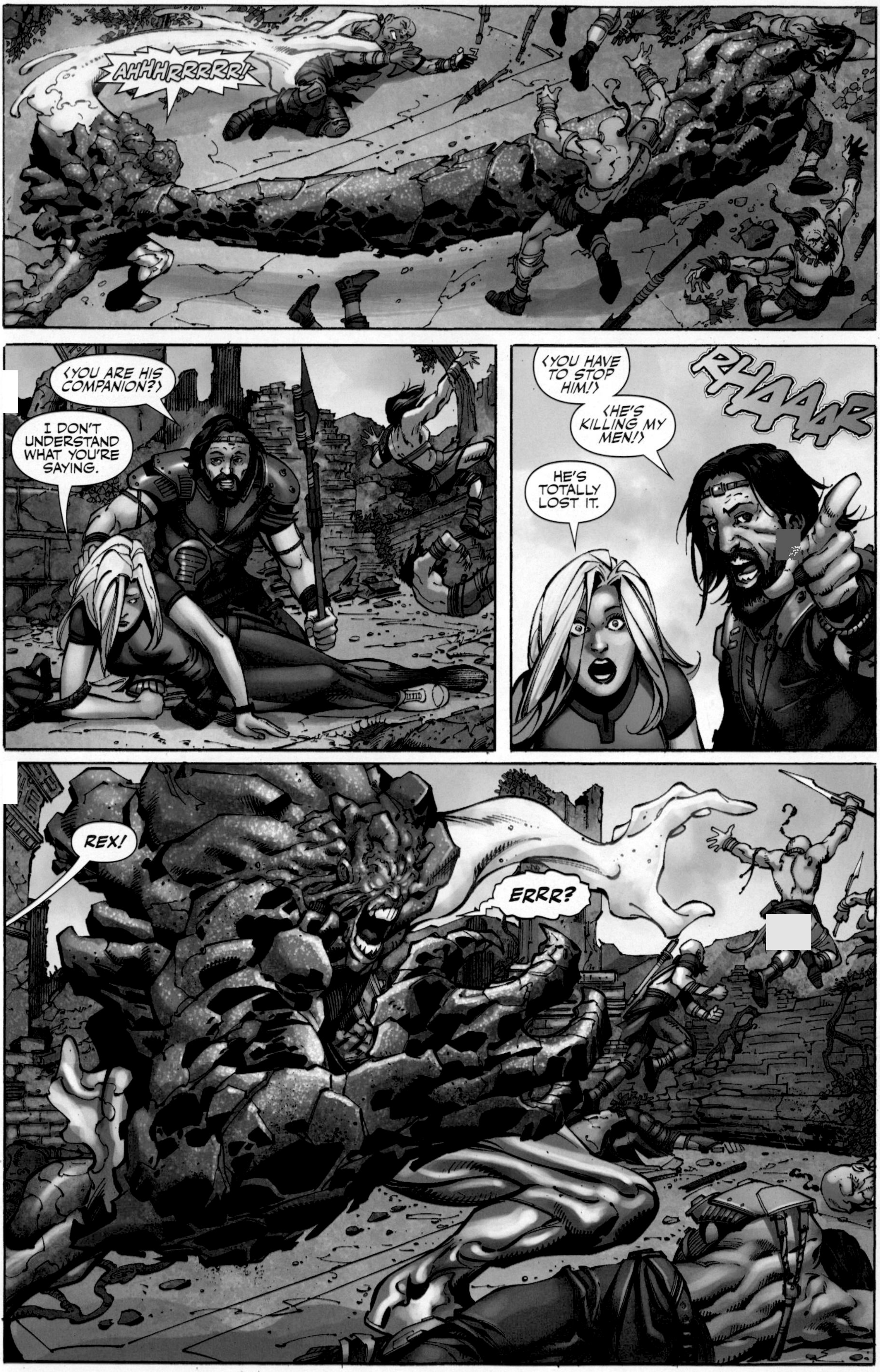
AHHHRRRRR!
‹YOU ARE HIS COMPANION?›
I DON'T UNDERSTAND WHAT YOU'RE SAYING.
‹YOU HAVE TO STOP HIM!›
‹HE'S KILLING MY MEN!›
RHAAAR
HE'S TOTALLY LOST IT.
REX!
ERRR?

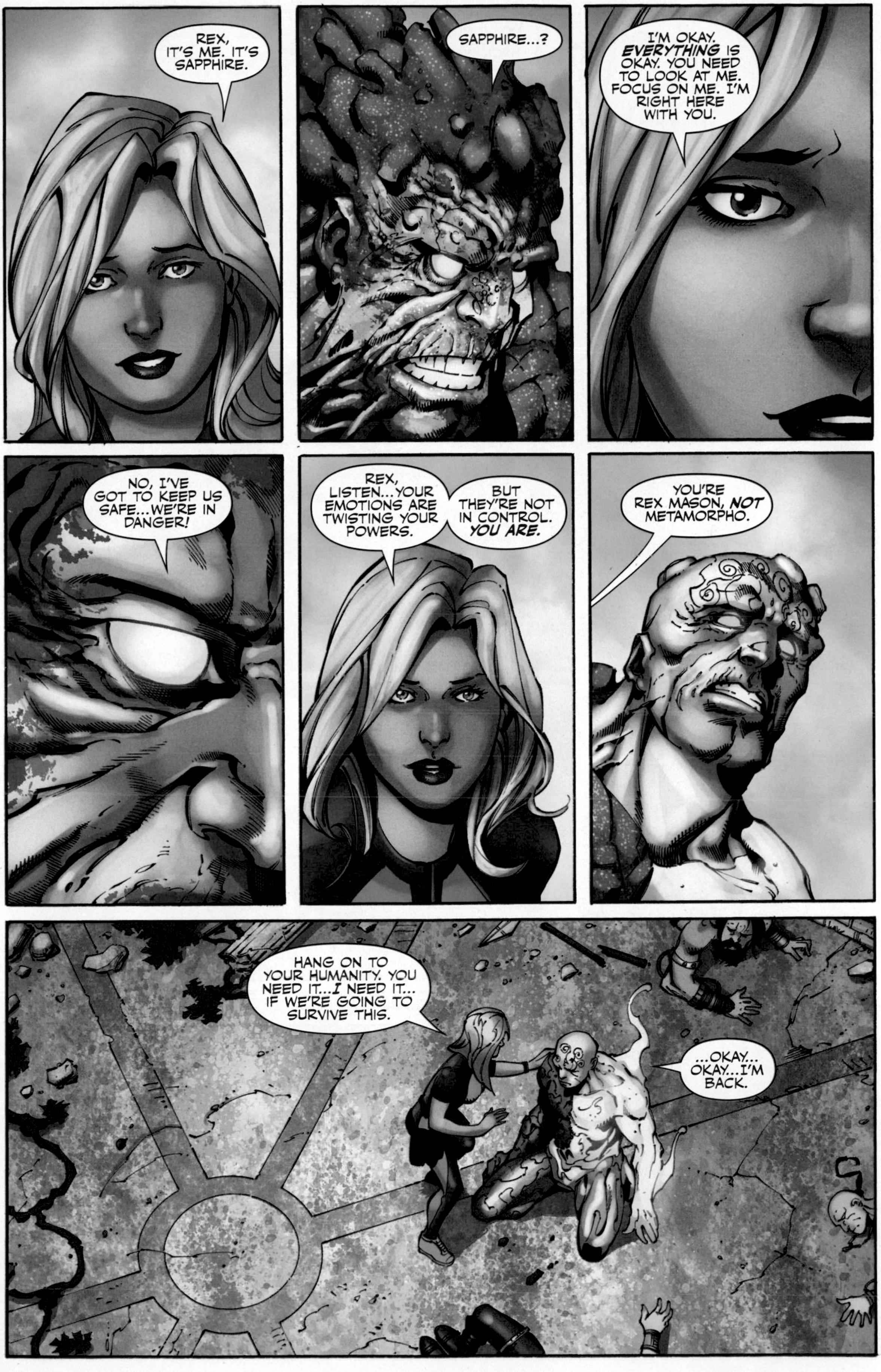
REX, IT'S ME. IT'S SAPPHIRE.
SAPPHIRE...?
I'M OKAY. *EVERYTHING* IS OKAY. YOU NEED TO LOOK AT ME. FOCUS ON ME. I'M RIGHT HERE WITH YOU.
NO, I'VE GOT TO KEEP US SAFE...WE'RE IN DANGER!
REX, LISTEN...YOUR EMOTIONS ARE TWISTING YOUR POWERS.
BUT THEY'RE NOT IN CONTROL. *YOU ARE.*
YOU'RE REX MASON, *NOT* METAMORPHO.
HANG ON TO YOUR HUMANITY. YOU NEED IT...*I* NEED IT... IF WE'RE GOING TO SURVIVE THIS.
...OKAY... OKAY...I'M BACK.

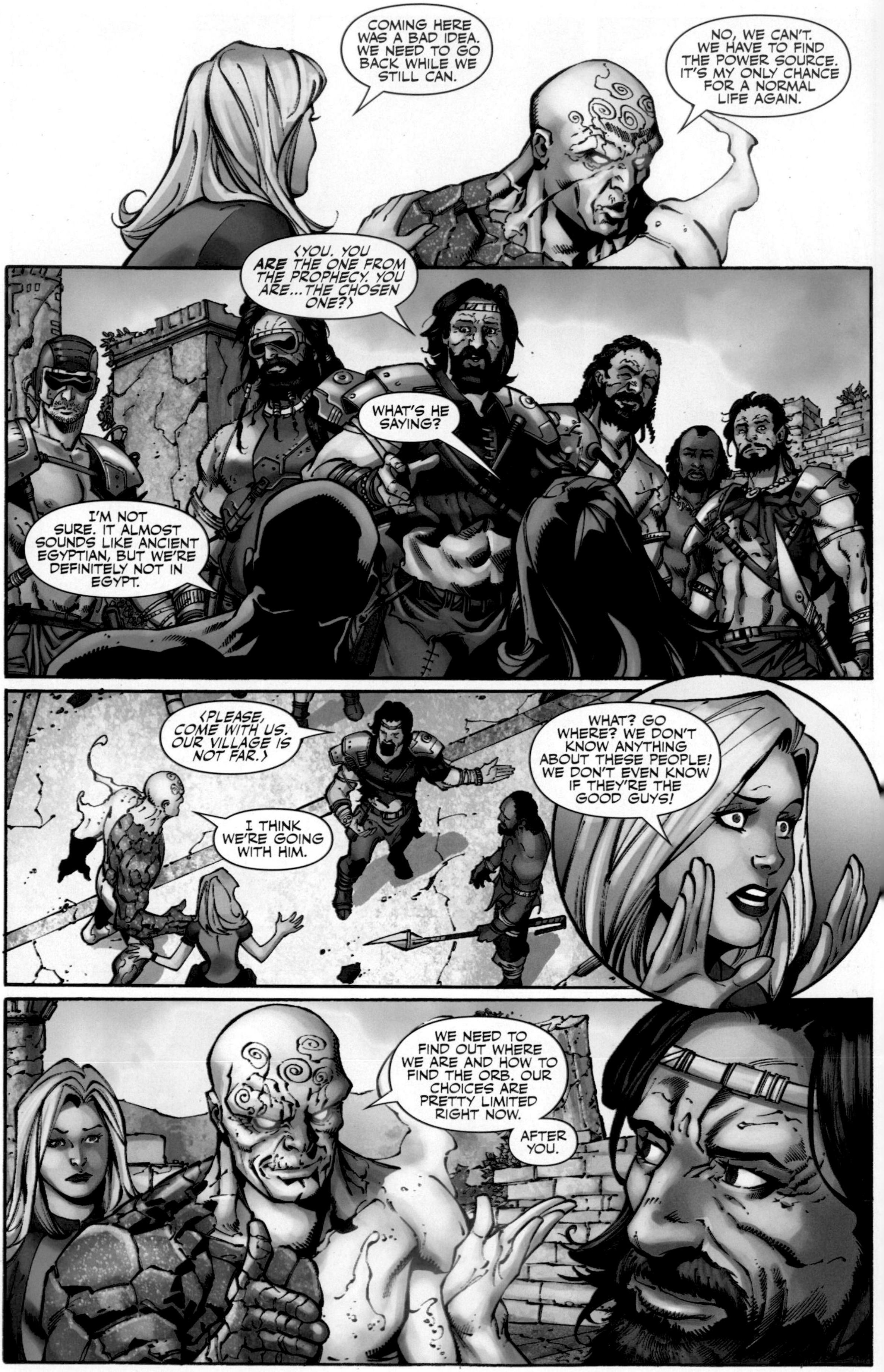
COMING HERE WAS A BAD IDEA. WE NEED TO GO BACK WHILE WE STILL CAN.
NO, WE CAN'T. WE HAVE TO FIND THE POWER SOURCE. IT'S MY ONLY CHANCE FOR A NORMAL LIFE AGAIN.
<YOU. YOU **ARE** THE ONE FROM THE PROPHECY. YOU ARE...THE CHOSEN ONE?>
WHAT'S HE SAYING?
I'M NOT SURE. IT ALMOST SOUNDS LIKE ANCIENT EGYPTIAN, BUT WE'RE DEFINITELY NOT IN EGYPT.
<PLEASE, COME WITH US. OUR VILLAGE IS NOT FAR.>
I THINK WE'RE GOING WITH HIM.
WHAT? GO WHERE? WE DON'T KNOW ANYTHING ABOUT THESE PEOPLE! WE DON'T EVEN KNOW IF THEY'RE THE GOOD GUYS!
WE NEED TO FIND OUT WHERE WE ARE AND HOW TO FIND THE ORB. OUR CHOICES ARE PRETTY LIMITED RIGHT NOW.
AFTER YOU.

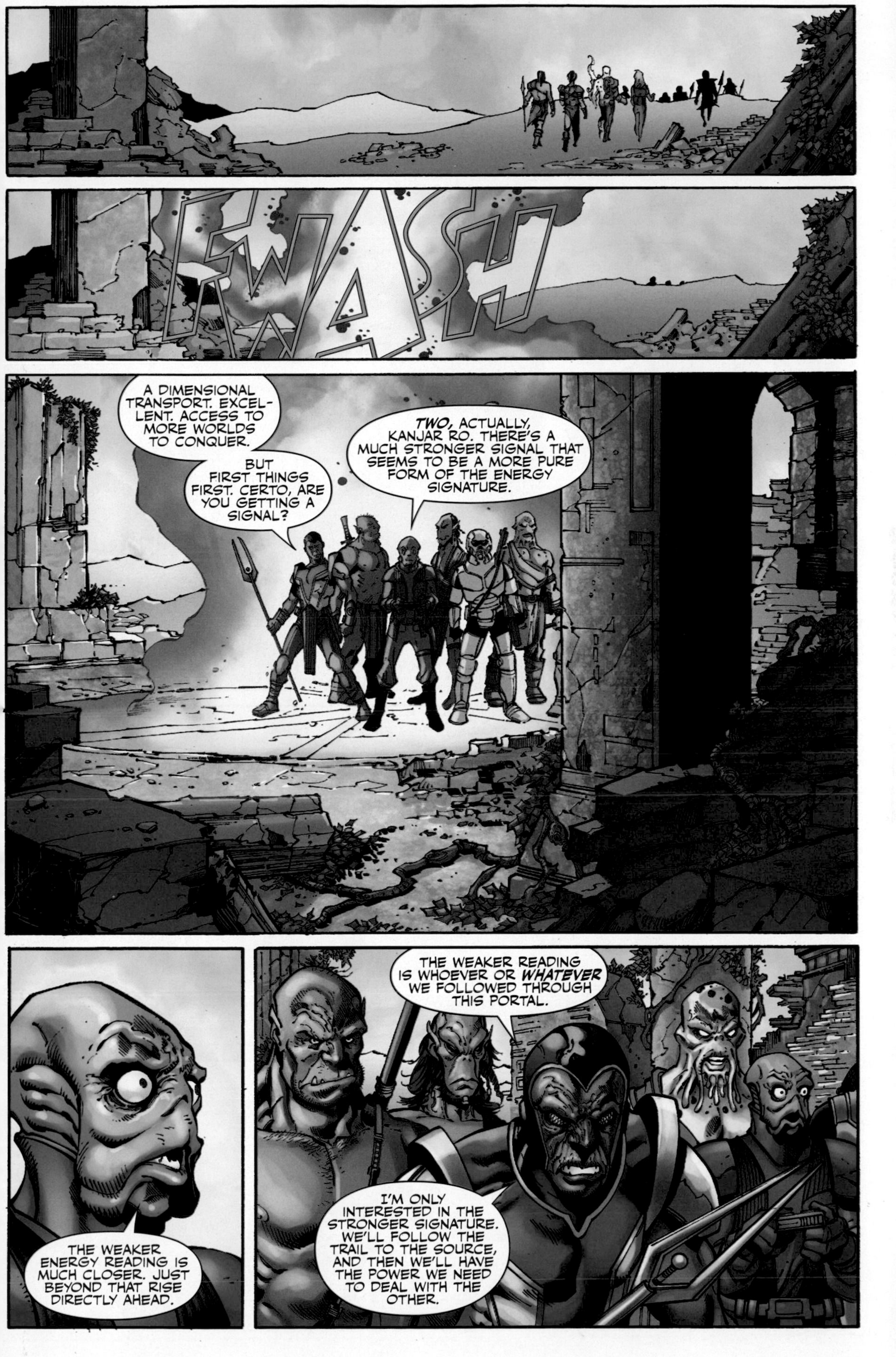
FWASH
A DIMENSIONAL TRANSPORT. EXCEL-LENT. ACCESS TO MORE WORLDS TO CONQUER.
BUT FIRST THINGS FIRST. CERTO, ARE YOU GETTING A SIGNAL?
TWO, ACTUALLY, KANJAR RO. THERE'S A MUCH STRONGER SIGNAL THAT SEEMS TO BE A MORE PURE FORM OF THE ENERGY SIGNATURE.
THE WEAKER ENERGY READING IS MUCH CLOSER. JUST BEYOND THAT RISE DIRECTLY AHEAD.
THE WEAKER READING IS WHOEVER OR *WHATEVER* WE FOLLOWED THROUGH THIS PORTAL.
I'M ONLY INTERESTED IN THE STRONGER SIGNATURE. WE'LL FOLLOW THE TRAIL TO THE SOURCE, AND THEN WE'LL HAVE THE POWER WE NEED TO DEAL WITH THE OTHER.

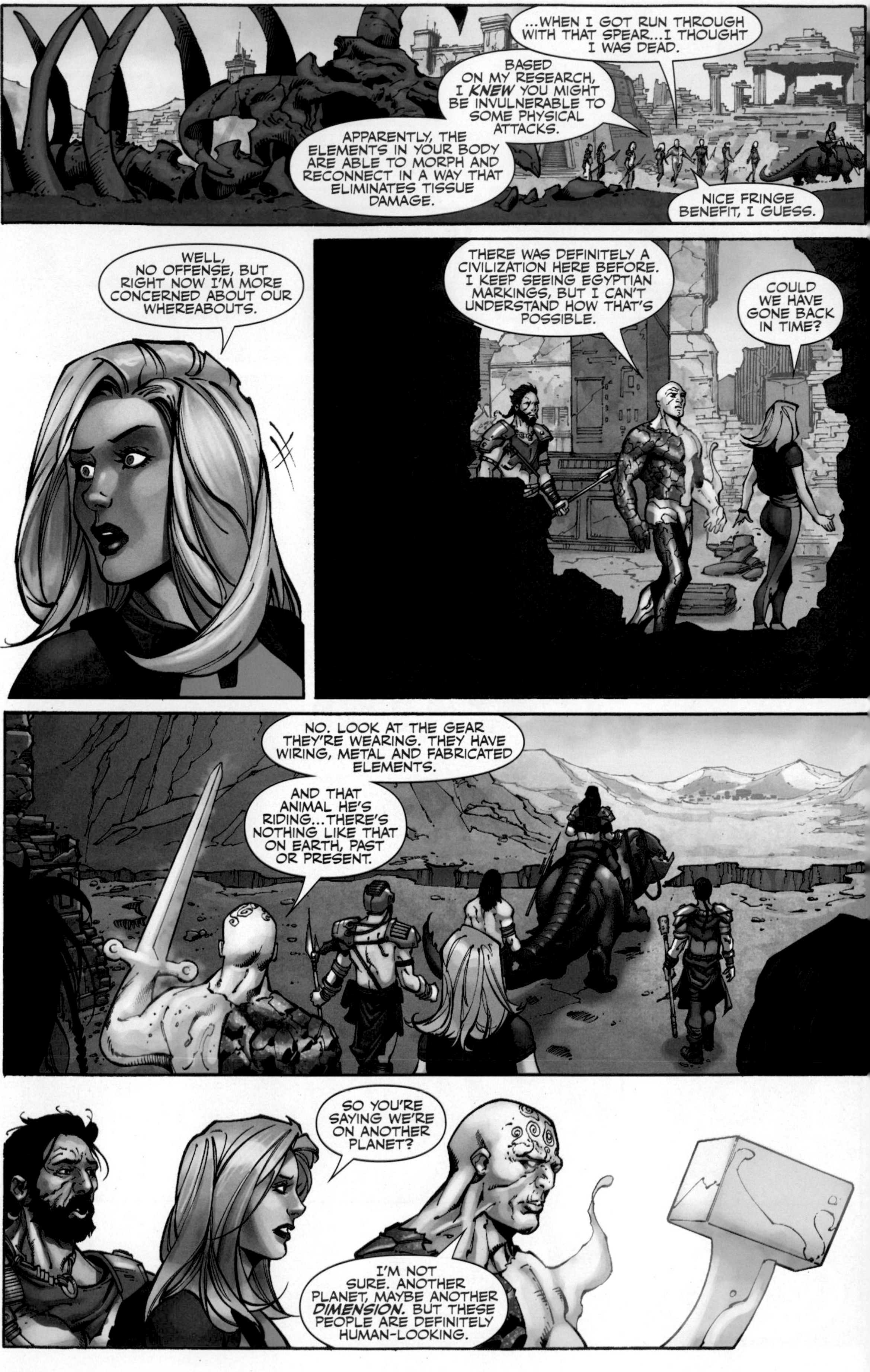
...WHEN I GOT RUN THROUGH WITH THAT SPEAR...I THOUGHT I WAS DEAD.
BASED ON MY RESEARCH, I *KNEW* YOU MIGHT BE INVULNERABLE TO SOME PHYSICAL ATTACKS.
APPARENTLY, THE ELEMENTS IN YOUR BODY ARE ABLE TO MORPH AND RECONNECT IN A WAY THAT ELIMINATES TISSUE DAMAGE.
NICE FRINGE BENEFIT, I GUESS.
WELL, NO OFFENSE, BUT RIGHT NOW I'M MORE CONCERNED ABOUT OUR WHEREABOUTS.
THERE WAS DEFINITELY A CIVILIZATION HERE BEFORE. I KEEP SEEING EGYPTIAN MARKINGS, BUT I CAN'T UNDERSTAND HOW THAT'S POSSIBLE.
COULD WE HAVE GONE BACK IN TIME?
NO. LOOK AT THE GEAR THEY'RE WEARING. THEY HAVE WIRING, METAL AND FABRICATED ELEMENTS.
AND THAT ANIMAL HE'S RIDING...THERE'S NOTHING LIKE THAT ON EARTH, PAST OR PRESENT.
SO YOU'RE SAYING WE'RE ON ANOTHER PLANET?
I'M NOT SURE. ANOTHER PLANET, MAYBE ANOTHER *DIMENSION.* BUT THESE PEOPLE ARE DEFINITELY HUMAN-LOOKING.

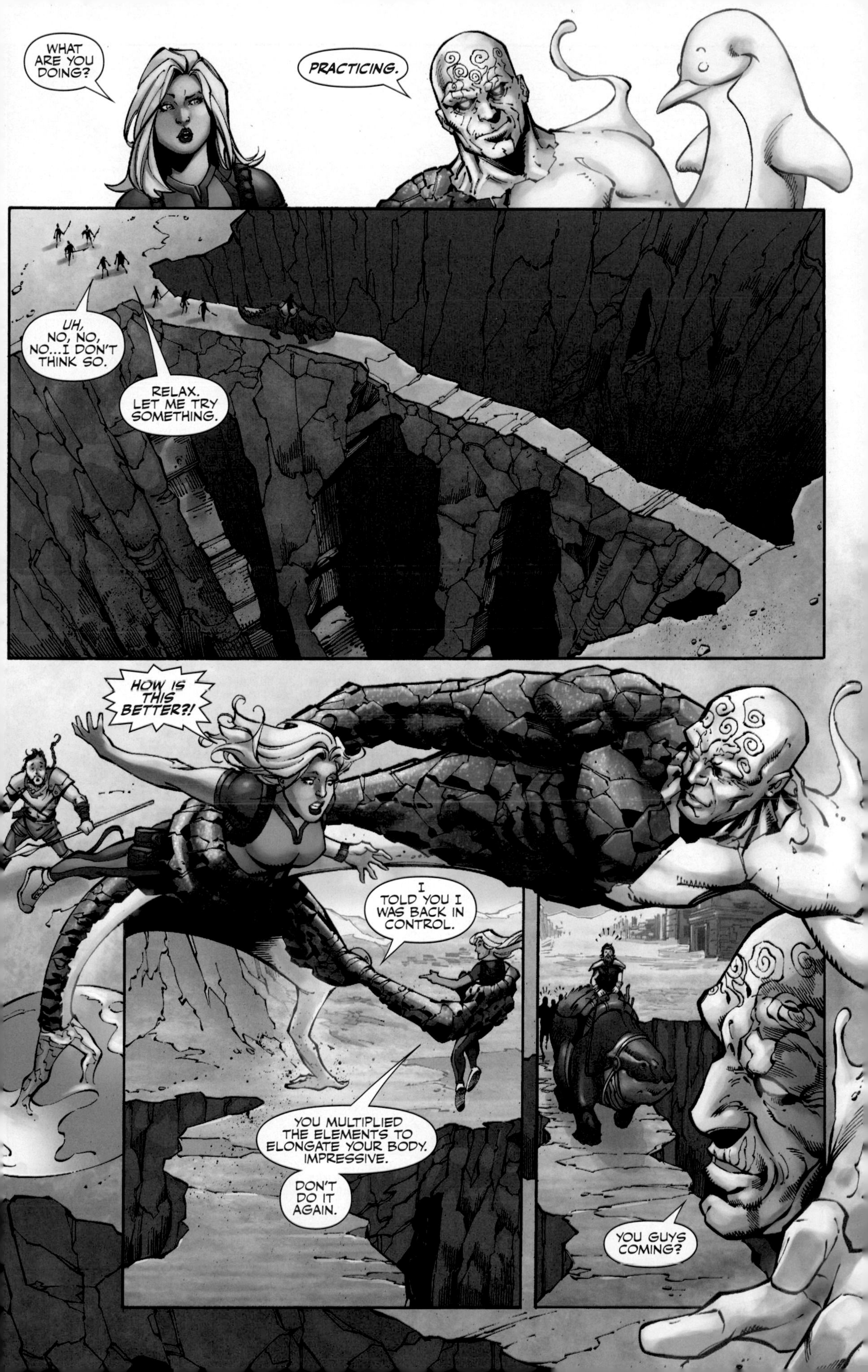
WHAT ARE YOU DOING?
PRACTICING.
UH, NO, NO, NO...I DON'T THINK SO.
RELAX. LET ME TRY SOMETHING.
HOW IS THIS BETTER?!
I TOLD YOU I WAS BACK IN CONTROL.
YOU MULTIPLIED THE ELEMENTS TO ELONGATE YOUR BODY. IMPRESSIVE.
DON'T DO IT AGAIN.
YOU GUYS COMING?

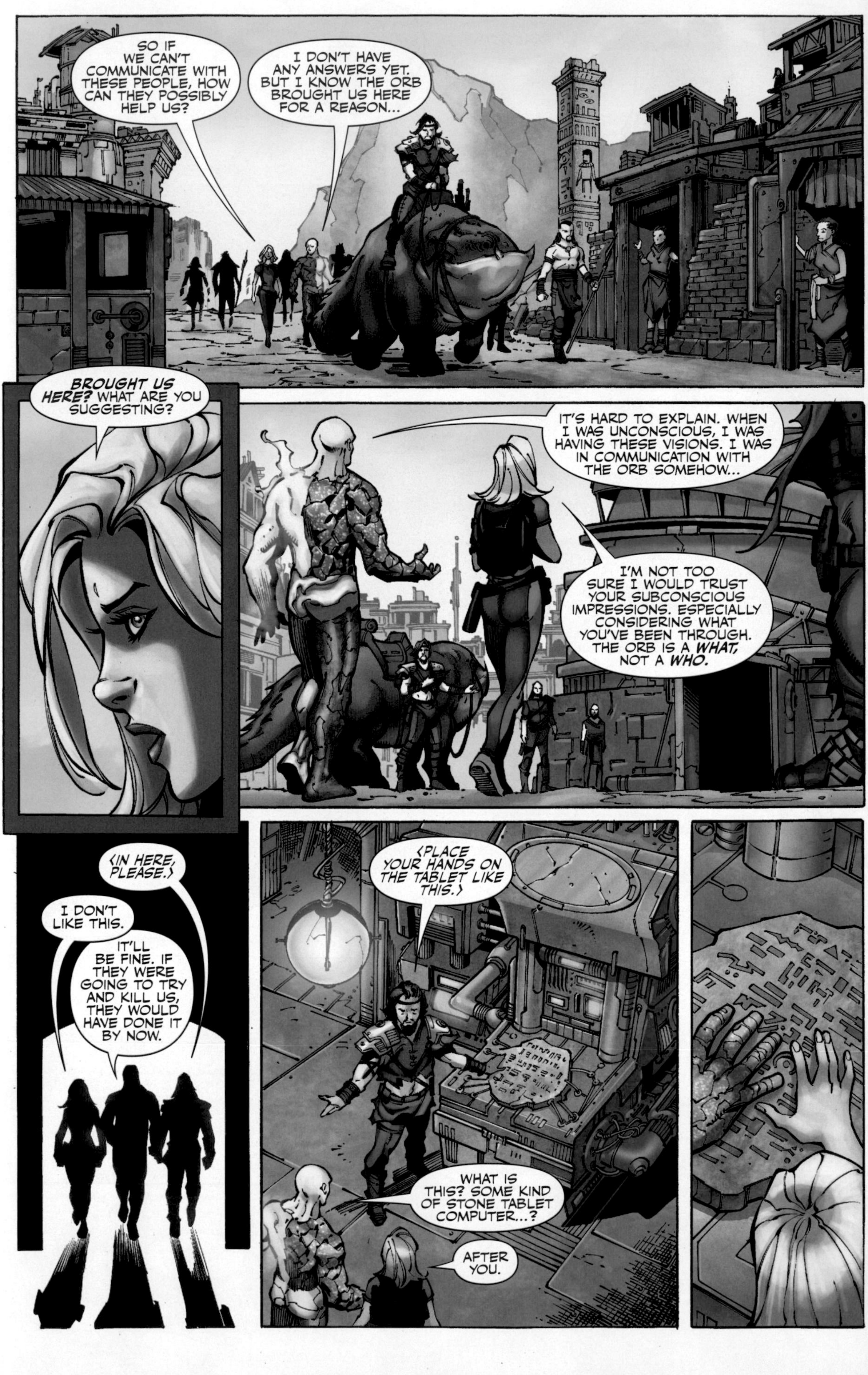
SO IF WE CAN'T COMMUNICATE WITH THESE PEOPLE, HOW CAN THEY POSSIBLY HELP US?
I DON'T HAVE ANY ANSWERS YET. BUT I KNOW THE ORB BROUGHT US HERE FOR A REASON...
BROUGHT US HERE? WHAT ARE YOU SUGGESTING?
IT'S HARD TO EXPLAIN. WHEN I WAS UNCONSCIOUS, I WAS HAVING THESE VISIONS. I WAS IN COMMUNICATION WITH THE ORB SOMEHOW...
I'M NOT TOO SURE I WOULD TRUST YOUR SUBCONSCIOUS IMPRESSIONS. ESPECIALLY CONSIDERING WHAT YOU'VE BEEN THROUGH. THE ORB IS A WHAT, NOT A WHO.
<IN HERE, PLEASE.>
I DON'T LIKE THIS.
IT'LL BE FINE. IF THEY WERE GOING TO TRY AND KILL US, THEY WOULD HAVE DONE IT BY NOW.
<PLACE YOUR HANDS ON THE TABLET LIKE THIS.>
WHAT IS THIS? SOME KIND OF STONE TABLET COMPUTER...?
AFTER YOU.

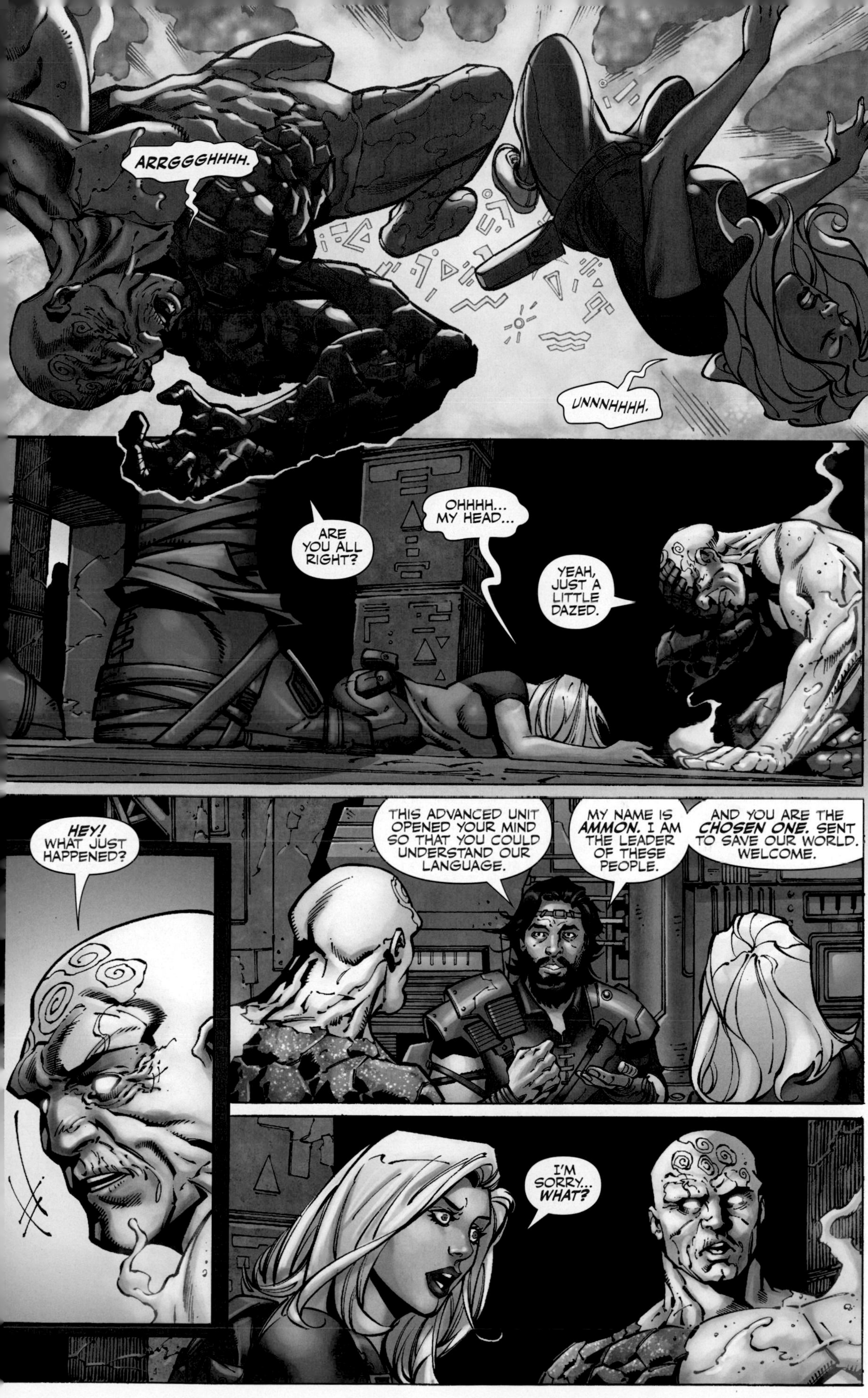

ARRGGGHHHH.
UNNNHHHH.
ARE YOU ALL RIGHT?
OHHHH... MY HEAD...
YEAH, JUST A LITTLE DAZED.
HEY! WHAT JUST HAPPENED?
THIS ADVANCED UNIT OPENED YOUR MIND SO THAT YOU COULD UNDERSTAND OUR LANGUAGE.
MY NAME IS AMMON. I AM THE LEADER OF THESE PEOPLE.
AND YOU ARE THE CHOSEN ONE. SENT TO SAVE OUR WORLD. WELCOME.
I'M SORRY... WHAT?

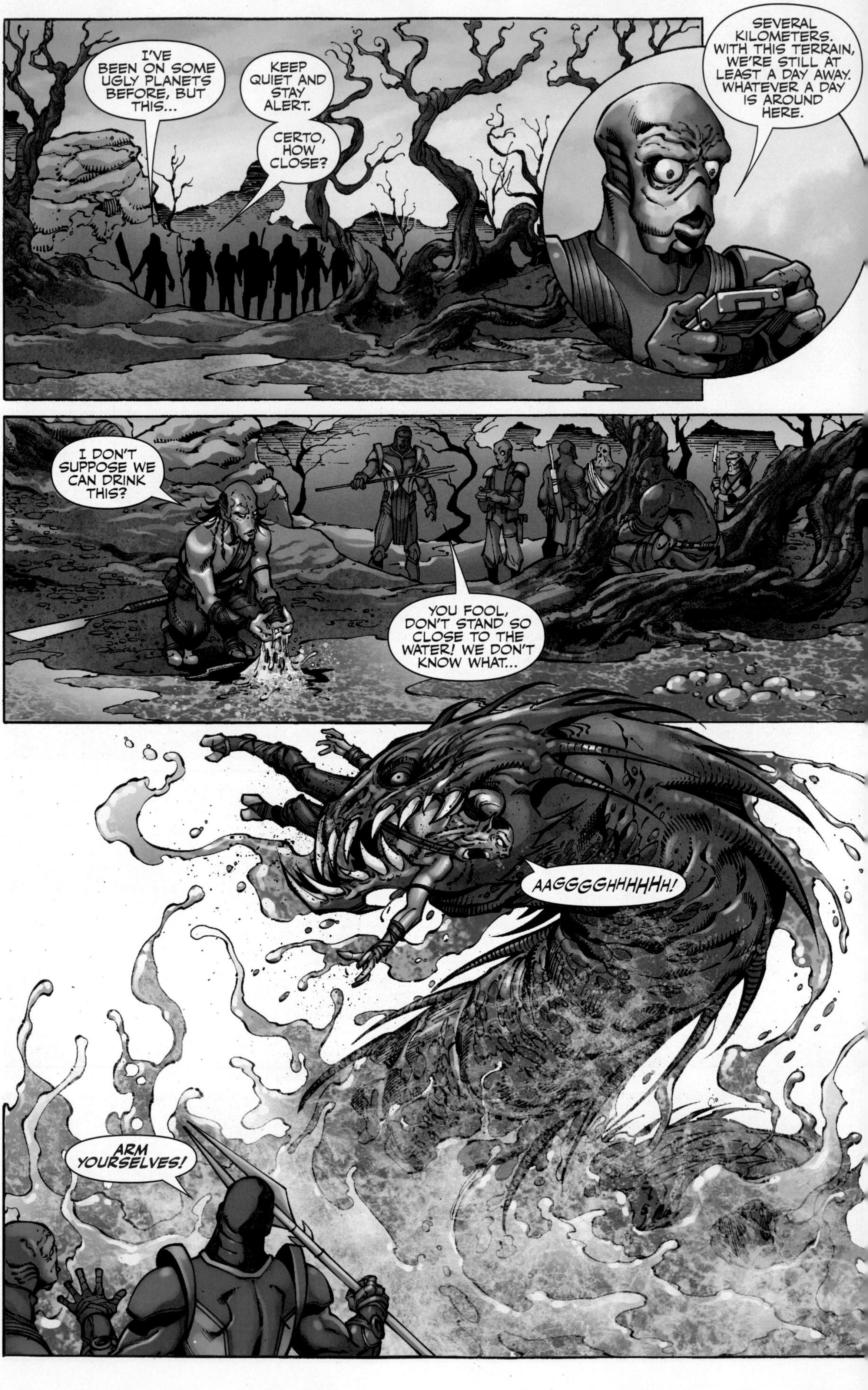
I'VE BEEN ON SOME UGLY PLANETS BEFORE, BUT THIS...
KEEP QUIET AND STAY ALERT.
CERTO, HOW CLOSE?
SEVERAL KILOMETERS. WITH THIS TERRAIN, WE'RE STILL AT LEAST A DAY AWAY. WHATEVER A DAY IS AROUND HERE.
I DON'T SUPPOSE WE CAN DRINK THIS?
YOU FOOL, DON'T STAND SO CLOSE TO THE WATER! WE DON'T KNOW WHAT...
AAGGGGHHHHHH!
ARM YOURSELVES!

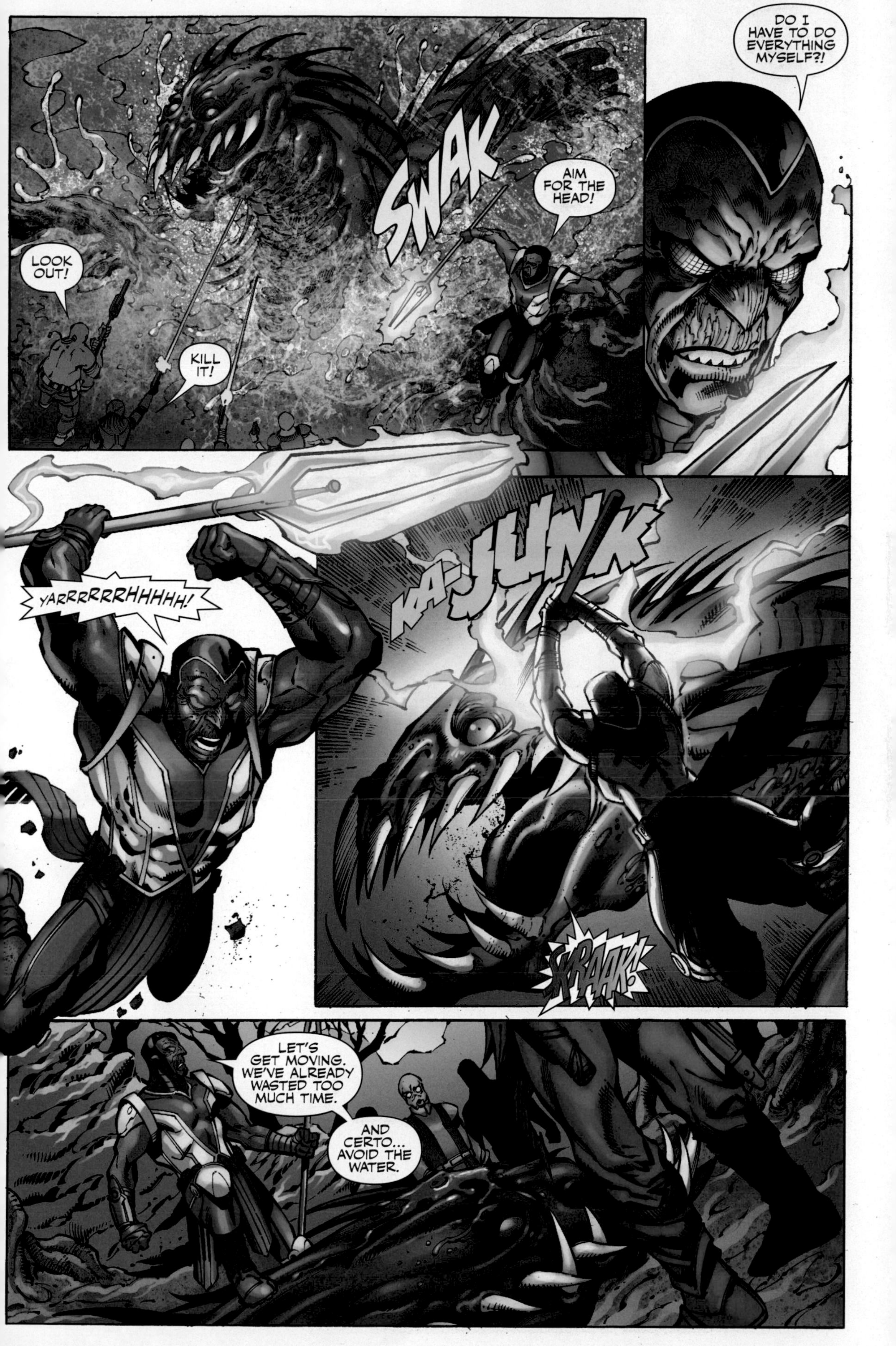
DO I HAVE TO DO EVERYTHING MYSELF?!
SWAK
AIM FOR THE HEAD!
LOOK OUT!
KILL IT!
YARRRRRRHHHHH!
KA-JUNK
SKRAAK!
LET'S GET MOVING. WE'VE ALREADY WASTED TOO MUCH TIME.
AND CERTO... AVOID THE WATER.

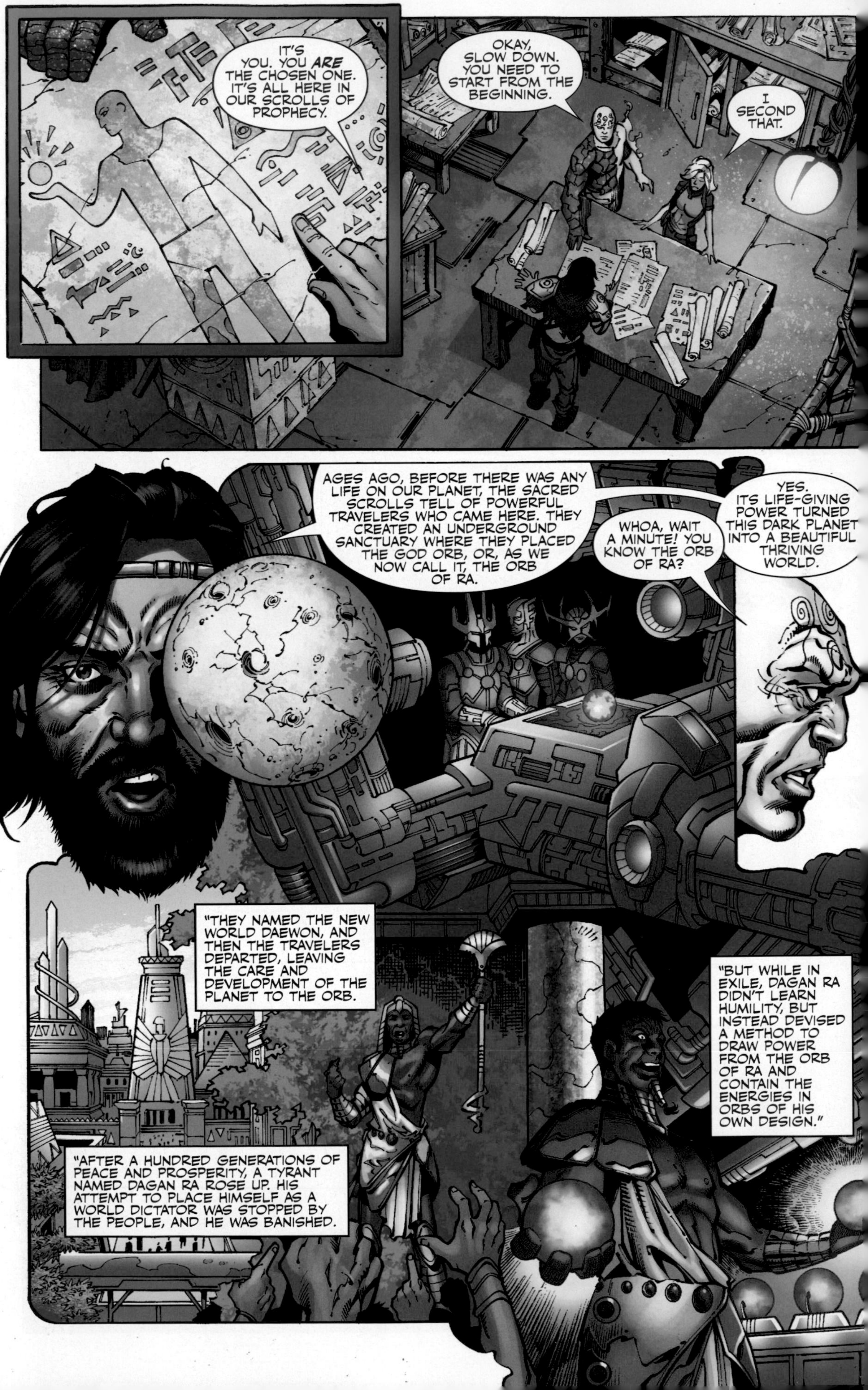
IT'S YOU. YOU *ARE* THE CHOSEN ONE. IT'S ALL HERE IN OUR SCROLLS OF PROPHECY.
OKAY, SLOW DOWN. YOU NEED TO START FROM THE BEGINNING.
I SECOND THAT.
AGES AGO, BEFORE THERE WAS ANY LIFE ON OUR PLANET, THE SACRED SCROLLS TELL OF POWERFUL TRAVELERS WHO CAME HERE. THEY CREATED AN UNDERGROUND SANCTUARY WHERE THEY PLACED THE GOD ORB, OR, AS WE NOW CALL IT, THE ORB OF RA.
WHOA, WAIT A MINUTE! YOU KNOW THE ORB OF RA?
YES. ITS LIFE-GIVING POWER TURNED THIS DARK PLANET INTO A BEAUTIFUL THRIVING WORLD.
"THEY NAMED THE NEW WORLD DAEWON, AND THEN THE TRAVELERS DEPARTED, LEAVING THE CARE AND DEVELOPMENT OF THE PLANET TO THE ORB.
"AFTER A HUNDRED GENERATIONS OF PEACE AND PROSPERITY, A TYRANT NAMED DAGAN RA ROSE UP. HIS ATTEMPT TO PLACE HIMSELF AS A WORLD DICTATOR WAS STOPPED BY THE PEOPLE, AND HE WAS BANISHED.
"BUT WHILE IN EXILE, DAGAN RA DIDN'T LEARN HUMILITY, BUT INSTEAD DEVISED A METHOD TO DRAW POWER FROM THE ORB OF RA AND CONTAIN THE ENERGIES IN ORBS OF HIS OWN DESIGN."

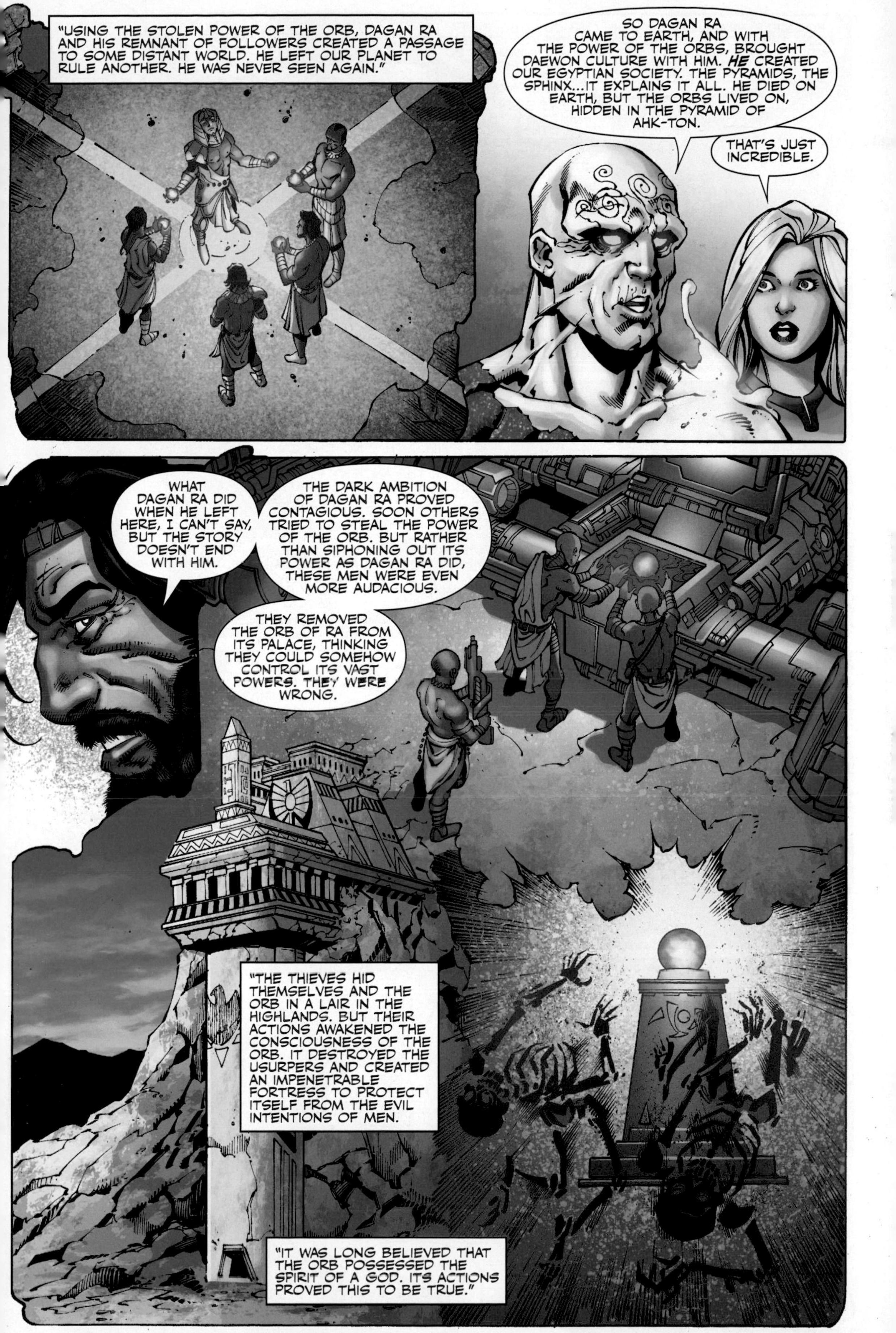
"USING THE STOLEN POWER OF THE ORB, DAGAN RA AND HIS REMNANT OF FOLLOWERS CREATED A PASSAGE TO SOME DISTANT WORLD. HE LEFT OUR PLANET TO RULE ANOTHER. HE WAS NEVER SEEN AGAIN."
SO DAGAN RA CAME TO EARTH, AND WITH THE POWER OF THE ORBS, BROUGHT DAEWON CULTURE WITH HIM. HE CREATED OUR EGYPTIAN SOCIETY. THE PYRAMIDS, THE SPHINX...IT EXPLAINS IT ALL. HE DIED ON EARTH, BUT THE ORBS LIVED ON, HIDDEN IN THE PYRAMID OF AHK-TON.
THAT'S JUST INCREDIBLE.
WHAT DAGAN RA DID WHEN HE LEFT HERE, I CAN'T SAY, BUT THE STORY DOESN'T END WITH HIM.
THE DARK AMBITION OF DAGAN RA PROVED CONTAGIOUS. SOON OTHERS TRIED TO STEAL THE POWER OF THE ORB. BUT RATHER THAN SIPHONING OUT ITS POWER AS DAGAN RA DID, THESE MEN WERE EVEN MORE AUDACIOUS.
THEY REMOVED THE ORB OF RA FROM ITS PALACE, THINKING THEY COULD SOMEHOW CONTROL ITS VAST POWERS. THEY WERE WRONG.
"THE THIEVES HID THEMSELVES AND THE ORB IN A LAIR IN THE HIGHLANDS. BUT THEIR ACTIONS AWAKENED THE CONSCIOUSNESS OF THE ORB. IT DESTROYED THE USURPERS AND CREATED AN IMPENETRABLE FORTRESS TO PROTECT ITSELF FROM THE EVIL INTENTIONS OF MEN.
"IT WAS LONG BELIEVED THAT THE ORB POSSESSED THE SPIRIT OF A GOD. ITS ACTIONS PROVED THIS TO BE TRUE."

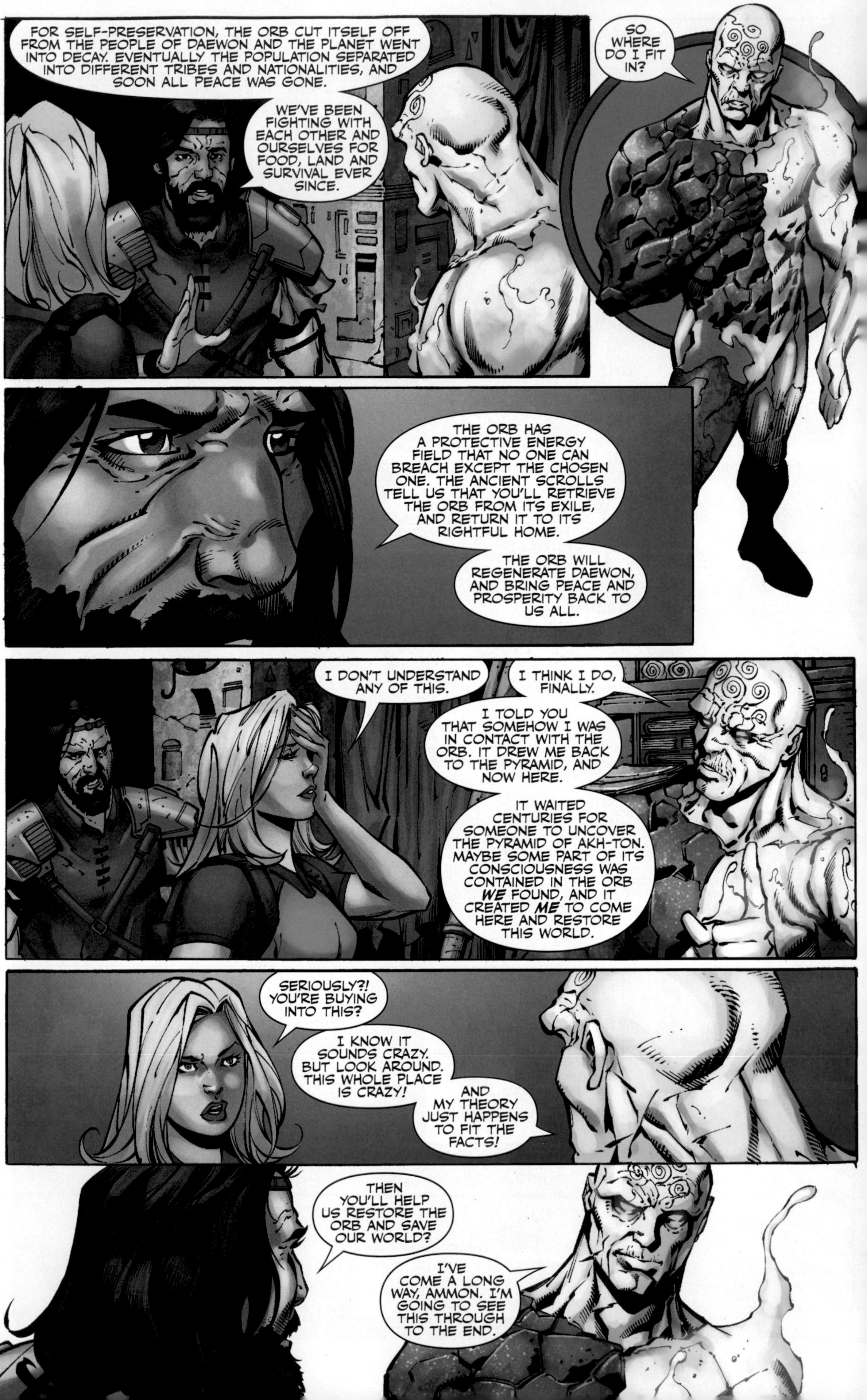
FOR SELF-PRESERVATION, THE ORB CUT ITSELF OFF FROM THE PEOPLE OF DAEWON AND THE PLANET WENT INTO DECAY. EVENTUALLY THE POPULATION SEPARATED INTO DIFFERENT TRIBES AND NATIONALITIES, AND SOON ALL PEACE WAS GONE.
WE'VE BEEN FIGHTING WITH EACH OTHER AND OURSELVES FOR FOOD, LAND AND SURVIVAL EVER SINCE.
SO WHERE DO I FIT IN?
THE ORB HAS A PROTECTIVE ENERGY FIELD THAT NO ONE CAN BREACH EXCEPT THE CHOSEN ONE. THE ANCIENT SCROLLS TELL US THAT YOU'LL RETRIEVE THE ORB FROM ITS EXILE, AND RETURN IT TO ITS RIGHTFUL HOME.
THE ORB WILL REGENERATE DAEWON, AND BRING PEACE AND PROSPERITY BACK TO US ALL.
I DON'T UNDERSTAND ANY OF THIS.
I THINK I DO, FINALLY.
I TOLD YOU THAT SOMEHOW I WAS IN CONTACT WITH THE ORB. IT DREW ME BACK TO THE PYRAMID, AND NOW HERE.
IT WAITED CENTURIES FOR SOMEONE TO UNCOVER THE PYRAMID OF AKH-TON. MAYBE SOME PART OF ITS CONSCIOUSNESS WAS CONTAINED IN THE ORB *WE* FOUND, AND IT CREATED *ME* TO COME HERE AND RESTORE THIS WORLD.
SERIOUSLY?! YOU'RE BUYING INTO THIS?
I KNOW IT SOUNDS CRAZY. BUT LOOK AROUND. THIS WHOLE PLACE IS CRAZY!
AND MY THEORY JUST HAPPENS TO FIT THE FACTS!
THEN YOU'LL HELP US RESTORE THE ORB AND SAVE OUR WORLD?
I'VE COME A LONG WAY, AMMON. I'M GOING TO SEE THIS THROUGH TO THE END.

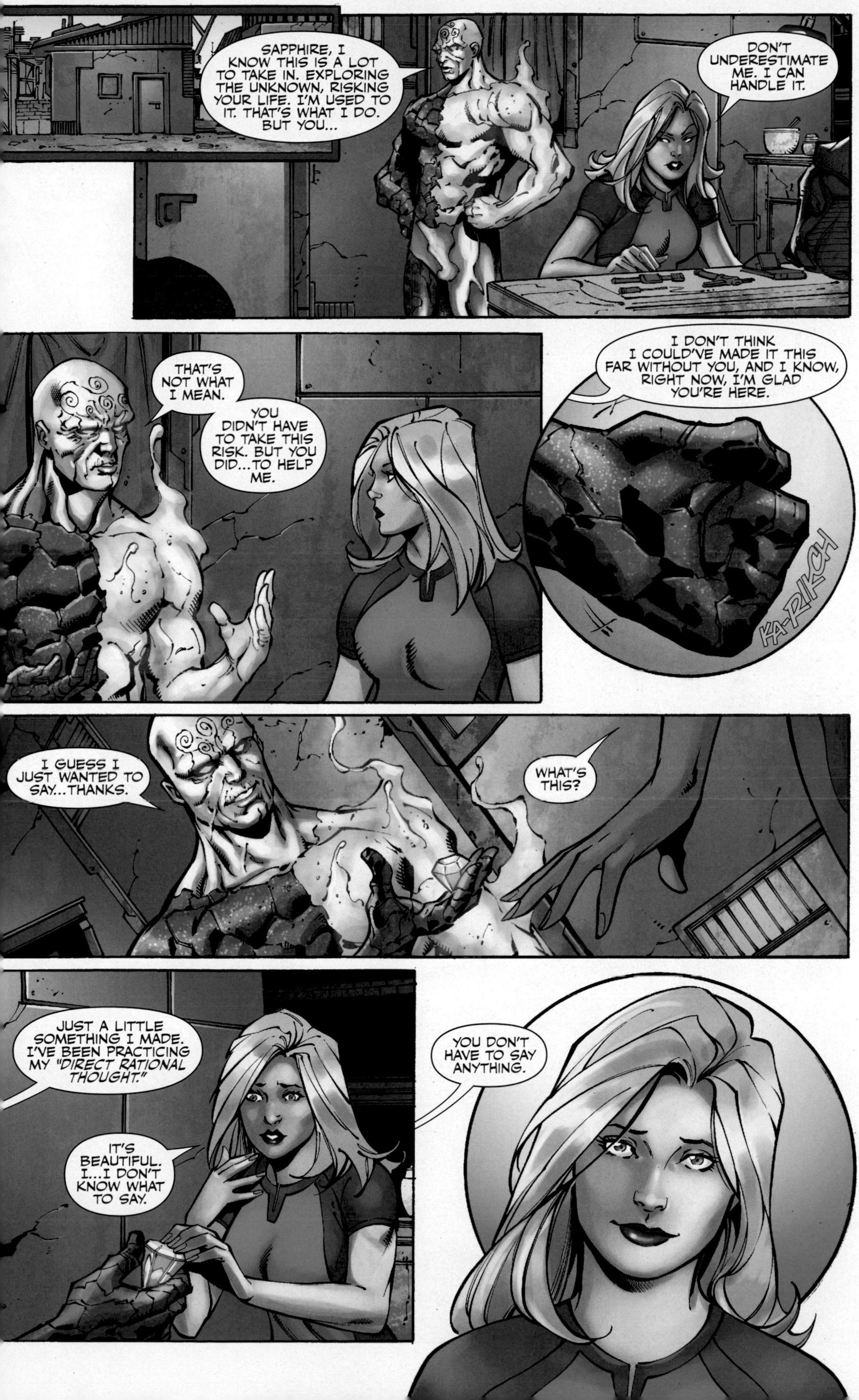
SAPPHIRE, I KNOW THIS IS A LOT TO TAKE IN. EXPLORING THE UNKNOWN, RISKING YOUR LIFE. I'M USED TO IT. THAT'S WHAT I DO. BUT YOU...
DON'T UNDERESTIMATE ME. I CAN HANDLE IT.
THAT'S NOT WHAT I MEAN.
YOU DIDN'T HAVE TO TAKE THIS RISK. BUT YOU DID...TO HELP ME.
I DON'T THINK I COULD'VE MADE IT THIS FAR WITHOUT YOU, AND I KNOW, RIGHT NOW, I'M GLAD YOU'RE HERE.
KA-RIKCH
I GUESS I JUST WANTED TO SAY...THANKS.
WHAT'S THIS?
JUST A LITTLE SOMETHING I MADE. I'VE BEEN PRACTICING MY "DIRECT RATIONAL THOUGHT."
IT'S BEAUTIFUL. I...I DON'T KNOW WHAT TO SAY.
YOU DON'T HAVE TO SAY ANYTHING.

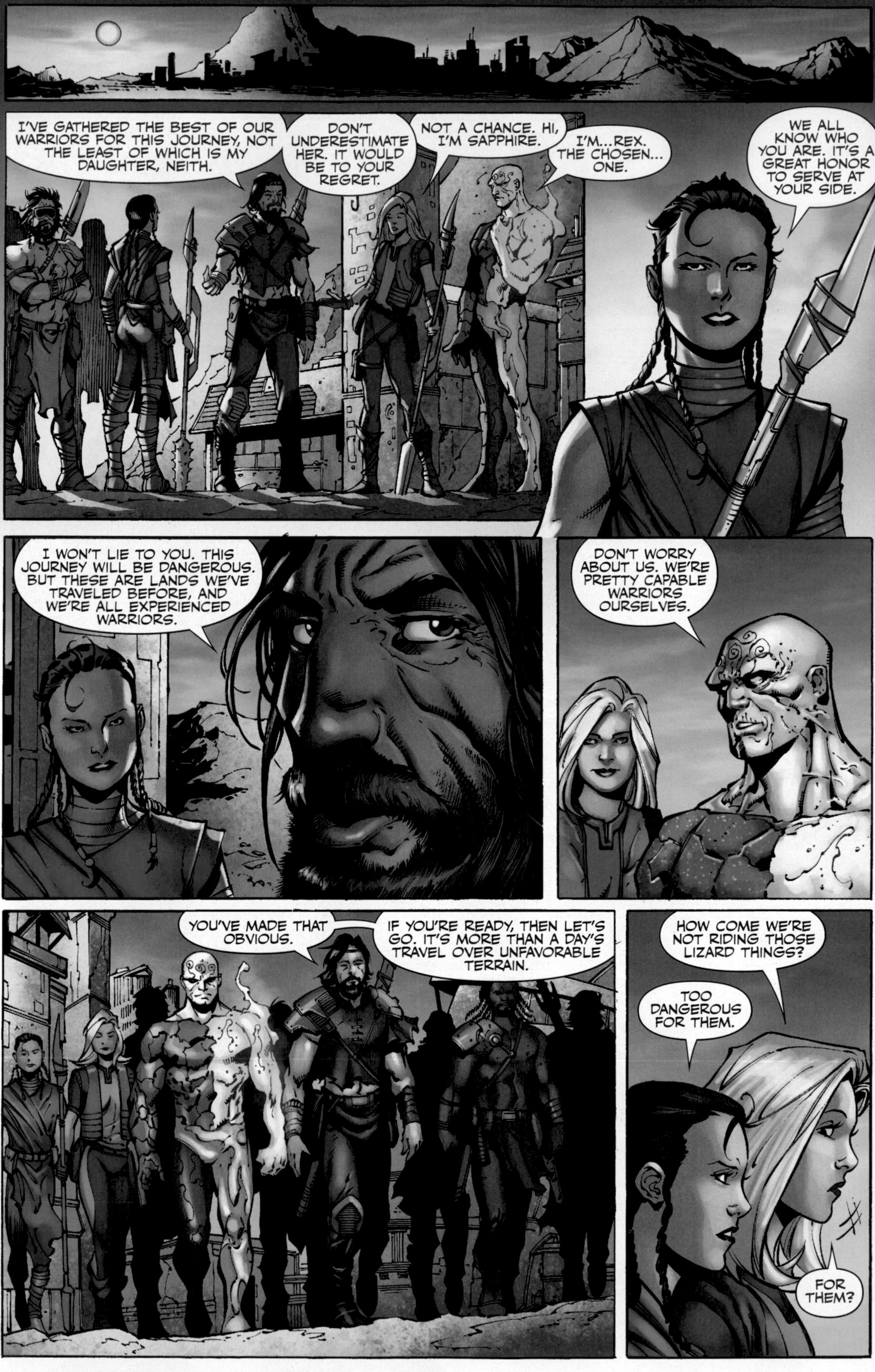
I'VE GATHERED THE BEST OF OUR WARRIORS FOR THIS JOURNEY, NOT THE LEAST OF WHICH IS MY DAUGHTER, NEITH.
DON'T UNDERESTIMATE HER. IT WOULD BE TO YOUR REGRET.
NOT A CHANCE. HI, I'M SAPPHIRE.
I'M...REX. THE CHOSEN... ONE.
WE ALL KNOW WHO YOU ARE. IT'S A GREAT HONOR TO SERVE AT YOUR SIDE.
I WON'T LIE TO YOU. THIS JOURNEY WILL BE DANGEROUS. BUT THESE ARE LANDS WE'VE TRAVELED BEFORE, AND WE'RE ALL EXPERIENCED WARRIORS.
DON'T WORRY ABOUT US. WE'RE PRETTY CAPABLE WARRIORS OURSELVES.
YOU'VE MADE THAT OBVIOUS.
IF YOU'RE READY, THEN LET'S GO. IT'S MORE THAN A DAY'S TRAVEL OVER UNFAVORABLE TERRAIN.
HOW COME WE'RE NOT RIDING THOSE LIZARD THINGS?
TOO DANGEROUS FOR THEM.
FOR THEM?

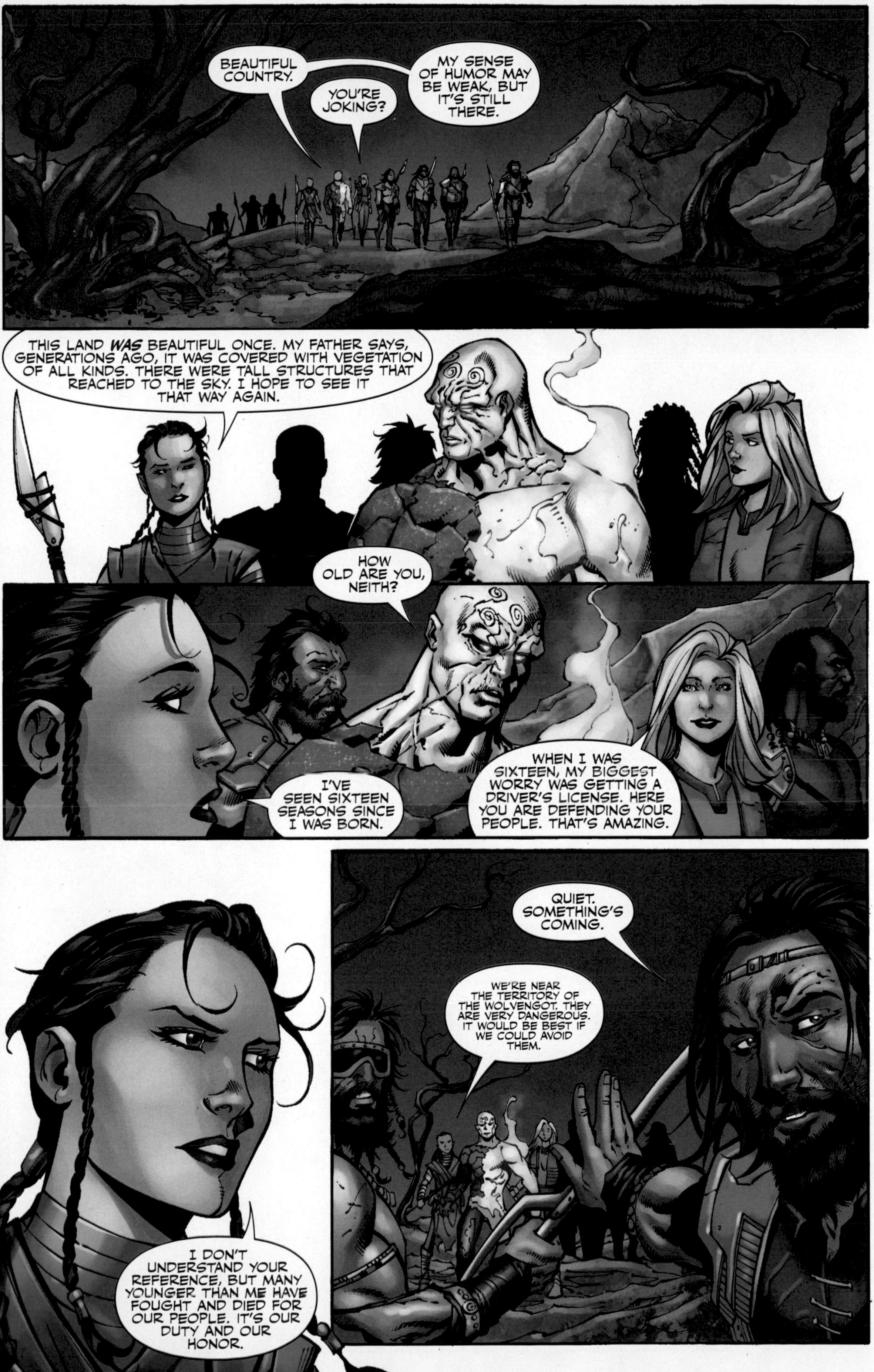
BEAUTIFUL COUNTRY.
YOU'RE JOKING?
MY SENSE OF HUMOR MAY BE WEAK, BUT IT'S STILL THERE.
THIS LAND WAS BEAUTIFUL ONCE. MY FATHER SAYS, GENERATIONS AGO, IT WAS COVERED WITH VEGETATION OF ALL KINDS. THERE WERE TALL STRUCTURES THAT REACHED TO THE SKY. I HOPE TO SEE IT THAT WAY AGAIN.
HOW OLD ARE YOU, NEITH?
I'VE SEEN SIXTEEN SEASONS SINCE I WAS BORN.
WHEN I WAS SIXTEEN, MY BIGGEST WORRY WAS GETTING A DRIVER'S LICENSE. HERE YOU ARE DEFENDING YOUR PEOPLE. THAT'S AMAZING.
I DON'T UNDERSTAND YOUR REFERENCE, BUT MANY YOUNGER THAN ME HAVE FOUGHT AND DIED FOR OUR PEOPLE. IT'S OUR DUTY AND OUR HONOR.
QUIET. SOMETHING'S COMING.
WE'RE NEAR THE TERRITORY OF THE WOLVENGOT. THEY ARE VERY DANGEROUS. IT WOULD BE BEST IF WE COULD AVOID THEM.

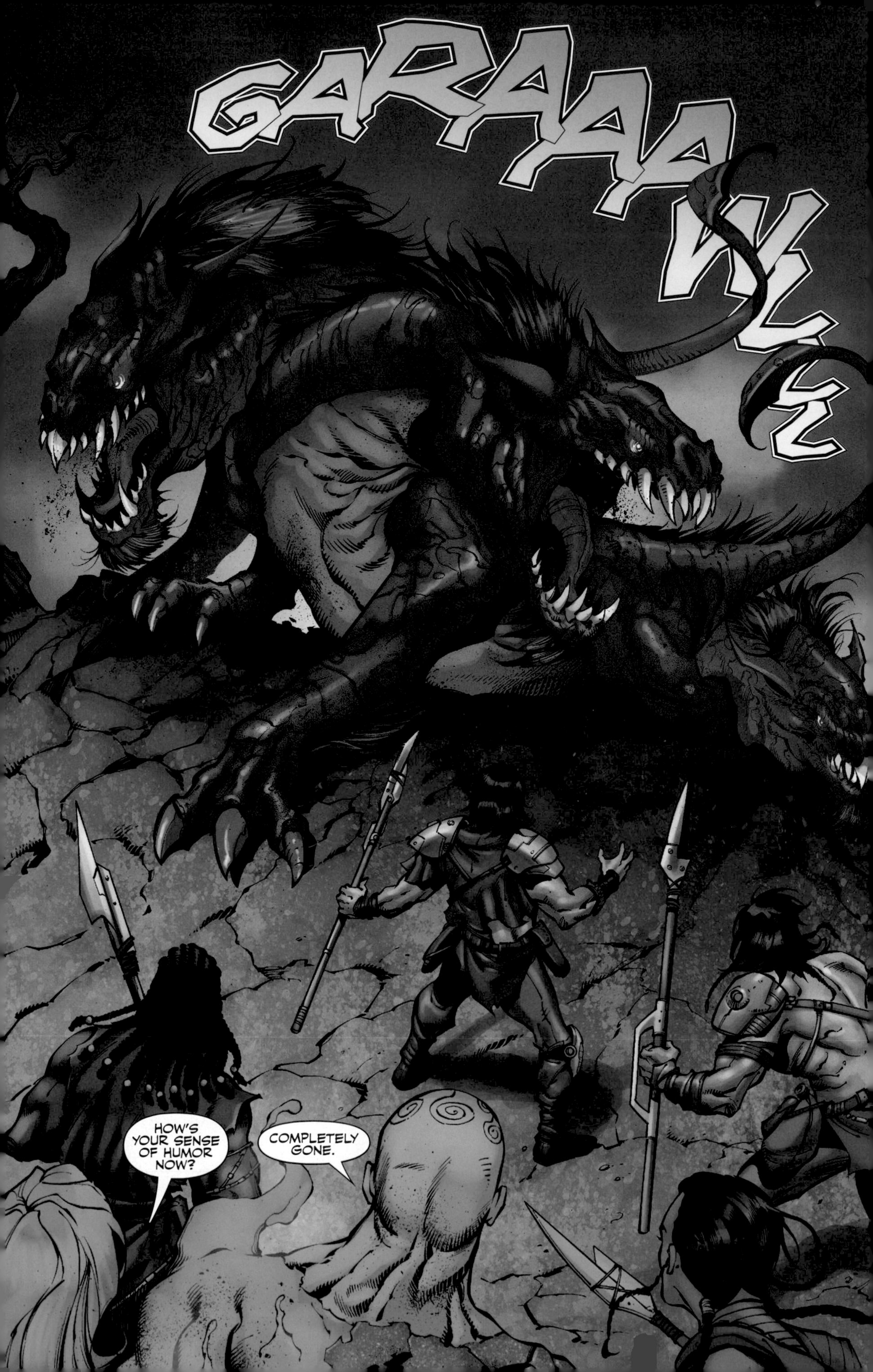
GARAAAWL
HOW'S YOUR SENSE OF HUMOR NOW?
COMPLETELY GONE.

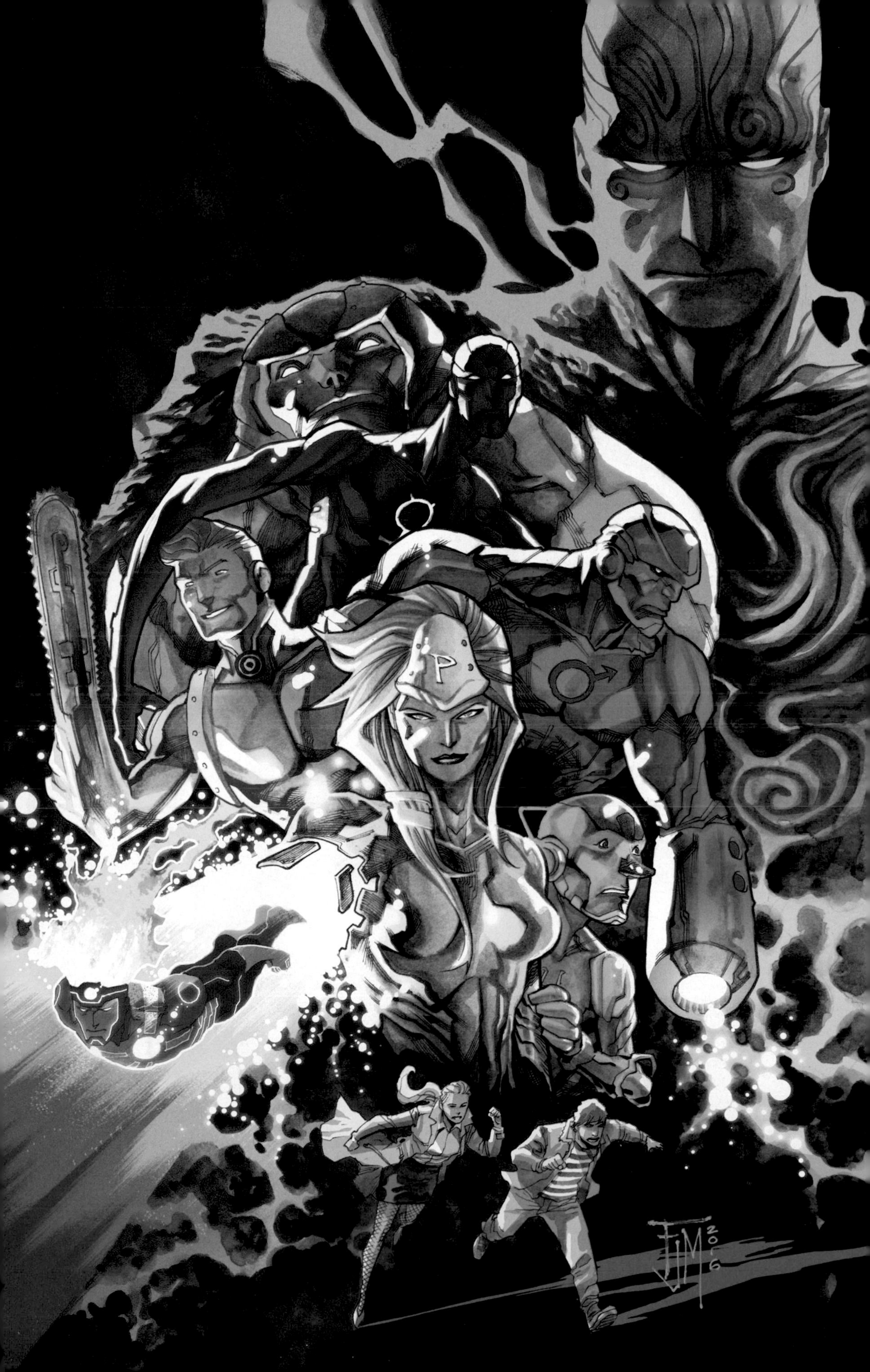

QUEST FOR POWER

AARON LOPRESTI writer/penciller AARON LOPRESTI and LIVESAY inkers CHRIS SOTOMAYOR colorist MICHAEL HEISLER letterer
FRANCIS MANAPUL cover

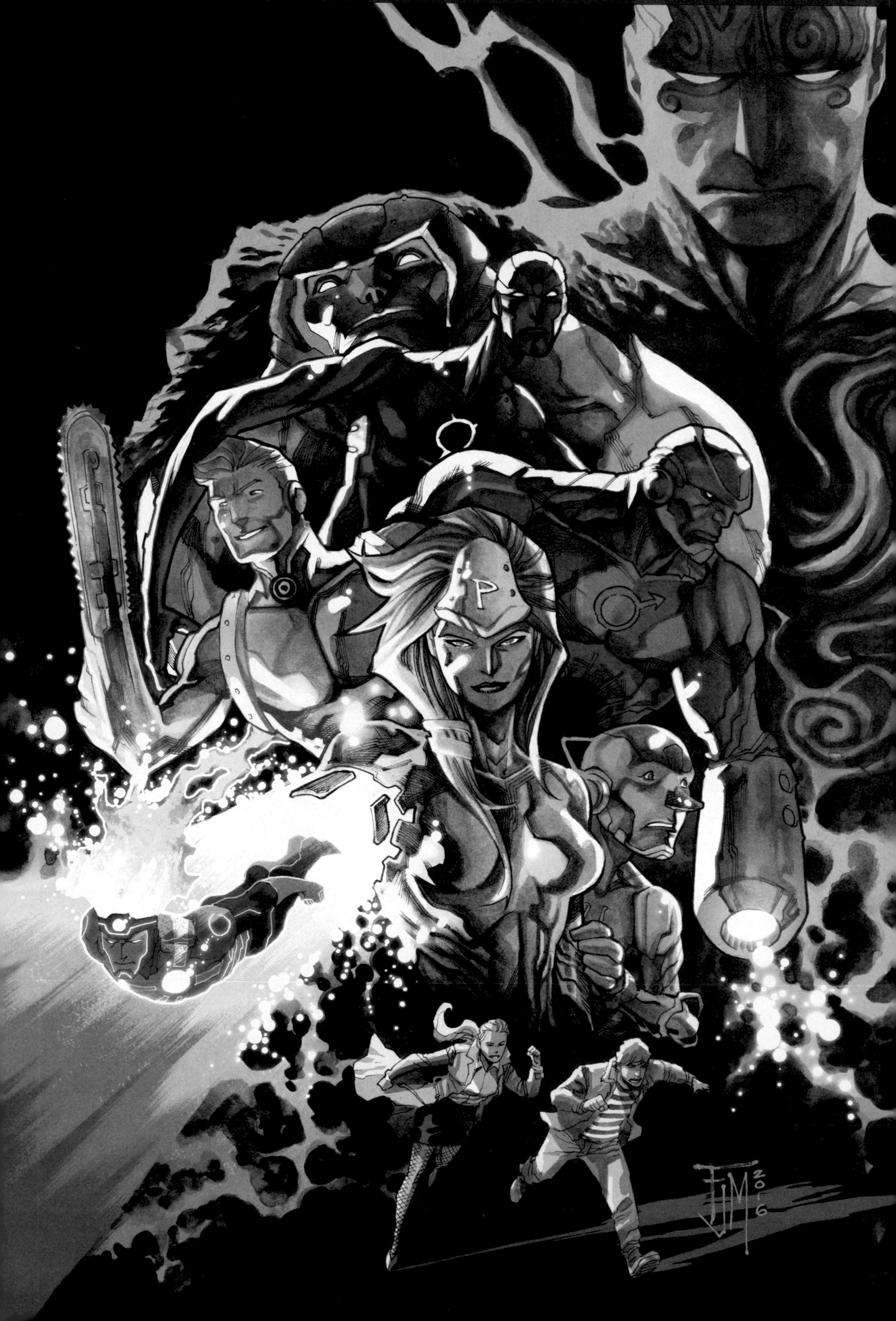
FJM
2016

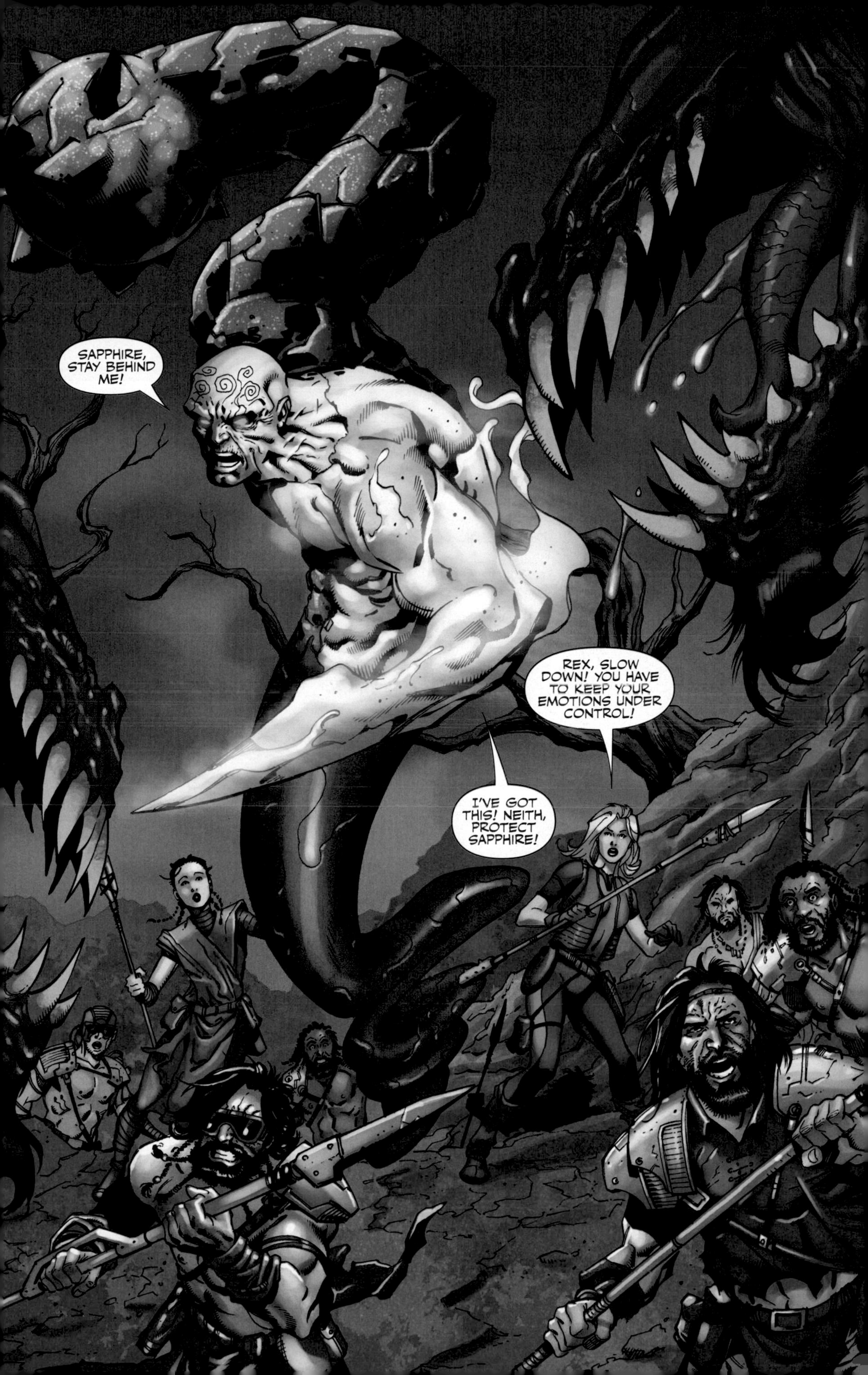
SAPPHIRE, STAY BEHIND ME!
REX, SLOW DOWN! YOU HAVE TO KEEP YOUR EMOTIONS UNDER CONTROL!
I'VE GOT THIS! NEITH, PROTECT SAPPHIRE!

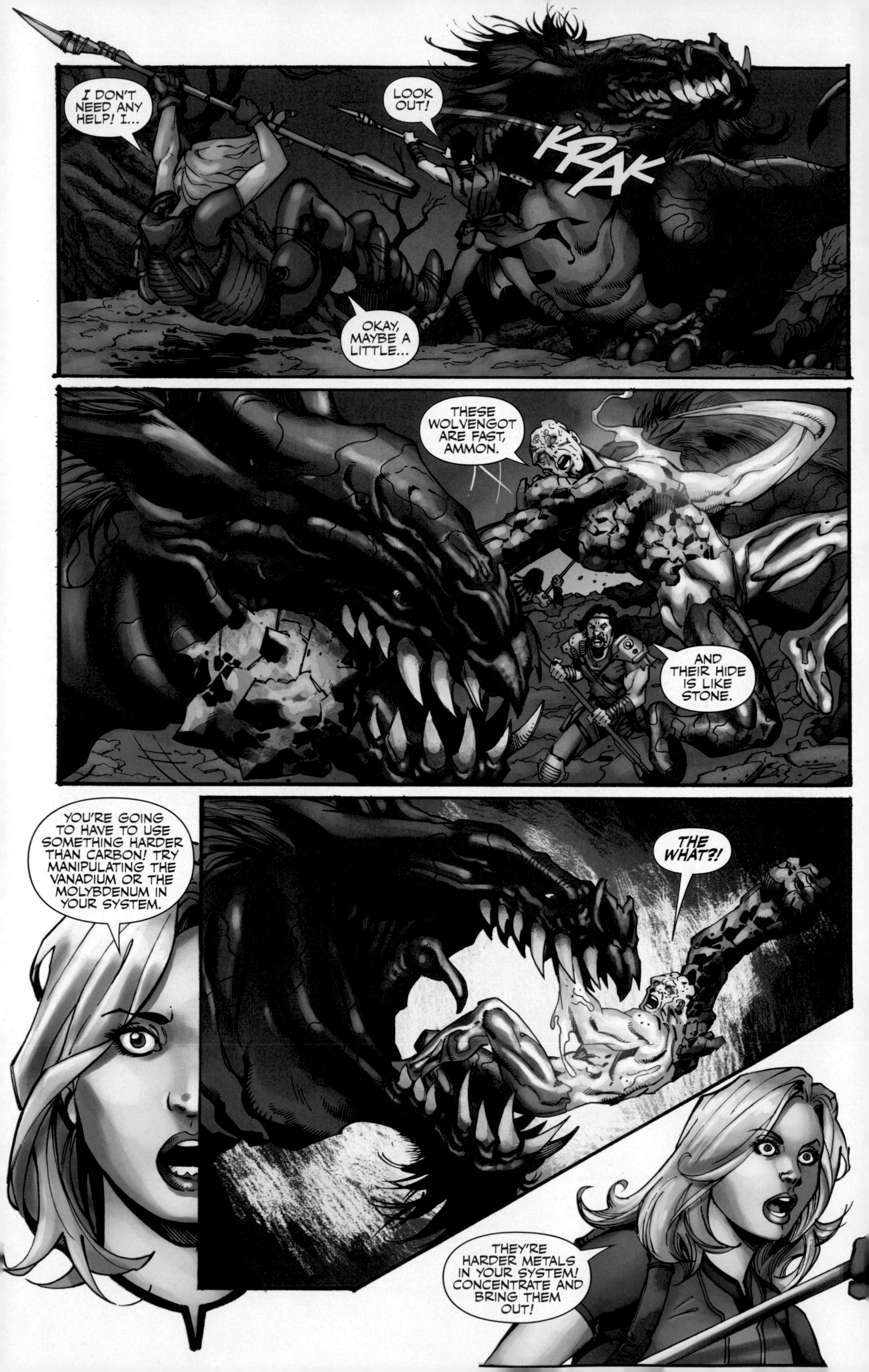
I DON'T NEED ANY HELP! I...
LOOK OUT!
KRAK
OKAY, MAYBE A LITTLE...
THESE WOLVENGOT ARE FAST, AMMON.
AND THEIR HIDE IS LIKE STONE.
YOU'RE GOING TO HAVE TO USE SOMETHING HARDER THAN CARBON! TRY MANIPULATING THE VANADIUM OR THE MOLYBDENUM IN YOUR SYSTEM.
THE WHAT?!
THEY'RE HARDER METALS IN YOUR SYSTEM! CONCENTRATE AND BRING THEM OUT!

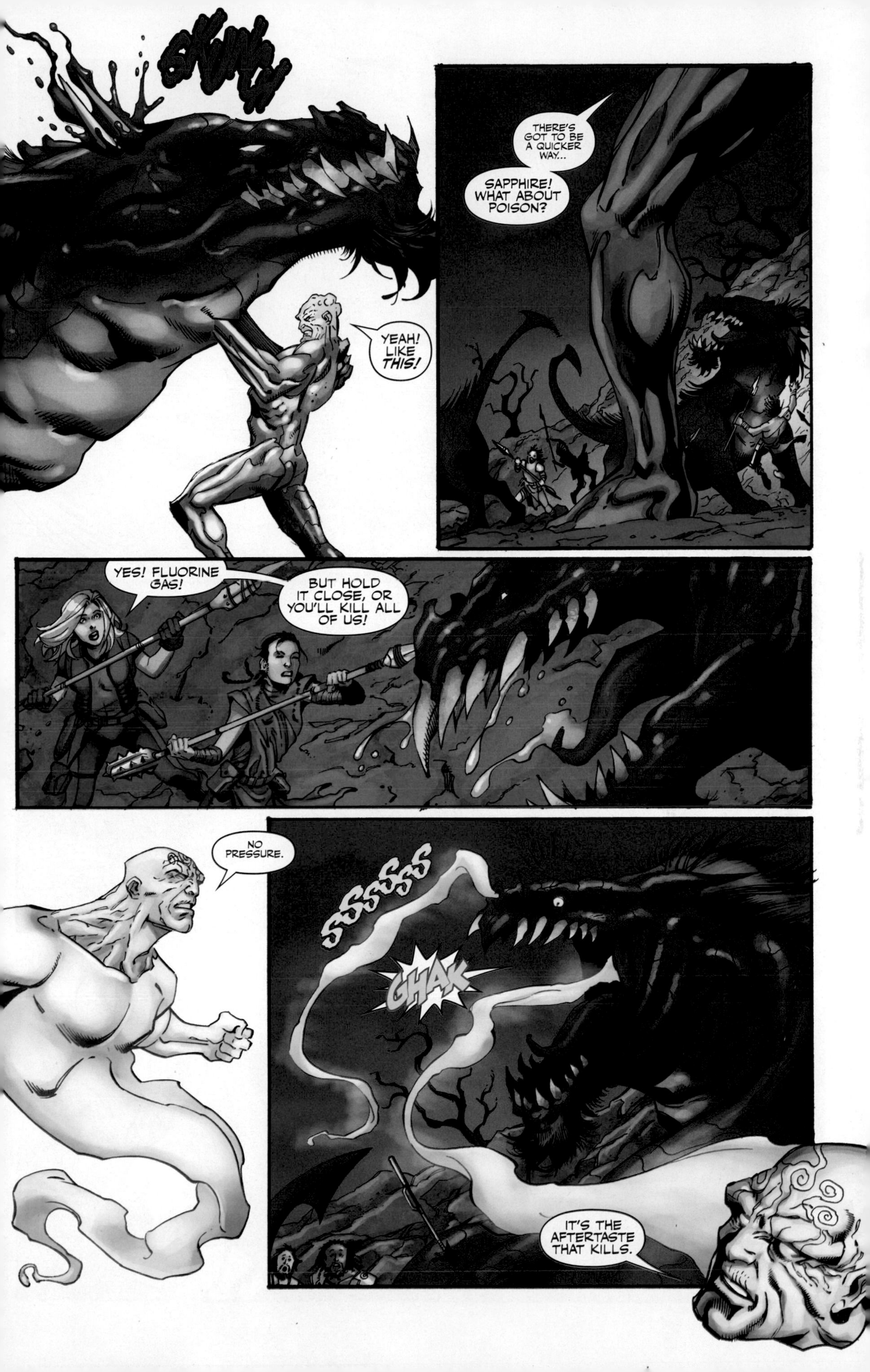
SKLNCH
YEAH! LIKE THIS!
THERE'S GOT TO BE A QUICKER WAY...
SAPPHIRE! WHAT ABOUT POISON?
YES! FLUORINE GAS!
BUT HOLD IT CLOSE, OR YOU'LL KILL ALL OF US!
NO PRESSURE.
SSSSSS
GHAK
IT'S THE AFTERTASTE THAT KILLS.

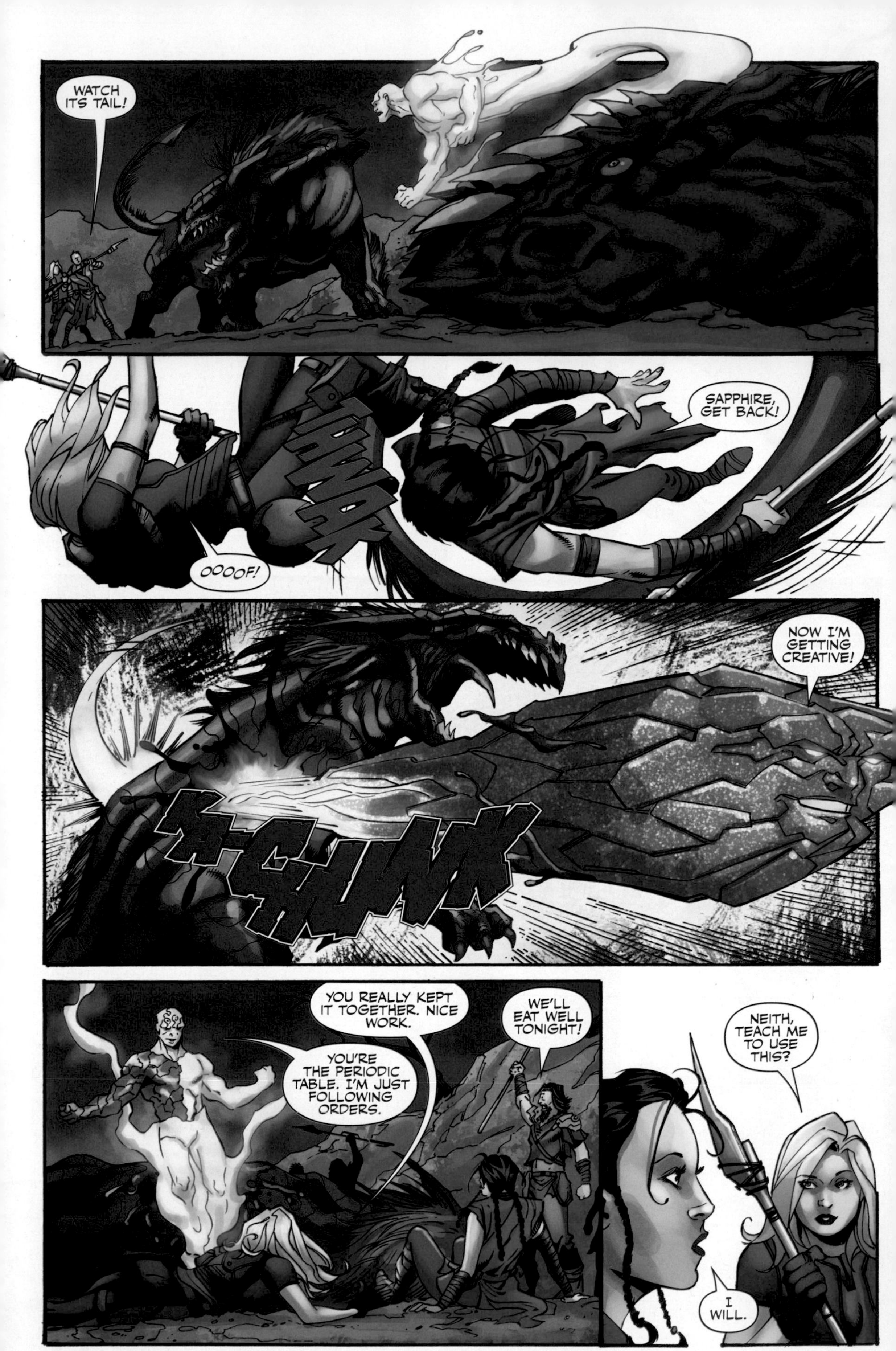
WATCH ITS TAIL!
SAPPHIRE, GET BACK!
THWAK
OOOOF!
NOW I'M GETTING CREATIVE!
K-CHUNK
YOU REALLY KEPT IT TOGETHER. NICE WORK.
YOU'RE THE PERIODIC TABLE. I'M JUST FOLLOWING ORDERS.
WE'LL EAT WELL TONIGHT!
NEITH, TEACH ME TO USE THIS?
I WILL.

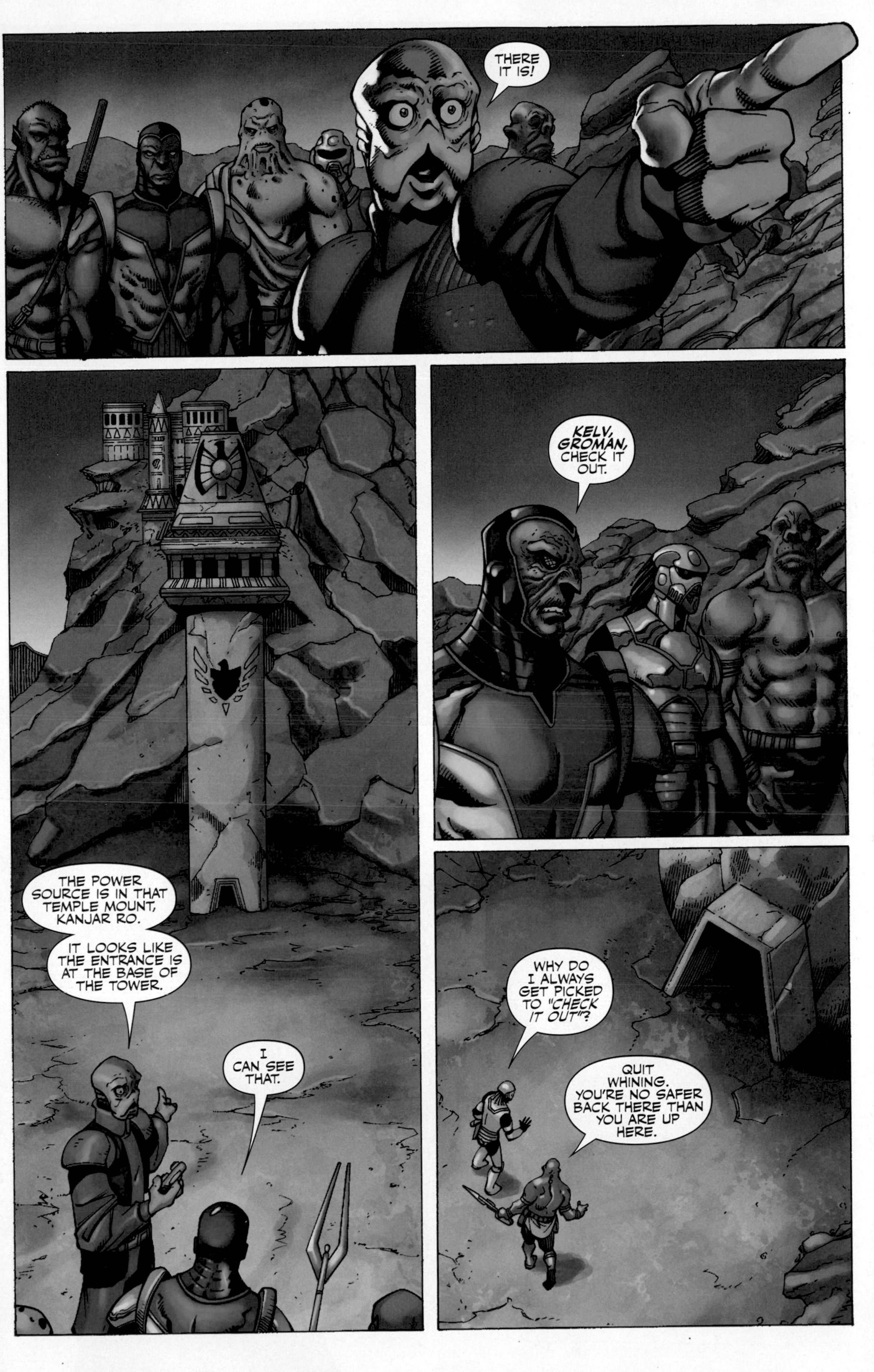
THERE IT IS!
KELV, GROMAN, CHECK IT OUT.
THE POWER SOURCE IS IN THAT TEMPLE MOUNT, KANJAR RO.
IT LOOKS LIKE THE ENTRANCE IS AT THE BASE OF THE TOWER.
I CAN SEE THAT.
WHY DO I ALWAYS GET PICKED TO "CHECK IT OUT"?
QUIT WHINING. YOU'RE NO SAFER BACK THERE THAN YOU ARE UP HERE.

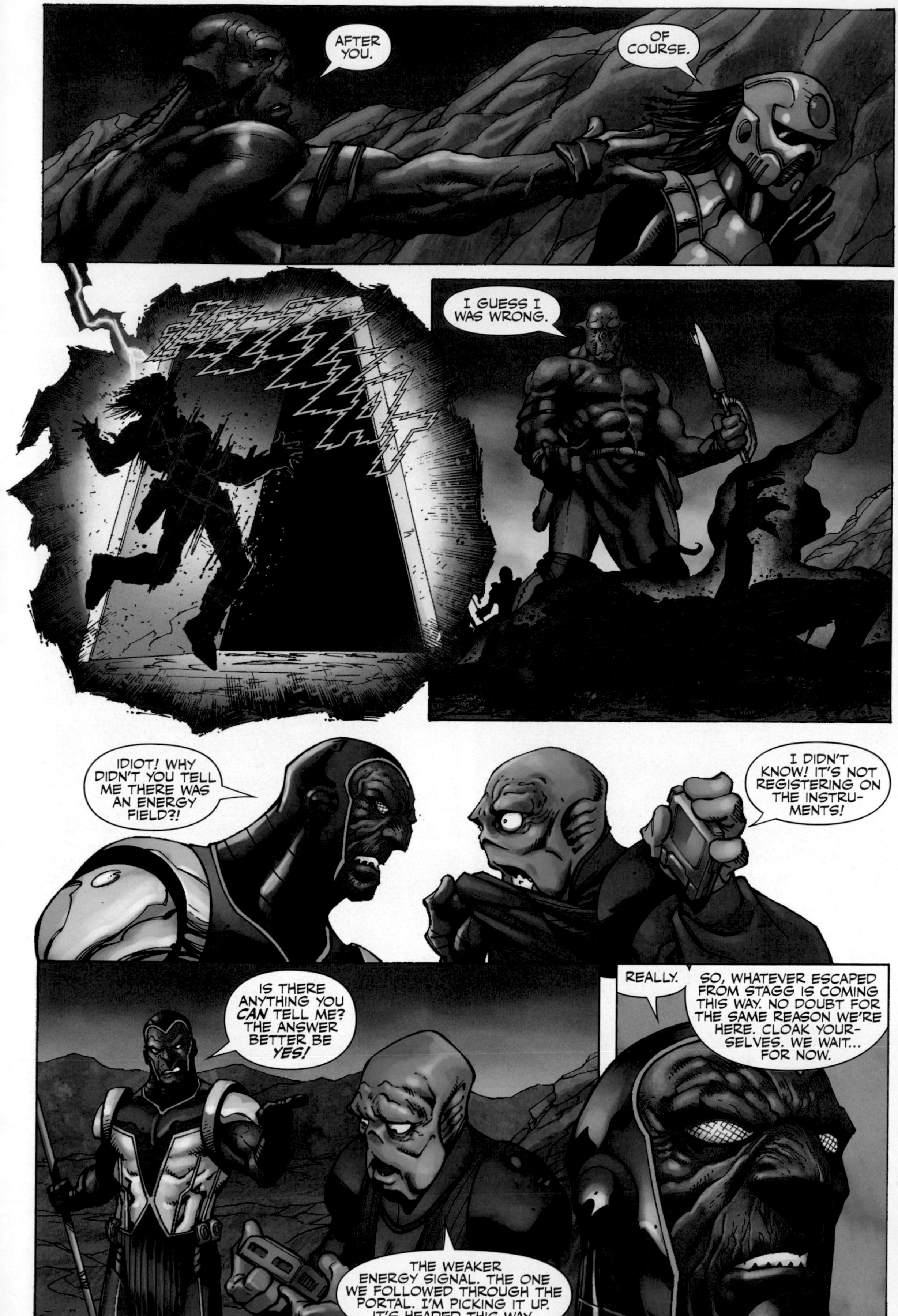
AFTER YOU.
OF COURSE.
I GUESS I WAS WRONG.
IDIOT! WHY DIDN'T YOU TELL ME THERE WAS AN ENERGY FIELD?!
I DIDN'T KNOW! IT'S NOT REGISTERING ON THE INSTRU-MENTS!
IS THERE ANYTHING YOU CAN TELL ME? THE ANSWER BETTER BE YES!
THE WEAKER ENERGY SIGNAL. THE ONE WE FOLLOWED THROUGH THE PORTAL. I'M PICKING IT UP. IT'S HEADED THIS WAY.
REALLY.
SO, WHATEVER ESCAPED FROM STAGG IS COMING THIS WAY. NO DOUBT FOR THE SAME REASON WE'RE HERE. CLOAK YOUR-SELVES. WE WAIT... FOR NOW.

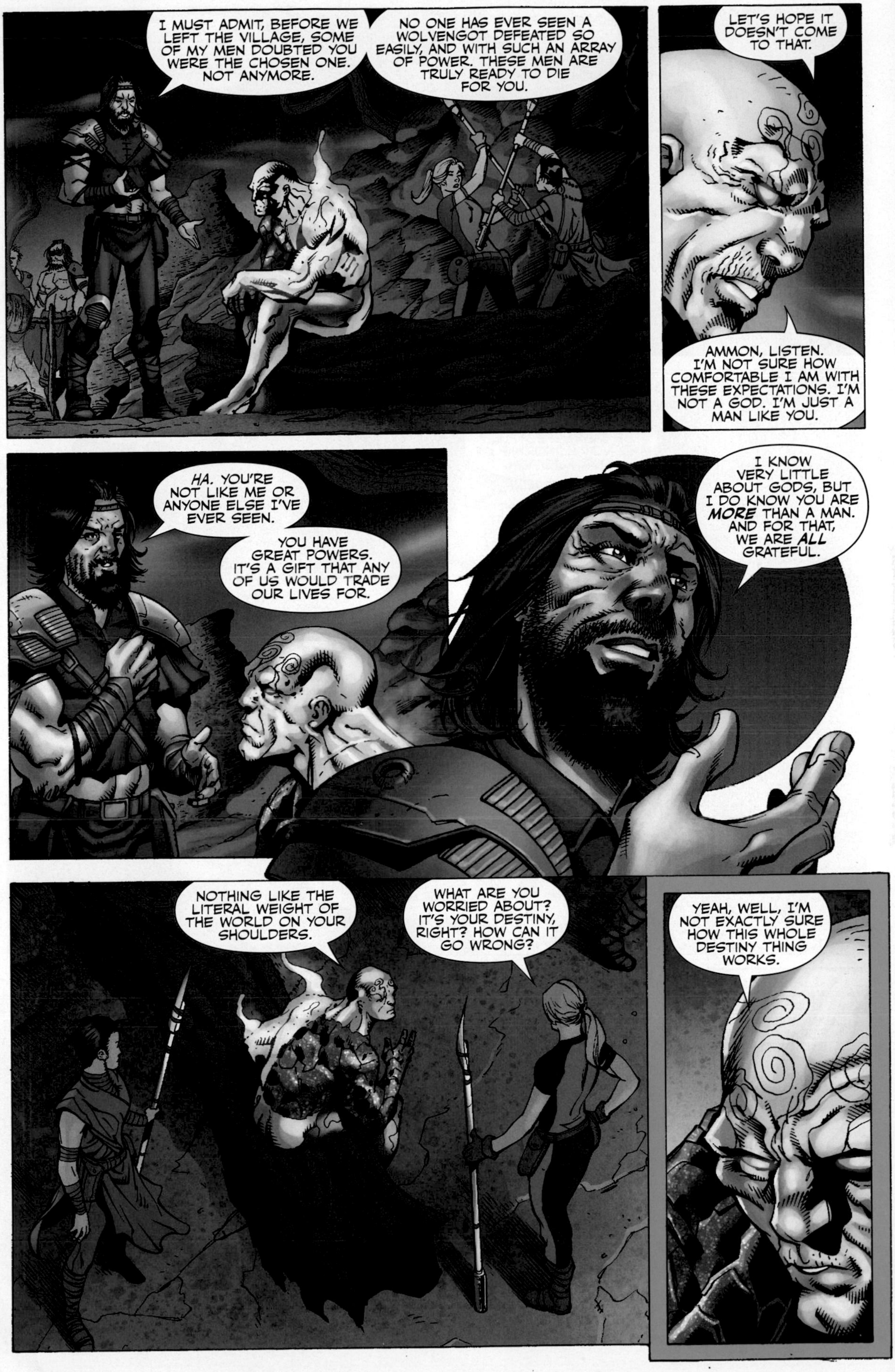
I MUST ADMIT, BEFORE WE LEFT THE VILLAGE, SOME OF MY MEN DOUBTED YOU WERE THE CHOSEN ONE. NOT ANYMORE.
NO ONE HAS EVER SEEN A WOLVENGOT DEFEATED SO EASILY, AND WITH SUCH AN ARRAY OF POWER. THESE MEN ARE TRULY READY TO DIE FOR YOU.
LET'S HOPE IT DOESN'T COME TO THAT.
AMMON, LISTEN. I'M NOT SURE HOW COMFORTABLE I AM WITH THESE EXPECTATIONS. I'M NOT A GOD. I'M JUST A MAN LIKE YOU.
HA. YOU'RE NOT LIKE ME OR ANYONE ELSE I'VE EVER SEEN.
YOU HAVE GREAT POWERS. IT'S A GIFT THAT ANY OF US WOULD TRADE OUR LIVES FOR.
I KNOW VERY LITTLE ABOUT GODS, BUT I DO KNOW YOU ARE ***MORE*** THAN A MAN. AND FOR THAT, WE ARE ***ALL*** GRATEFUL.
NOTHING LIKE THE LITERAL WEIGHT OF THE WORLD ON YOUR SHOULDERS.
WHAT ARE YOU WORRIED ABOUT? IT'S YOUR DESTINY, RIGHT? HOW CAN IT GO WRONG?
YEAH, WELL, I'M NOT EXACTLY SURE HOW THIS WHOLE DESTINY THING WORKS.

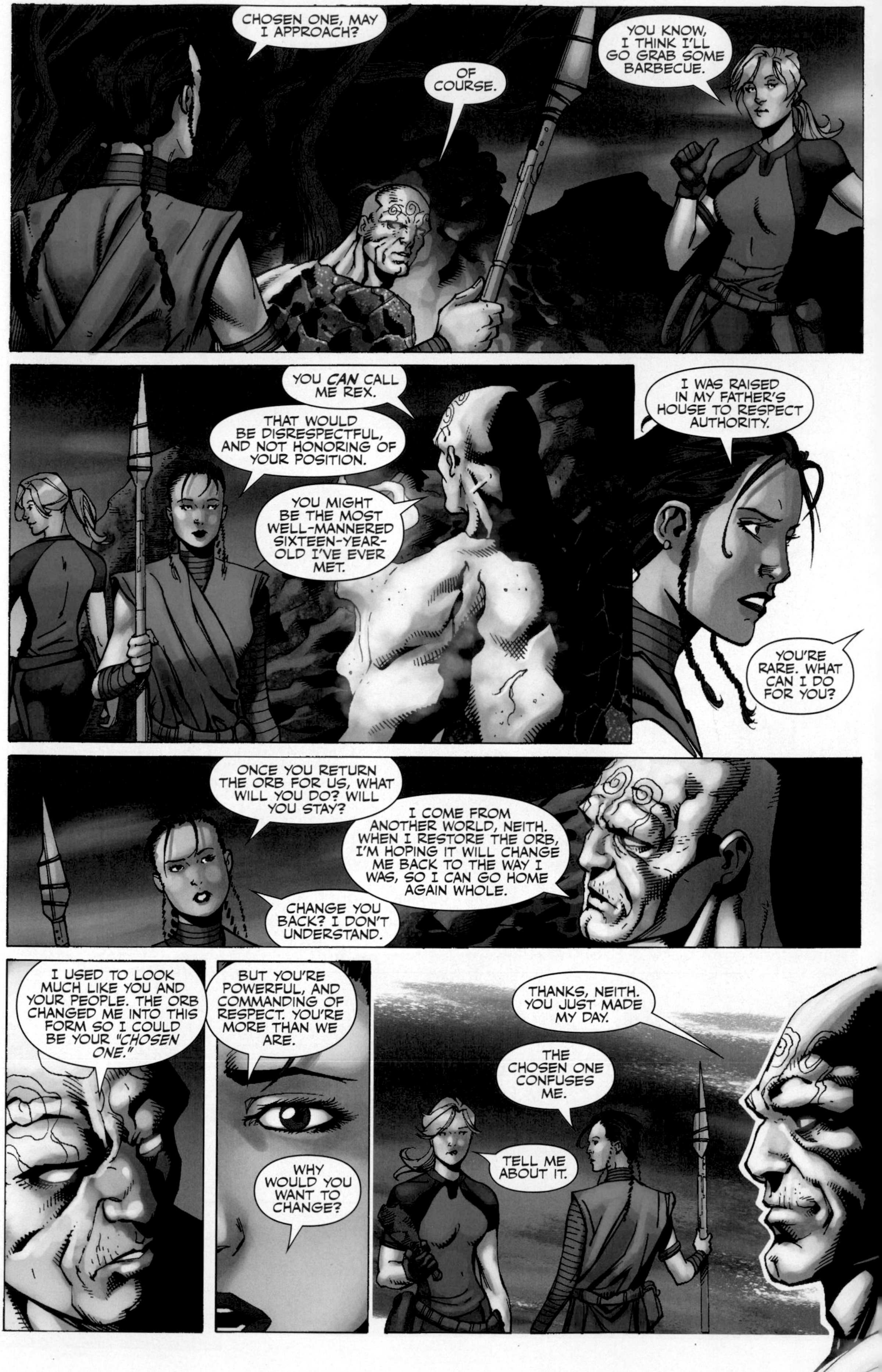
CHOSEN ONE, MAY I APPROACH?
OF COURSE.
YOU KNOW, I THINK I'LL GO GRAB SOME BARBECUE.
YOU CAN CALL ME REX.
THAT WOULD BE DISRESPECTFUL, AND NOT HONORING OF YOUR POSITION.
YOU MIGHT BE THE MOST WELL-MANNERED SIXTEEN-YEAR-OLD I'VE EVER MET.
I WAS RAISED IN MY FATHER'S HOUSE TO RESPECT AUTHORITY.
YOU'RE RARE. WHAT CAN I DO FOR YOU?
ONCE YOU RETURN THE ORB FOR US, WHAT WILL YOU DO? WILL YOU STAY?
I COME FROM ANOTHER WORLD, NEITH. WHEN I RESTORE THE ORB, I'M HOPING IT WILL CHANGE ME BACK TO THE WAY I WAS, SO I CAN GO HOME AGAIN WHOLE.
CHANGE YOU BACK? I DON'T UNDERSTAND.
I USED TO LOOK MUCH LIKE YOU AND YOUR PEOPLE. THE ORB CHANGED ME INTO THIS FORM SO I COULD BE YOUR "CHOSEN ONE."
BUT YOU'RE POWERFUL, AND COMMANDING OF RESPECT. YOU'RE MORE THAN WE ARE.
WHY WOULD YOU WANT TO CHANGE?
THANKS, NEITH. YOU JUST MADE MY DAY.
THE CHOSEN ONE CONFUSES ME.
TELL ME ABOUT IT.

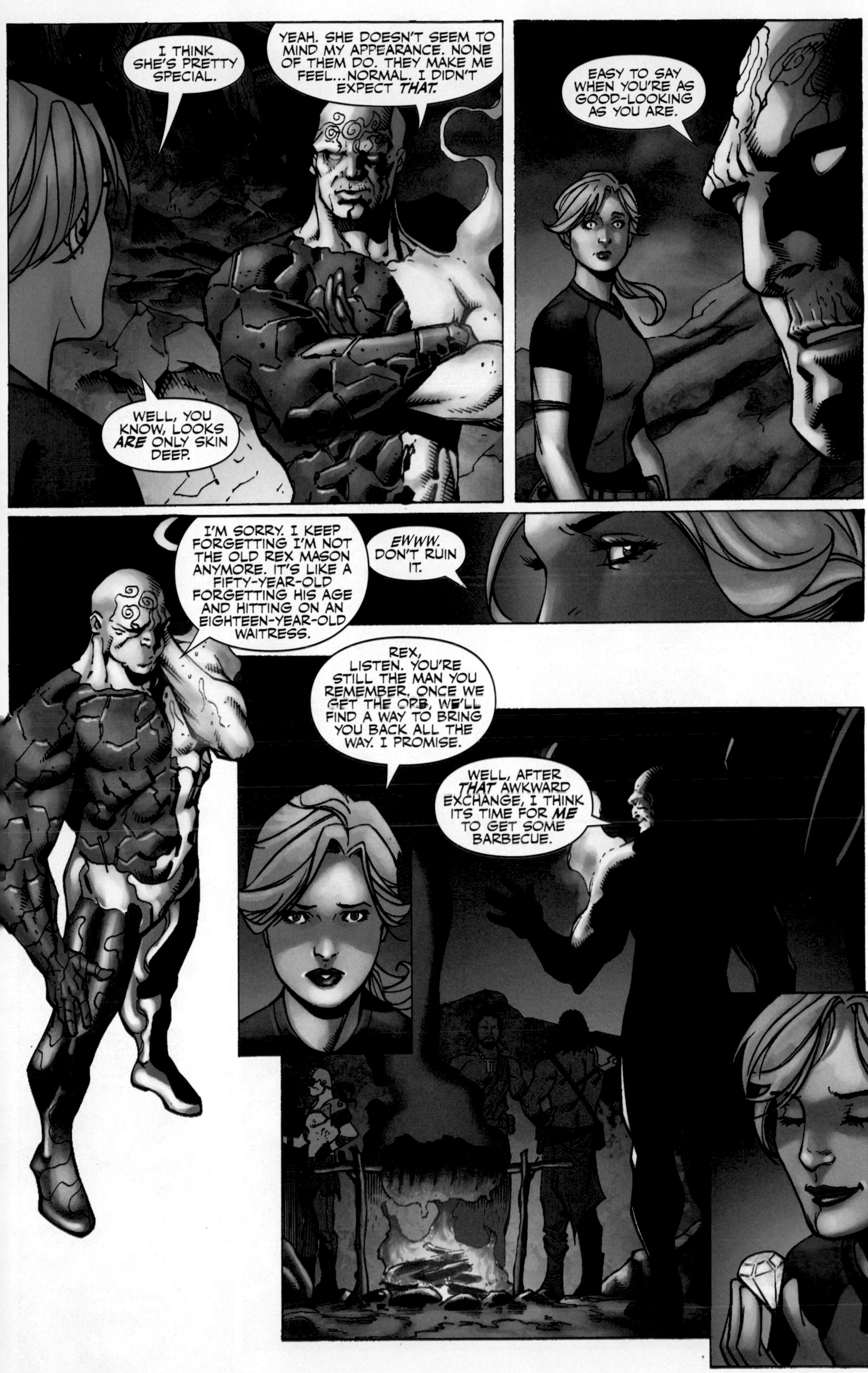
I THINK SHE'S PRETTY SPECIAL.
YEAH. SHE DOESN'T SEEM TO MIND MY APPEARANCE. NONE OF THEM DO. THEY MAKE ME FEEL...NORMAL. I DIDN'T EXPECT *THAT.*
WELL, YOU KNOW, LOOKS *ARE* ONLY SKIN DEEP.
EASY TO SAY WHEN YOU'RE AS GOOD-LOOKING AS YOU ARE.
I'M SORRY. I KEEP FORGETTING I'M NOT THE OLD REX MASON ANYMORE. IT'S LIKE A FIFTY-YEAR-OLD FORGETTING HIS AGE AND HITTING ON AN EIGHTEEN-YEAR-OLD WAITRESS.
EWWW. DON'T RUIN IT.
REX, LISTEN. YOU'RE STILL THE MAN YOU REMEMBER. ONCE WE GET THE ORB, WE'LL FIND A WAY TO BRING YOU BACK ALL THE WAY. I PROMISE.
WELL, AFTER *THAT* AWKWARD EXCHANGE, I THINK ITS TIME FOR *ME* TO GET SOME BARBECUE.

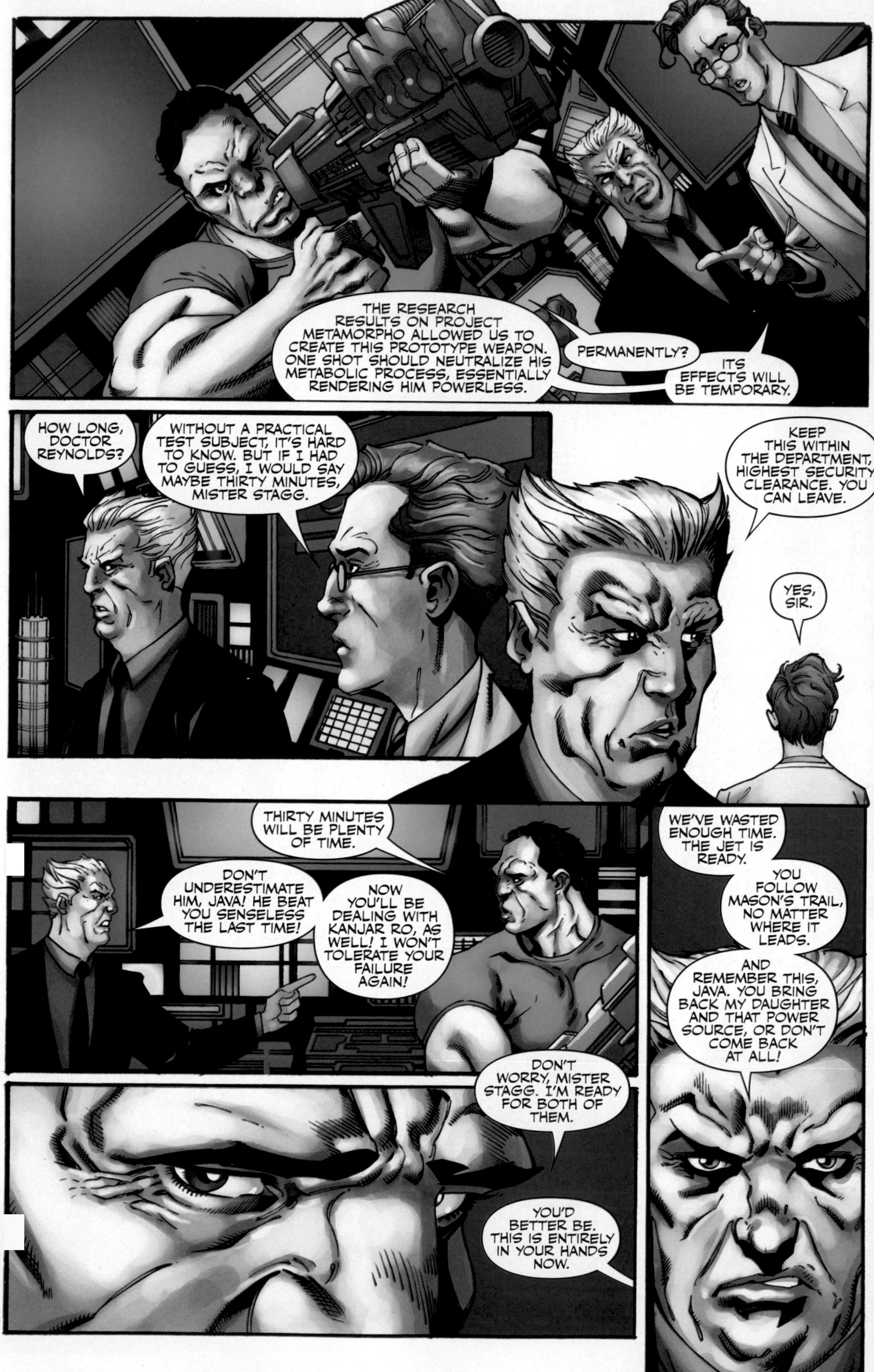
THE RESEARCH RESULTS ON PROJECT METAMORPHO ALLOWED US TO CREATE THIS PROTOTYPE WEAPON. ONE SHOT SHOULD NEUTRALIZE HIS METABOLIC PROCESS, ESSENTIALLY RENDERING HIM POWERLESS.
PERMANENTLY?
ITS EFFECTS WILL BE TEMPORARY.
HOW LONG, DOCTOR REYNOLDS?
WITHOUT A PRACTICAL TEST SUBJECT, IT'S HARD TO KNOW. BUT IF I HAD TO GUESS, I WOULD SAY MAYBE THIRTY MINUTES, MISTER STAGG.
KEEP THIS WITHIN THE DEPARTMENT, HIGHEST SECURITY CLEARANCE. YOU CAN LEAVE.
YES, SIR.
THIRTY MINUTES WILL BE PLENTY OF TIME.
DON'T UNDERESTIMATE HIM, JAVA! HE BEAT YOU SENSELESS THE LAST TIME!
NOW YOU'LL BE DEALING WITH KANJAR RO, AS WELL! I WON'T TOLERATE YOUR FAILURE AGAIN!
WE'VE WASTED ENOUGH TIME. THE JET IS READY.
YOU FOLLOW MASON'S TRAIL, NO MATTER WHERE IT LEADS.
AND REMEMBER THIS, JAVA. YOU BRING BACK MY DAUGHTER AND THAT POWER SOURCE, OR DON'T COME BACK AT ALL!
DON'T WORRY, MISTER STAGG. I'M READY FOR BOTH OF THEM.
YOU'D BETTER BE. THIS IS ENTIRELY IN YOUR HANDS NOW.

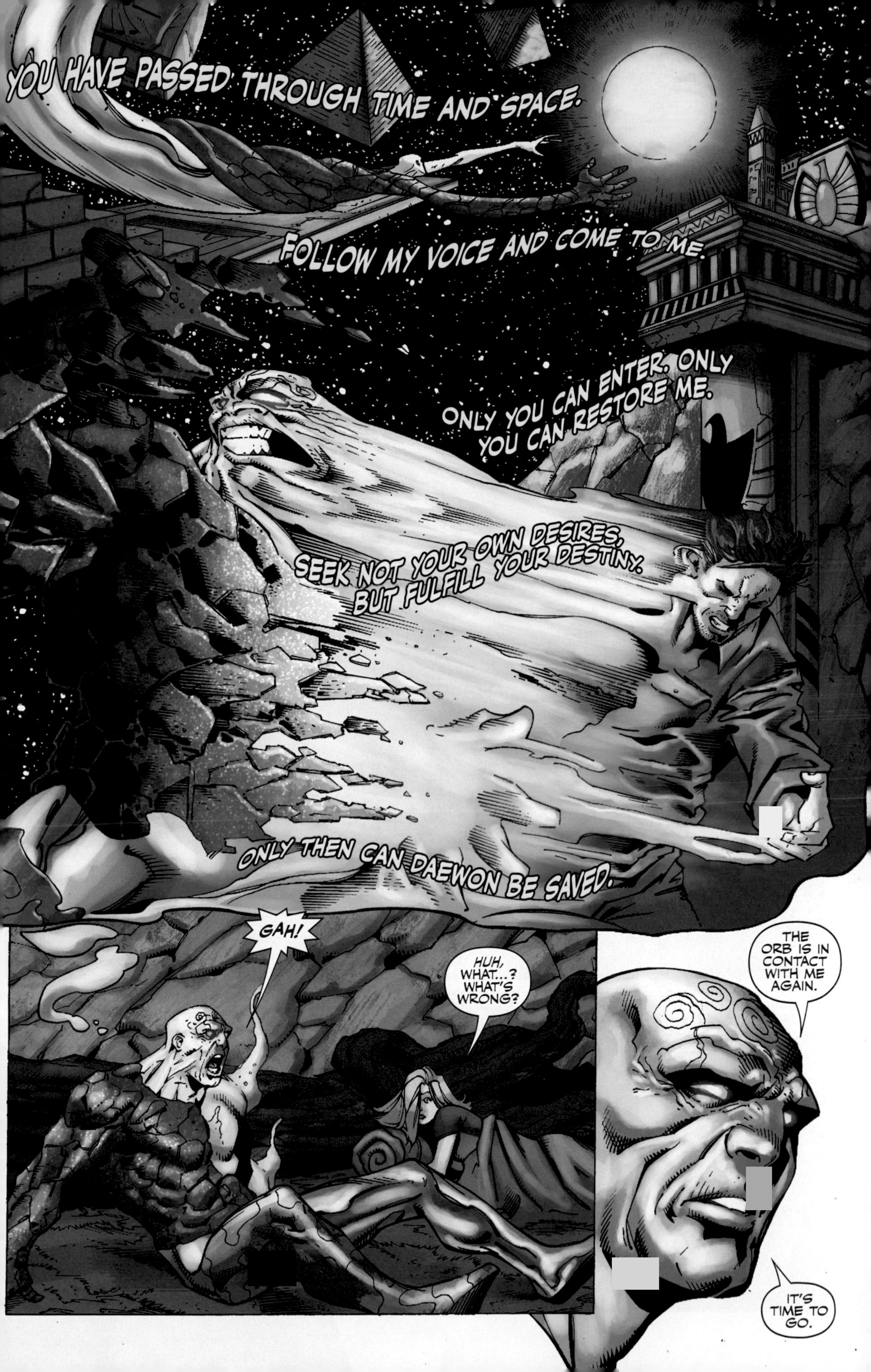

YOU HAVE PASSED THROUGH TIME AND SPACE.
FOLLOW MY VOICE AND COME TO ME.
ONLY YOU CAN ENTER. ONLY YOU CAN RESTORE ME.
SEEK NOT YOUR OWN DESIRES, BUT FULFILL YOUR DESTINY.
ONLY THEN CAN DAEWON BE SAVED.
GAH!
HUH, WHAT...? WHAT'S WRONG?
THE ORB IS IN CONTACT WITH ME AGAIN.
IT'S TIME TO GO.

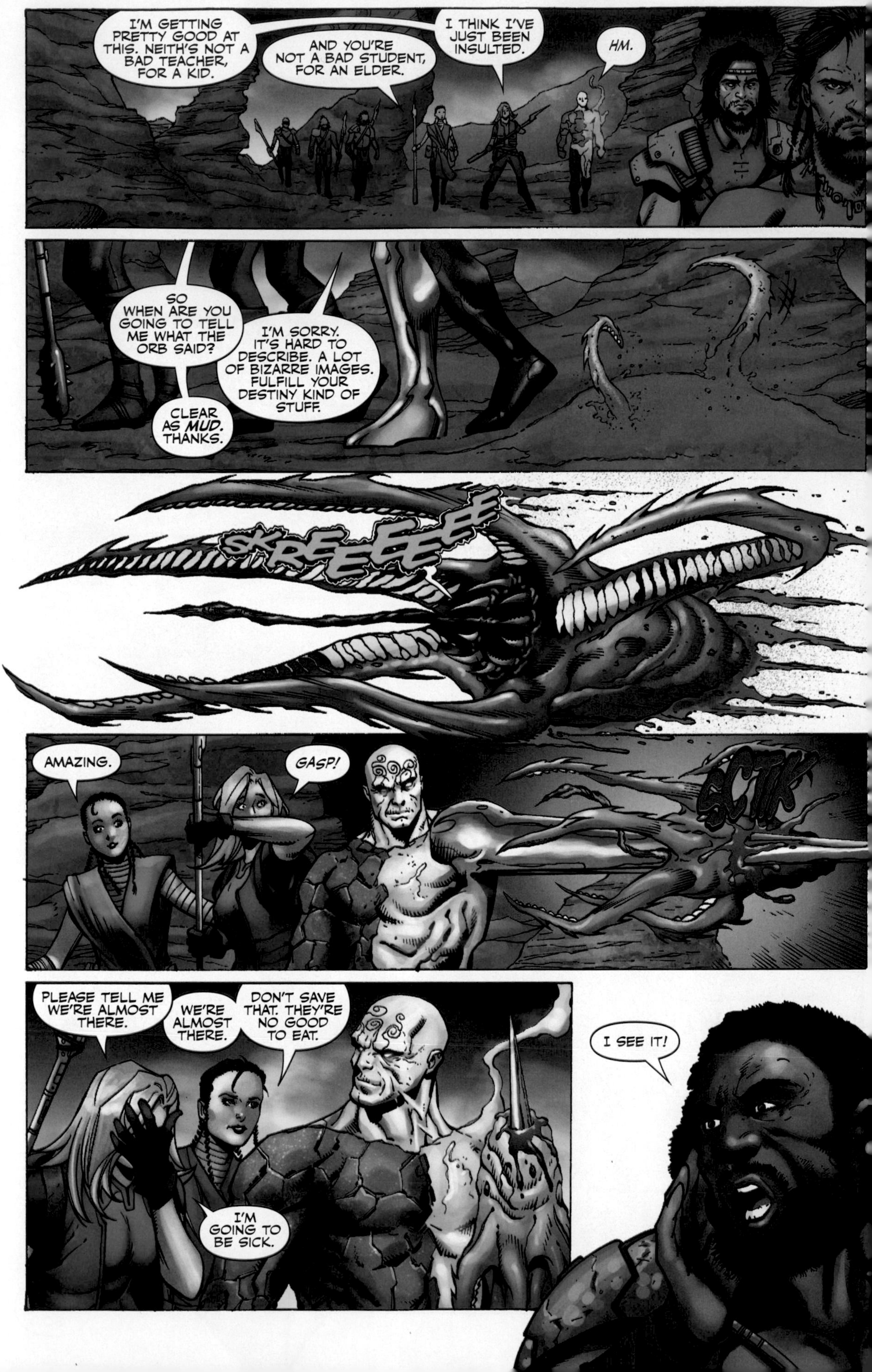

I'M GETTING PRETTY GOOD AT THIS. NEITH'S NOT A BAD TEACHER, FOR A KID.
AND YOU'RE NOT A BAD STUDENT, FOR AN ELDER.
I THINK I'VE JUST BEEN INSULTED.
HM.
SO WHEN ARE YOU GOING TO TELL ME WHAT THE ORB SAID?
I'M SORRY. IT'S HARD TO DESCRIBE. A LOT OF BIZARRE IMAGES. FULFILL YOUR DESTINY KIND OF STUFF.
CLEAR AS MUD. THANKS.
SKREEEEEEEE
AMAZING.
GASP!
SCTK
PLEASE TELL ME WE'RE ALMOST THERE.
WE'RE ALMOST THERE.
DON'T SAVE THAT. THEY'RE NO GOOD TO EAT.
I'M GOING TO BE SICK.
I SEE IT!

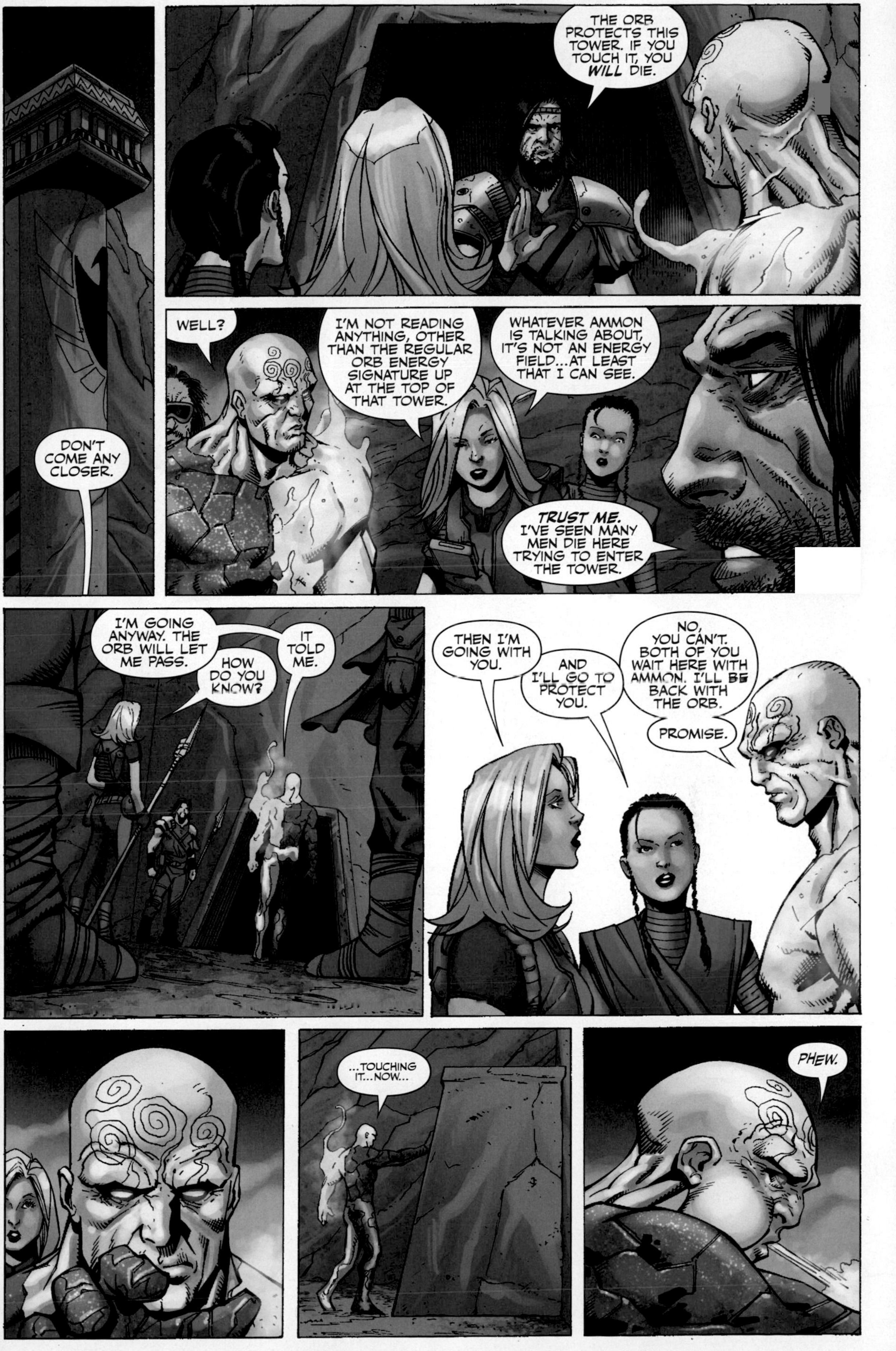
THE ORB PROTECTS THIS TOWER. IF YOU TOUCH IT, YOU *WILL* DIE.
DON'T COME ANY CLOSER.
WELL?
I'M NOT READING ANYTHING, OTHER THAN THE REGULAR ORB ENERGY SIGNATURE UP AT THE TOP OF THAT TOWER.
WHATEVER AMMON IS TALKING ABOUT, IT'S NOT AN ENERGY FIELD...AT LEAST THAT I CAN SEE.
TRUST ME. I'VE SEEN MANY MEN DIE HERE TRYING TO ENTER THE TOWER.
I'M GOING ANYWAY. THE ORB WILL LET ME PASS.
HOW DO YOU KNOW?
IT TOLD ME.
THEN I'M GOING WITH YOU.
AND I'LL GO TO PROTECT YOU.
NO, YOU CAN'T. BOTH OF YOU WAIT HERE WITH AMMON. I'LL BE BACK WITH THE ORB.
PROMISE.
...TOUCHING IT...NOW...
PHEW.

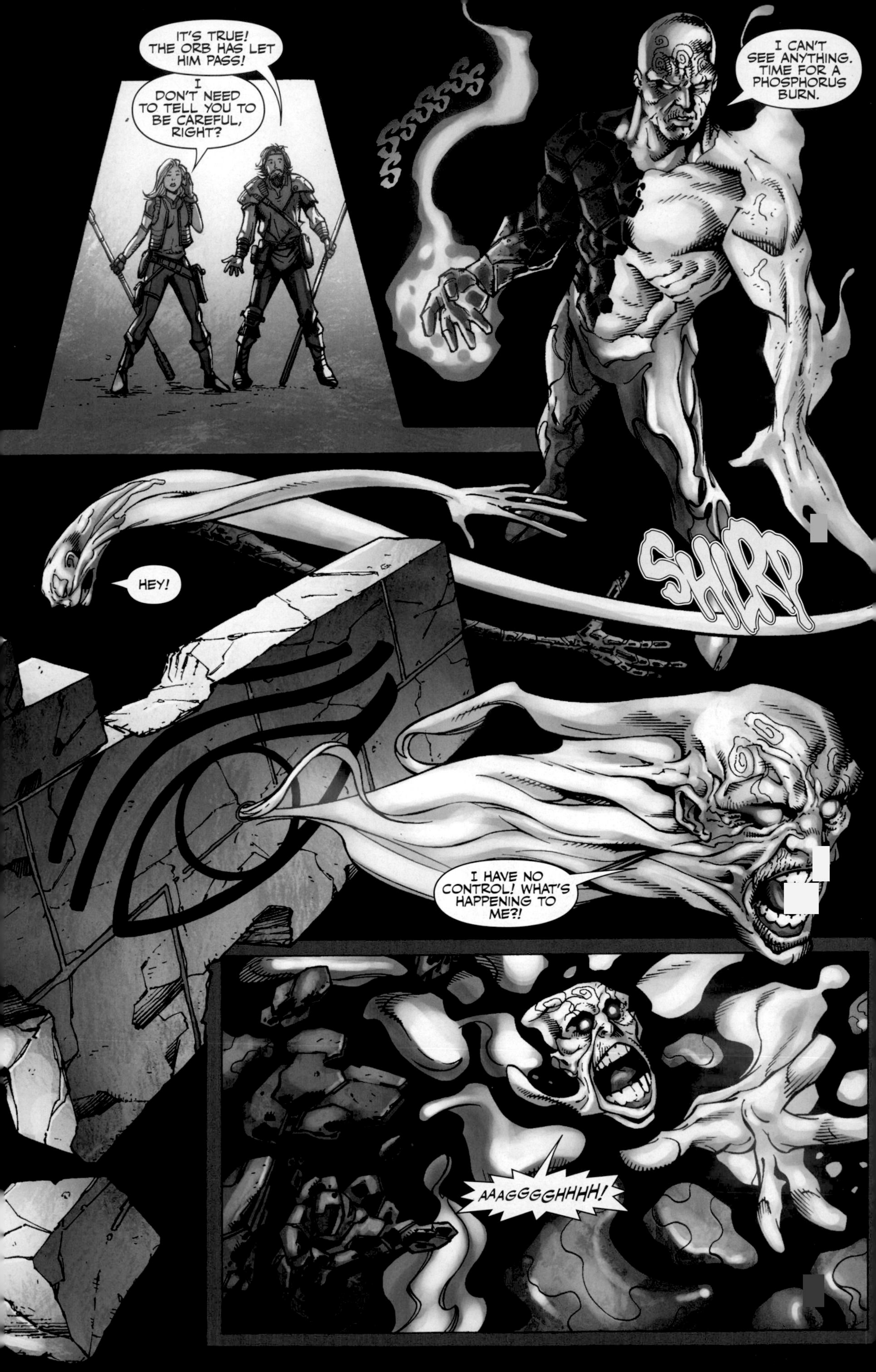
IT'S TRUE! THE ORB HAS LET HIM PASS!
I DON'T NEED TO TELL YOU TO BE CAREFUL, RIGHT?
SSSSSSS
I CAN'T SEE ANYTHING. TIME FOR A PHOSPHORUS BURN.
SHLRP
HEY!
I HAVE NO CONTROL! WHAT'S HAPPENING TO ME?!
AAAGGGGHHHH!

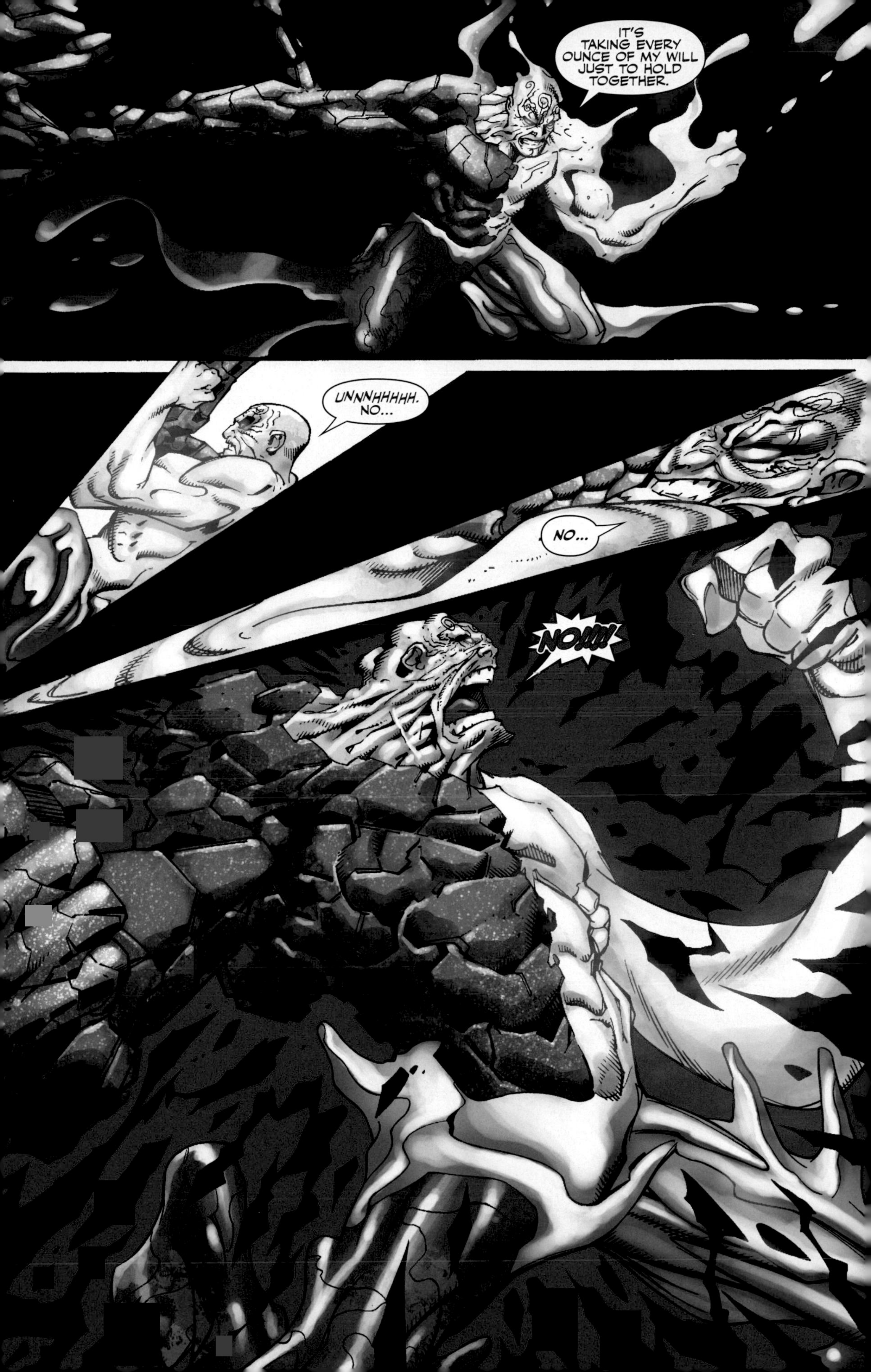
IT'S TAKING EVERY OUNCE OF MY WILL JUST TO HOLD TOGETHER.
UNNHHHHH. NO...
NO...
NO!!!!

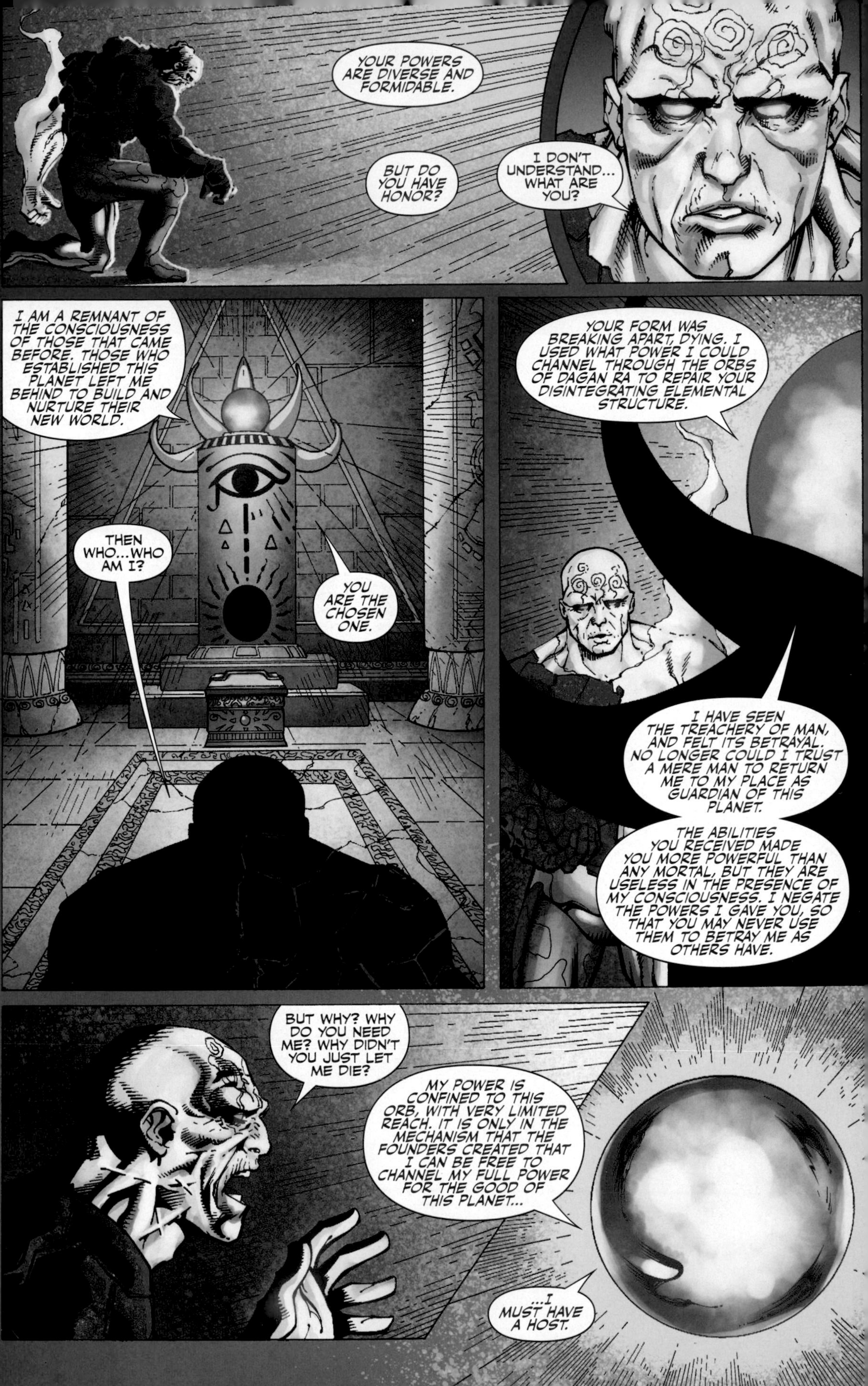
YOUR POWERS ARE DIVERSE AND FORMIDABLE.
BUT DO YOU HAVE HONOR?
I DON'T UNDERSTAND... WHAT ARE YOU?
I AM A REMNANT OF THE CONSCIOUSNESS OF THOSE THAT CAME BEFORE. THOSE WHO ESTABLISHED THIS PLANET LEFT ME BEHIND TO BUILD AND NURTURE THEIR NEW WORLD.
THEN WHO...WHO AM I?
YOU ARE THE CHOSEN ONE.
YOUR FORM WAS BREAKING APART, DYING. I USED WHAT POWER I COULD CHANNEL THROUGH THE ORBS OF DAGAN RA TO REPAIR YOUR DISINTEGRATING ELEMENTAL STRUCTURE.
I HAVE SEEN THE TREACHERY OF MAN, AND FELT ITS BETRAYAL. NO LONGER COULD I TRUST A MERE MAN TO RETURN ME TO MY PLACE AS GUARDIAN OF THIS PLANET.
THE ABILITIES YOU RECEIVED MADE YOU MORE POWERFUL THAN ANY MORTAL, BUT THEY ARE USELESS IN THE PRESENCE OF MY CONSCIOUSNESS. I NEGATE THE POWERS I GAVE YOU, SO THAT YOU MAY NEVER USE THEM TO BETRAY ME AS OTHERS HAVE.
BUT WHY? WHY DO YOU NEED ME? WHY DIDN'T YOU JUST LET ME DIE?
MY POWER IS CONFINED TO THIS ORB, WITH VERY LIMITED REACH. IT IS ONLY IN THE MECHANISM THAT THE FOUNDERS CREATED THAT I CAN BE FREE TO CHANNEL MY FULL POWER FOR THE GOOD OF THIS PLANET...
...I MUST HAVE A HOST.

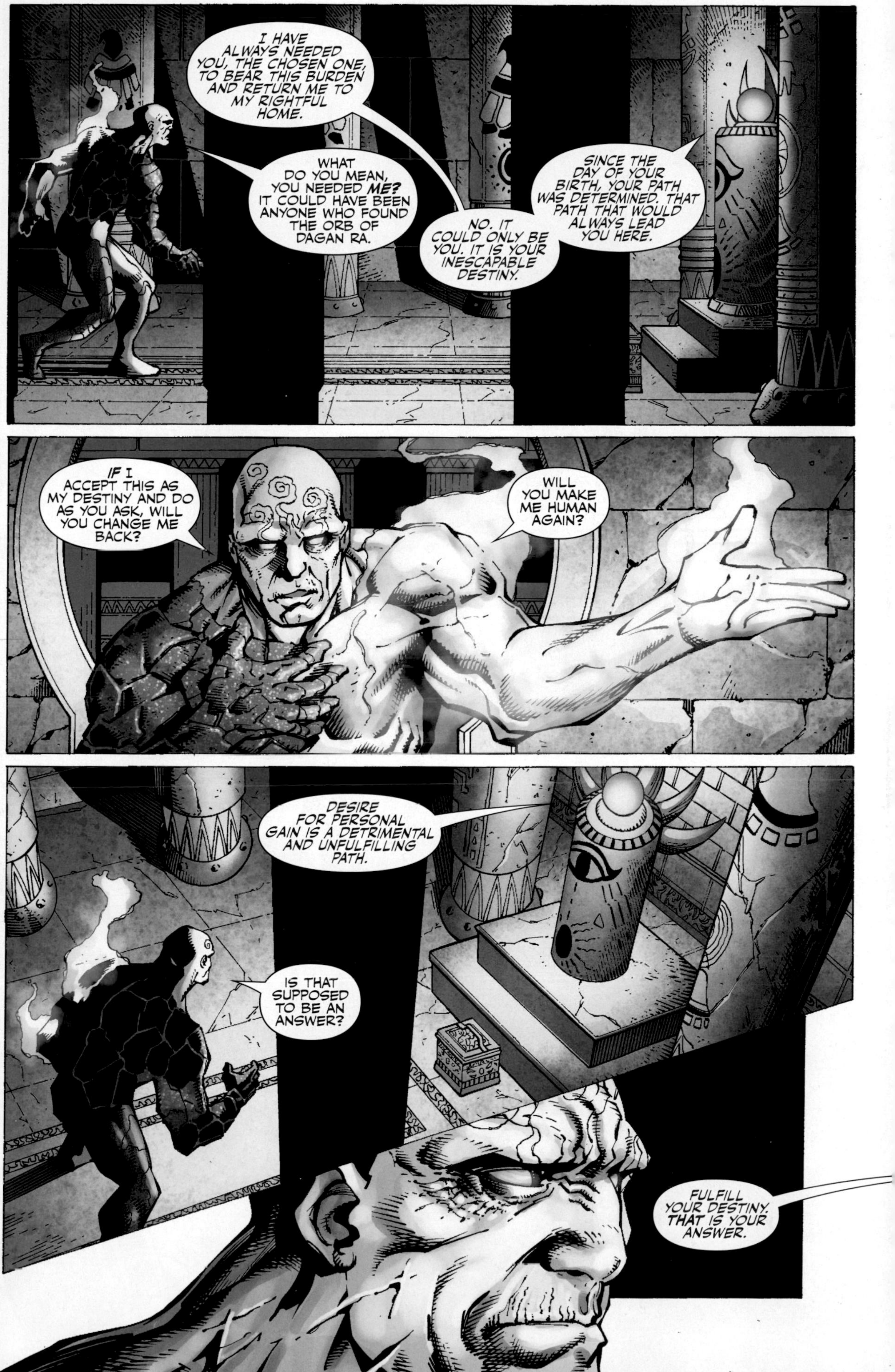
I HAVE ALWAYS NEEDED YOU, THE CHOSEN ONE, TO BEAR THIS BURDEN AND RETURN ME TO MY RIGHTFUL HOME.
WHAT DO YOU MEAN, YOU NEEDED ME? IT COULD HAVE BEEN ANYONE WHO FOUND THE ORB OF DAGAN RA.
NO. IT COULD ONLY BE YOU. IT IS YOUR INESCAPABLE DESTINY.
SINCE THE DAY OF YOUR BIRTH, YOUR PATH WAS DETERMINED. THAT PATH THAT WOULD ALWAYS LEAD YOU HERE.
IF I ACCEPT THIS AS MY DESTINY AND DO AS YOU ASK, WILL YOU CHANGE ME BACK?
WILL YOU MAKE ME HUMAN AGAIN?
DESIRE FOR PERSONAL GAIN IS A DETRIMENTAL AND UNFULFILLING PATH.
IS THAT SUPPOSED TO BE AN ANSWER?
FULFILL YOUR DESTINY. THAT IS YOUR ANSWER.

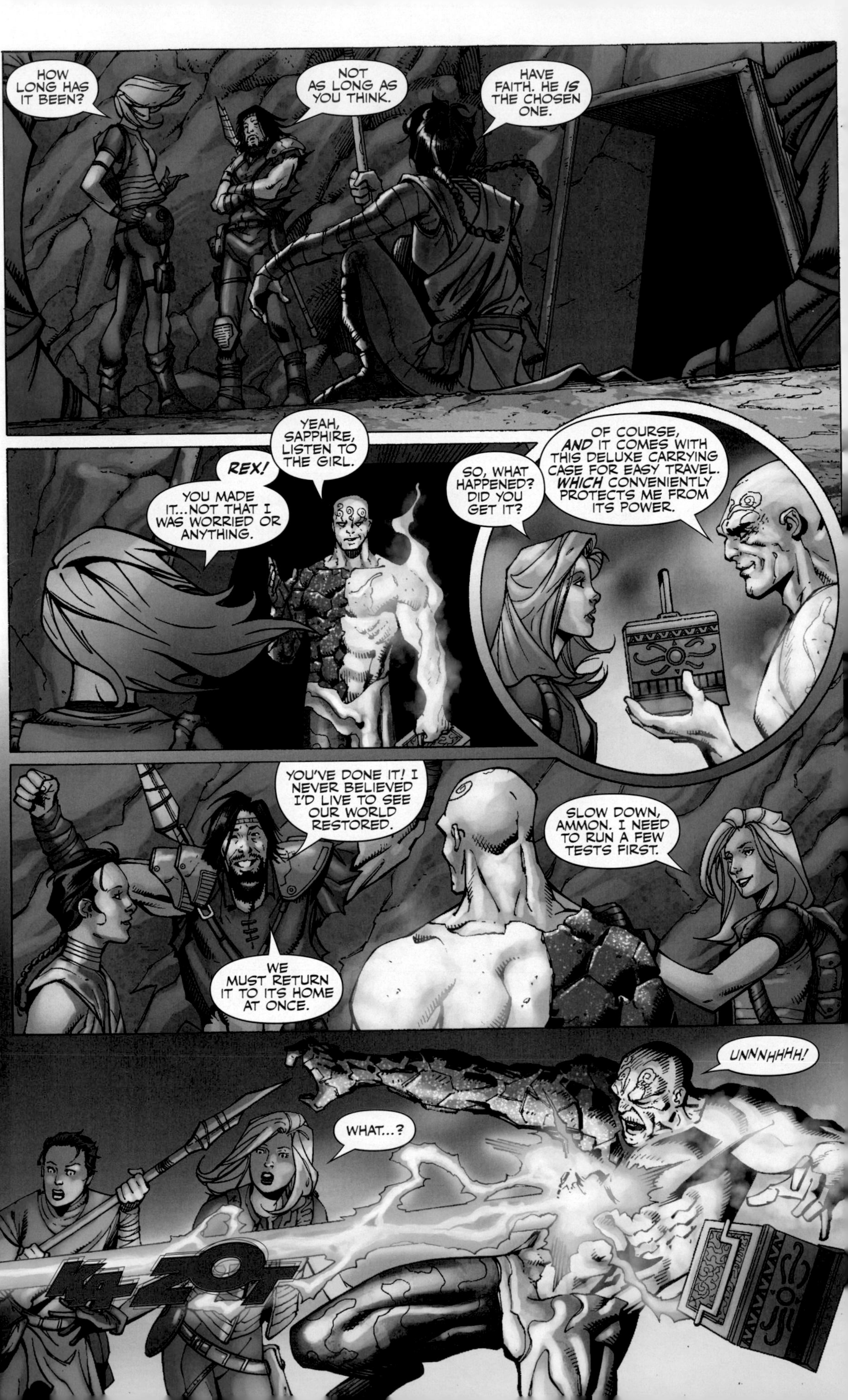
HOW LONG HAS IT BEEN?
NOT AS LONG AS YOU THINK.
HAVE FAITH. HE *IS* THE CHOSEN ONE.
YEAH, SAPPHIRE, LISTEN TO THE GIRL.
REX!
YOU MADE IT...NOT THAT I WAS WORRIED OR ANYTHING.
SO, WHAT HAPPENED? DID YOU GET IT?
OF COURSE, *AND* IT COMES WITH THIS DELUXE CARRYING CASE FOR EASY TRAVEL. *WHICH* CONVENIENTLY PROTECTS ME FROM ITS POWER.
YOU'VE DONE IT! I NEVER BELIEVED I'D LIVE TO SEE OUR WORLD RESTORED.
WE MUST RETURN IT TO ITS HOME AT ONCE.
SLOW DOWN, AMMON. I NEED TO RUN A FEW TESTS FIRST.
UNNNHHHH!
WHAT...?
KZOT

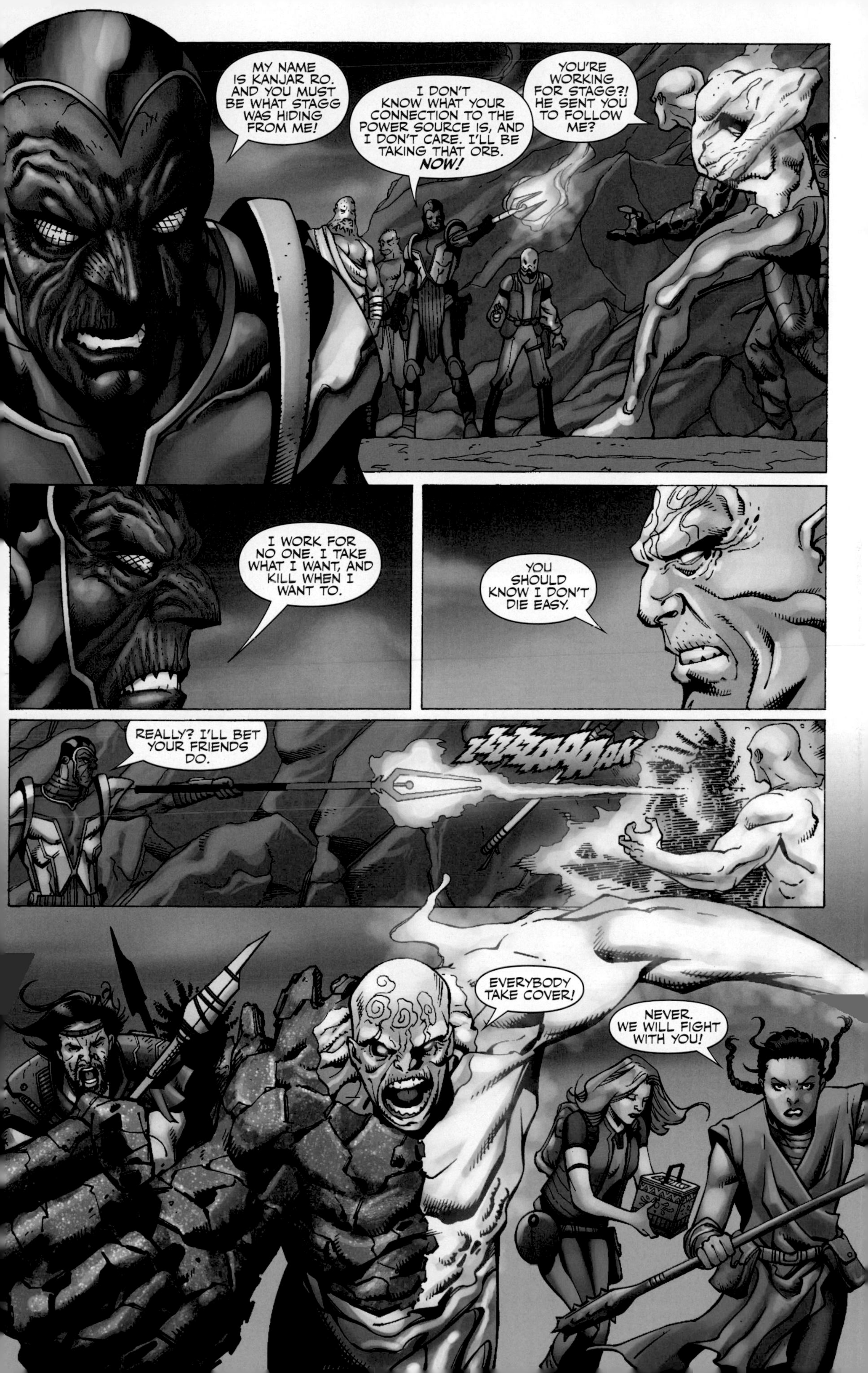
MY NAME IS KANJAR RO. AND YOU MUST BE WHAT STAGG WAS HIDING FROM ME!
YOU'RE WORKING FOR STAGG?! HE SENT YOU TO FOLLOW ME?
I DON'T KNOW WHAT YOUR CONNECTION TO THE POWER SOURCE IS, AND I DON'T CARE. I'LL BE TAKING THAT ORB. NOW!
I WORK FOR NO ONE. I TAKE WHAT I WANT, AND KILL WHEN I WANT TO.
YOU SHOULD KNOW I DON'T DIE EASY.
REALLY? I'LL BET YOUR FRIENDS DO.
ZZZZAAAAK
EVERYBODY TAKE COVER!
NEVER. WE WILL FIGHT WITH YOU!

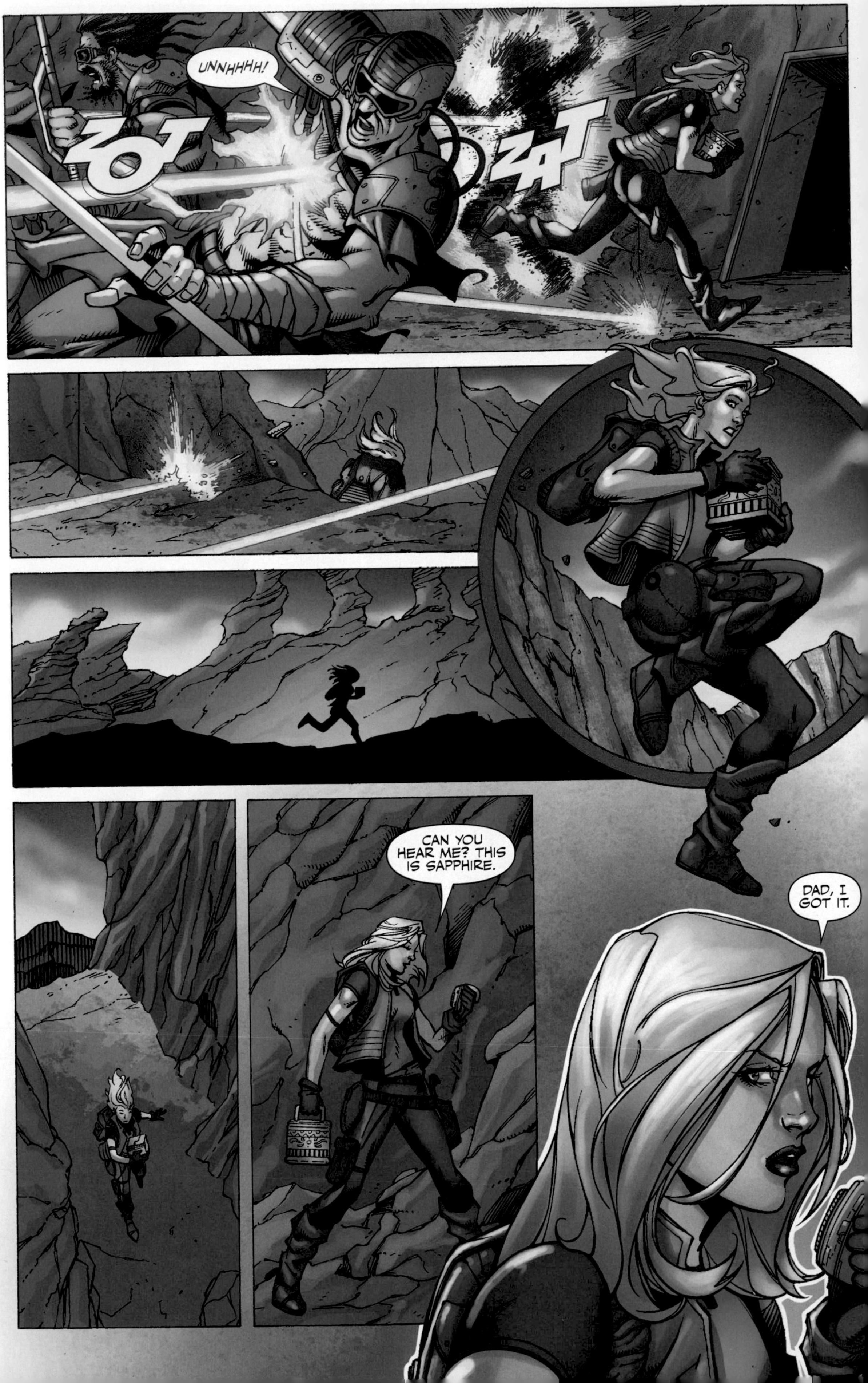
UNNHHHH!
ZOT
ZAT
CAN YOU HEAR ME? THIS IS SAPPHIRE.
DAD, I GOT IT.

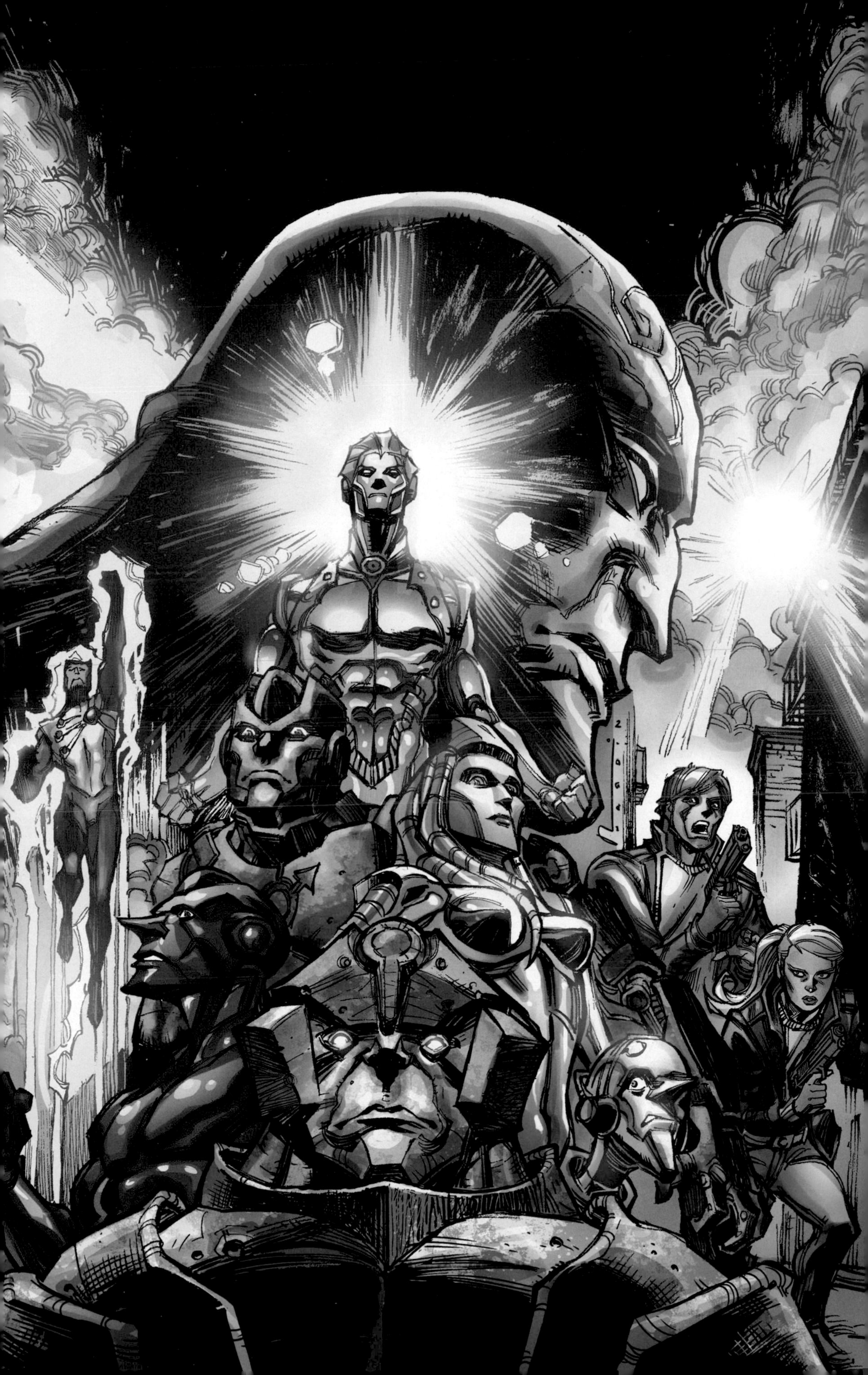

WHAT COMES AROUND...

AARON LOPRESTI writer/penciller LIVESAY inker CHRIS SOTOMAYOR colorist MICHAEL HEISLER letterer
CHAD HARDIN and PAUL MOUNTS cover

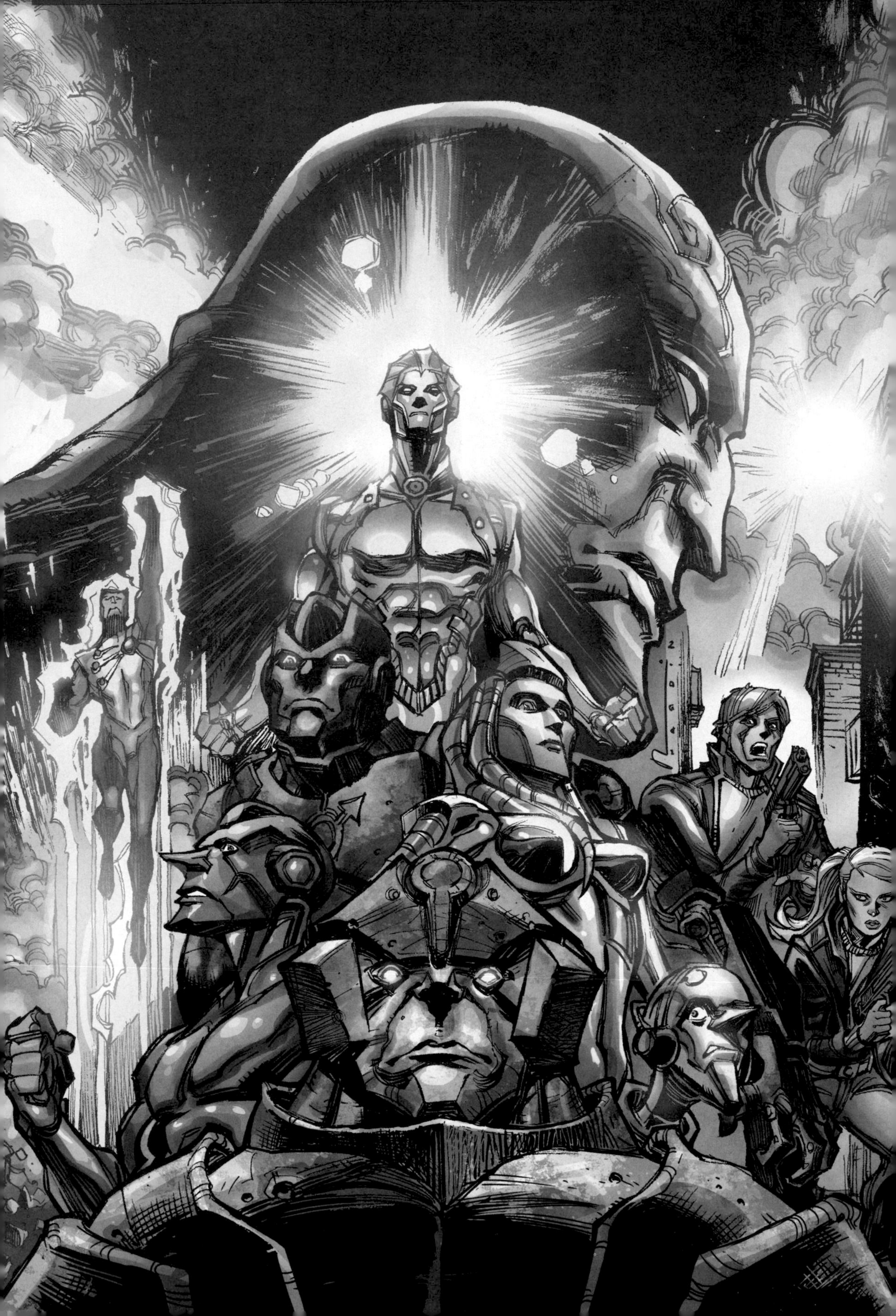

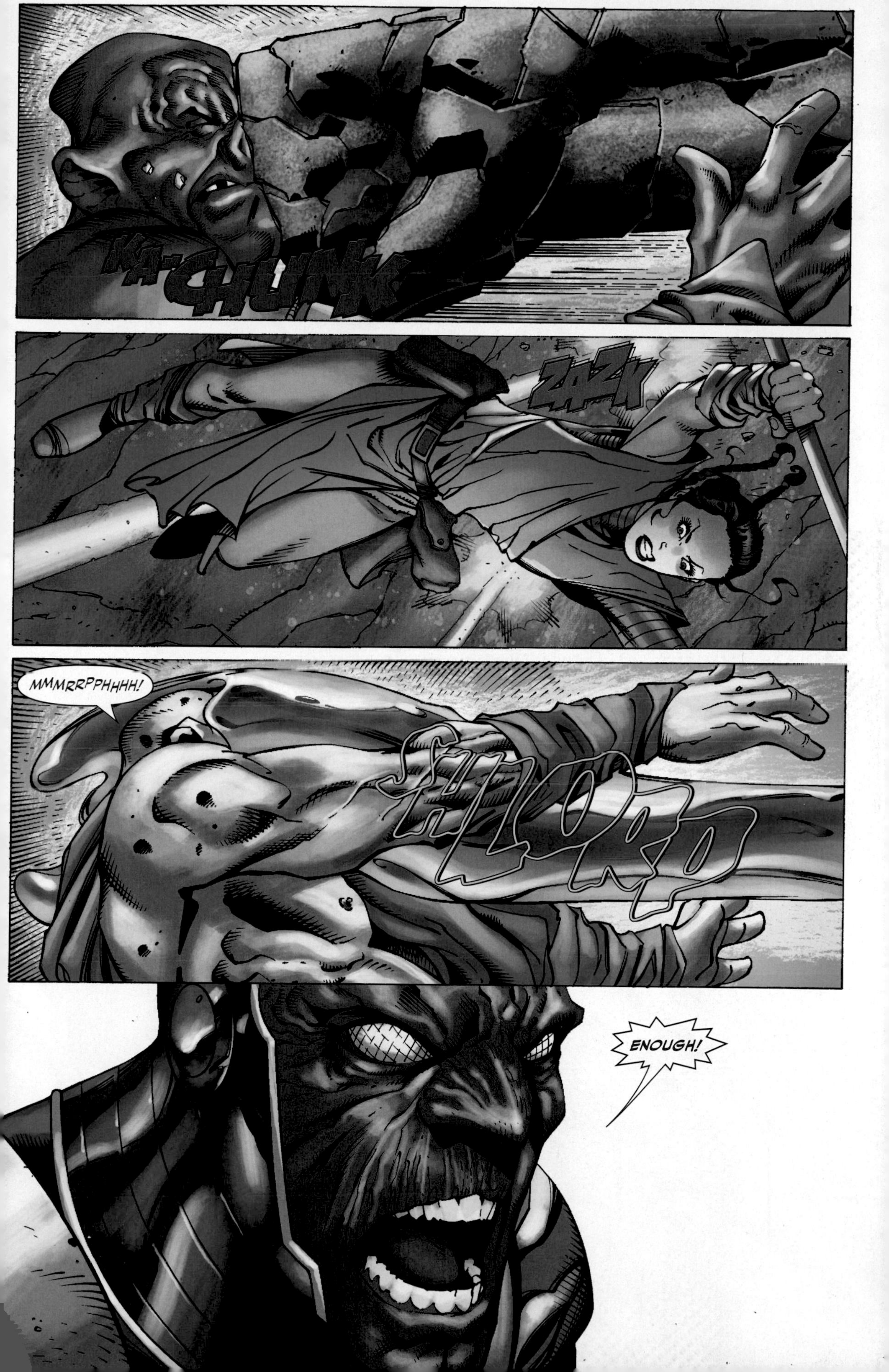
KA-CHUNK
ZAZK
MMMRRPPHHHH!
SHLORP
ENOUGH!

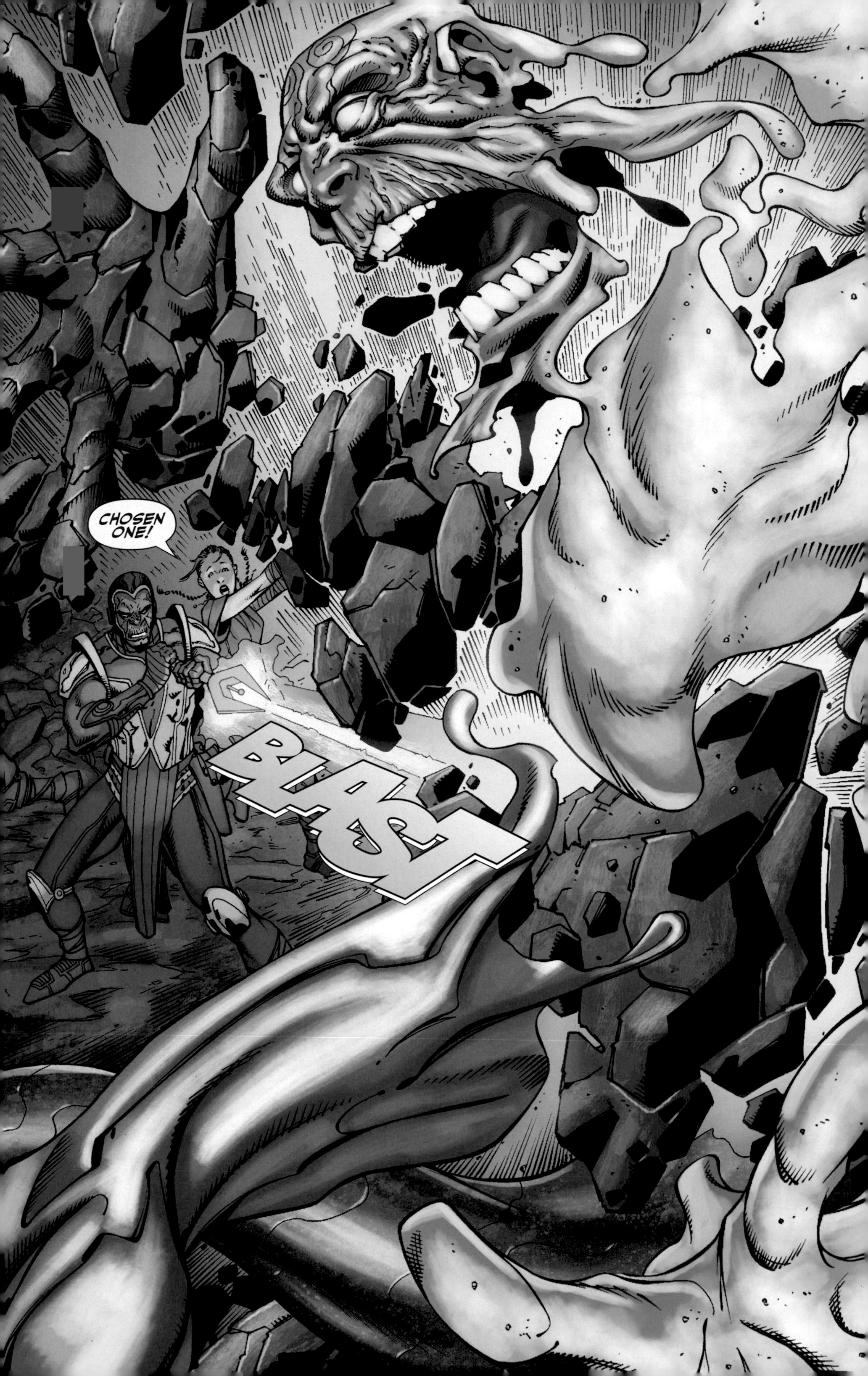
CHOSEN ONE!
BLAST

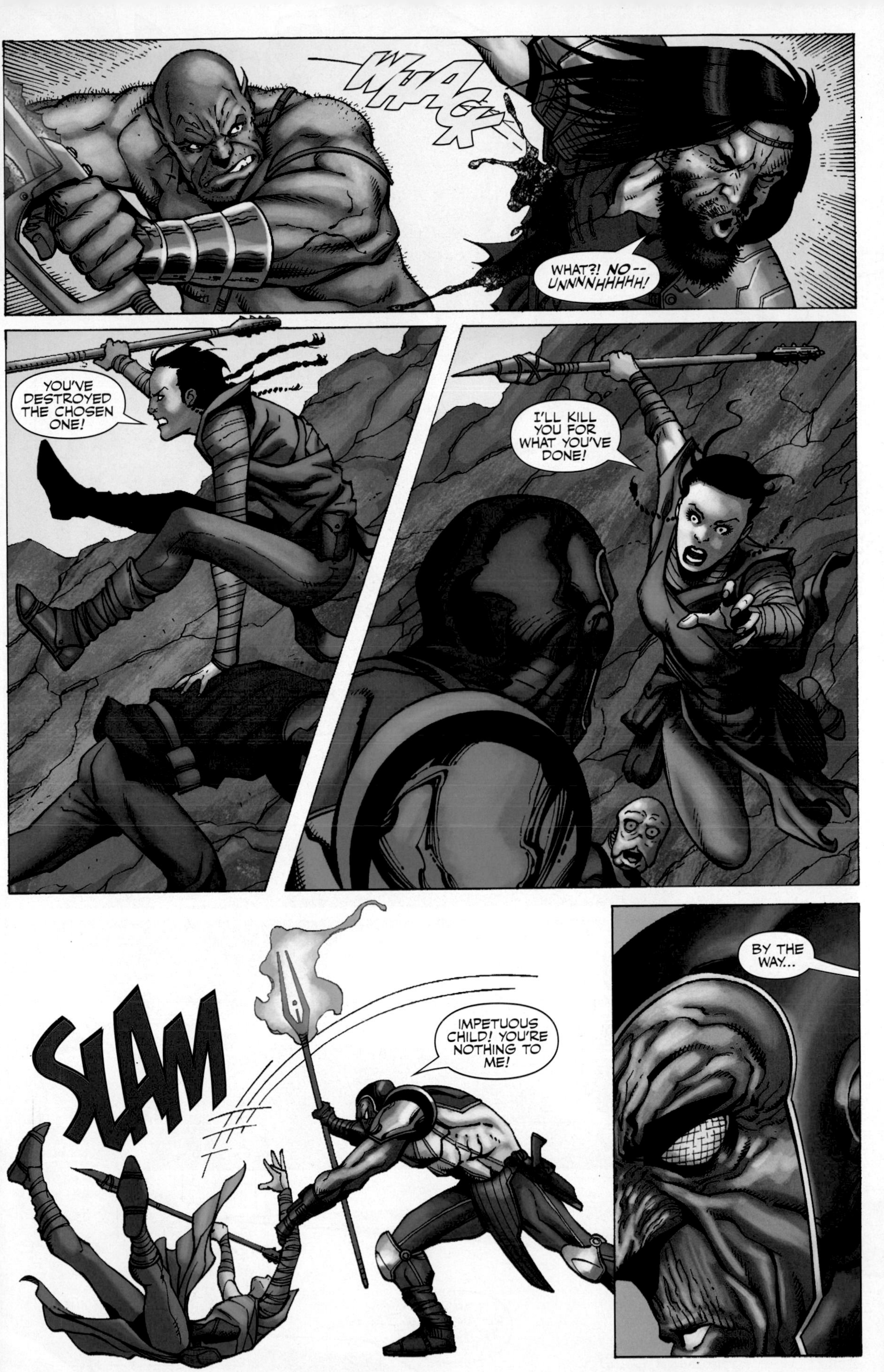
WHACK
WHAT?! NO-- UNNNNHHHHH!
YOU'VE DESTROYED THE CHOSEN ONE!
I'LL KILL YOU FOR WHAT YOU'VE DONE!
SLAM
IMPETUOUS CHILD! YOU'RE NOTHING TO ME!
BY THE WAY...

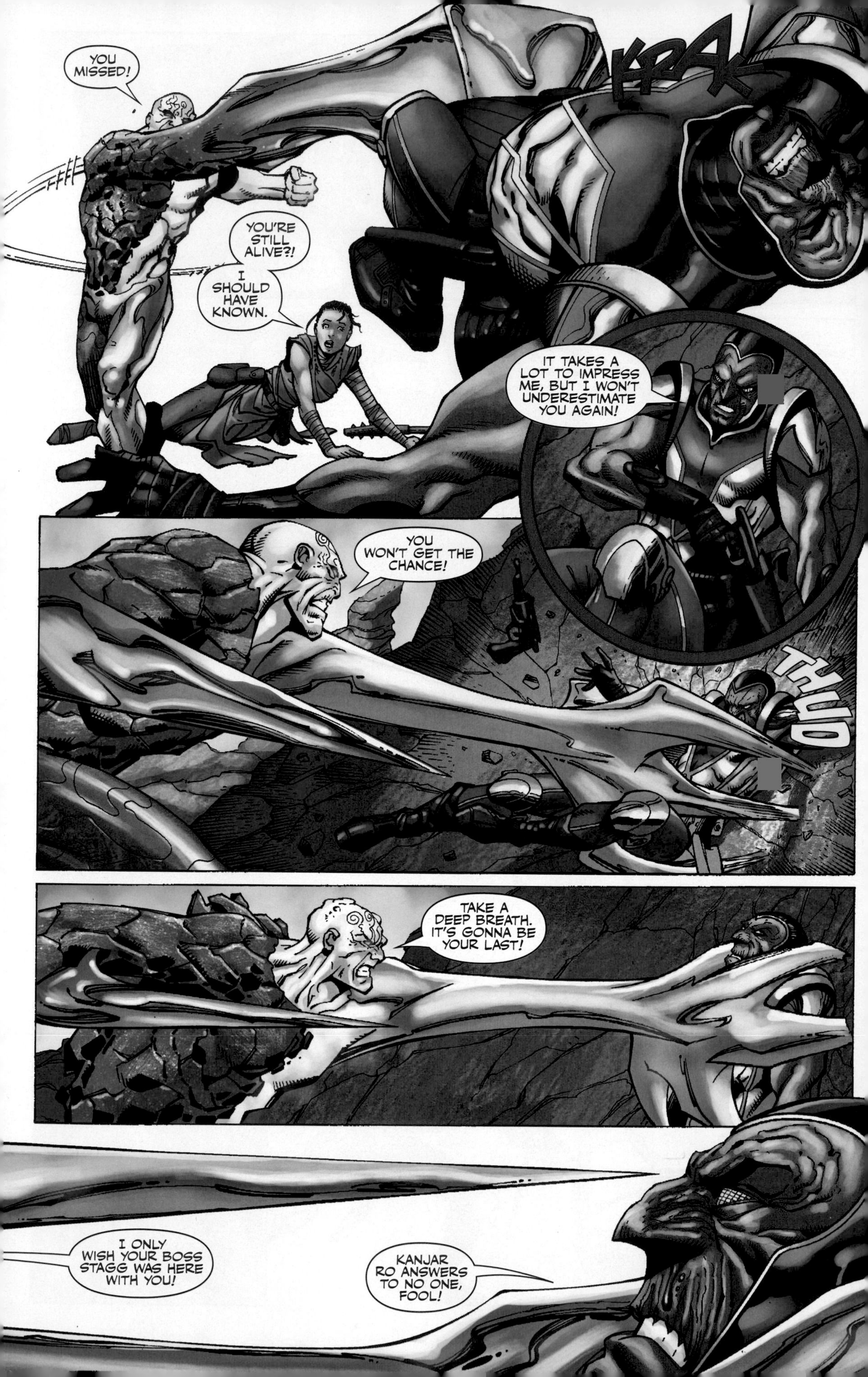
YOU MISSED!
KRAK
YOU'RE STILL ALIVE?!
I SHOULD HAVE KNOWN.
IT TAKES A LOT TO IMPRESS ME, BUT I WON'T UNDERESTIMATE YOU AGAIN!
YOU WON'T GET THE CHANCE!
THUD
TAKE A DEEP BREATH. IT'S GONNA BE YOUR LAST!
I ONLY WISH YOUR BOSS STAGG WAS HERE WITH YOU!
KANJAR RO ANSWERS TO NO ONE, FOOL!

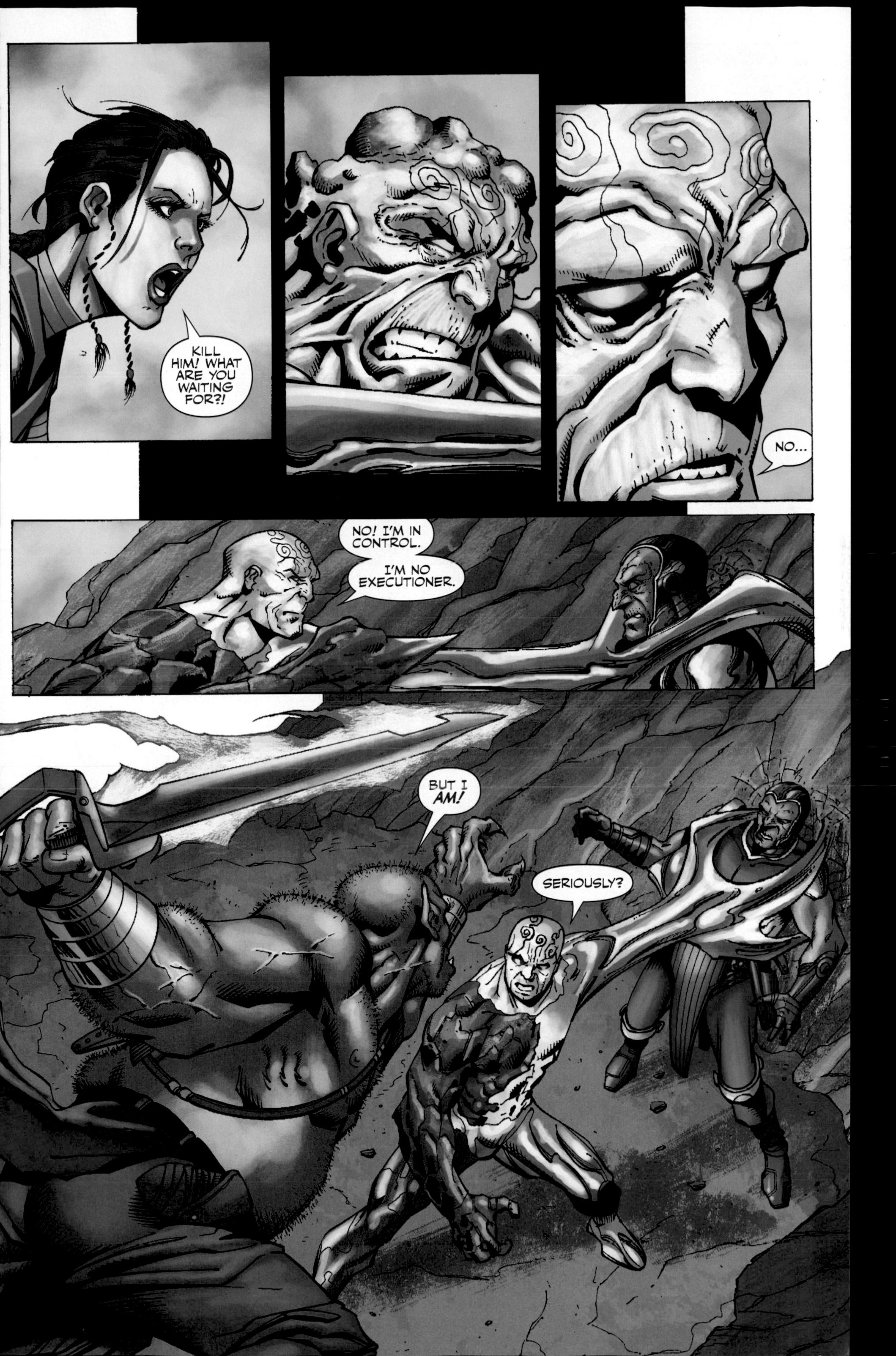
KILL HIM! WHAT ARE YOU WAITING FOR?!
NO...
NO! I'M IN CONTROL.
I'M NO EXECUTIONER.
BUT I AM!
SERIOUSLY?

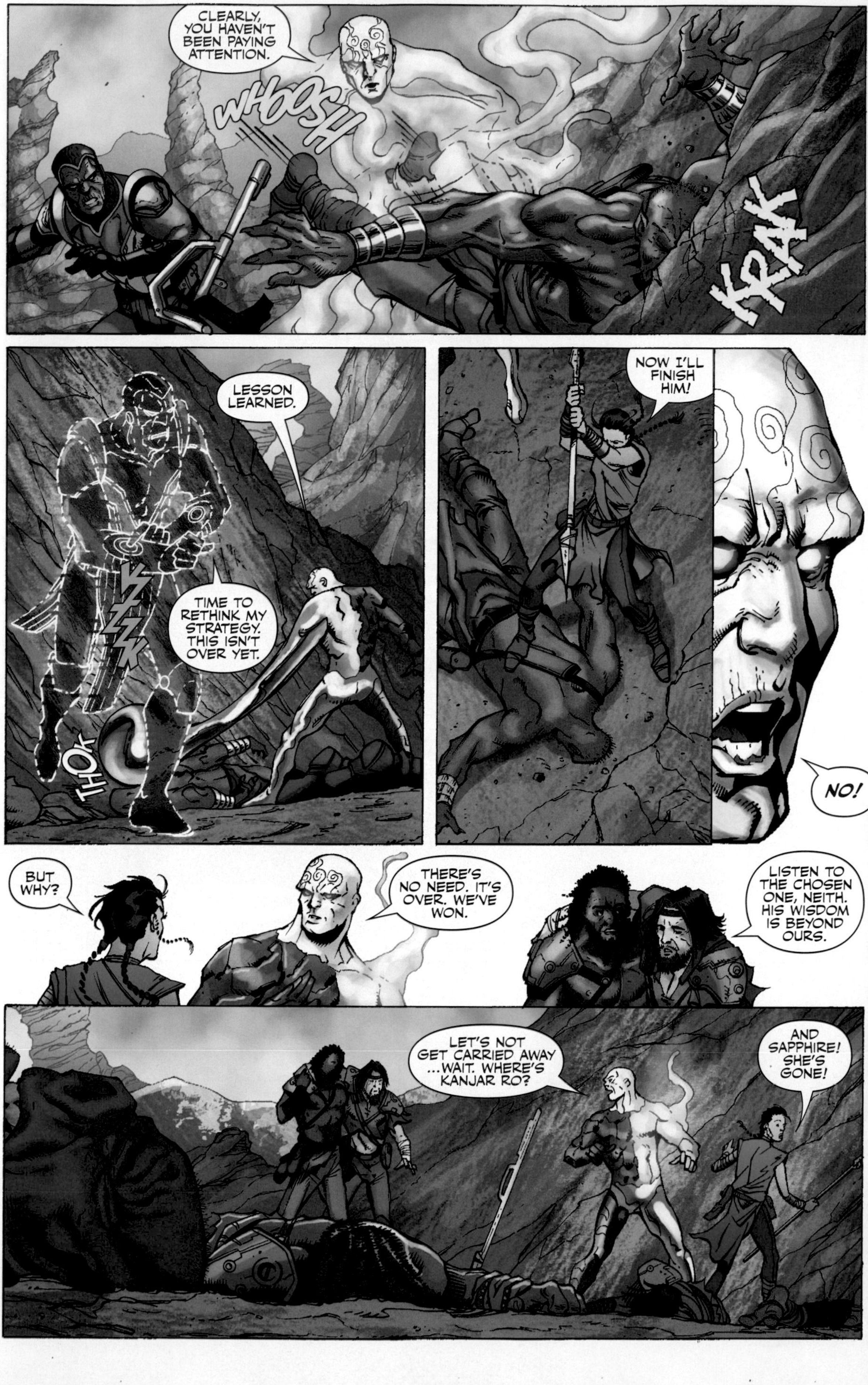
CLEARLY, YOU HAVEN'T BEEN PAYING ATTENTION.
WHOOSH
KRAK
LESSON LEARNED.
TIME TO RETHINK MY STRATEGY. THIS ISN'T OVER YET.
VZZK
THOK
NOW I'LL FINISH HIM!
NO!
BUT WHY?
THERE'S NO NEED. IT'S OVER. WE'VE WON.
LISTEN TO THE CHOSEN ONE, NEITH. HIS WISDOM IS BEYOND OURS.
LET'S NOT GET CARRIED AWAY ...WAIT. WHERE'S KANJAR RO?
AND SAPPHIRE! SHE'S GONE!

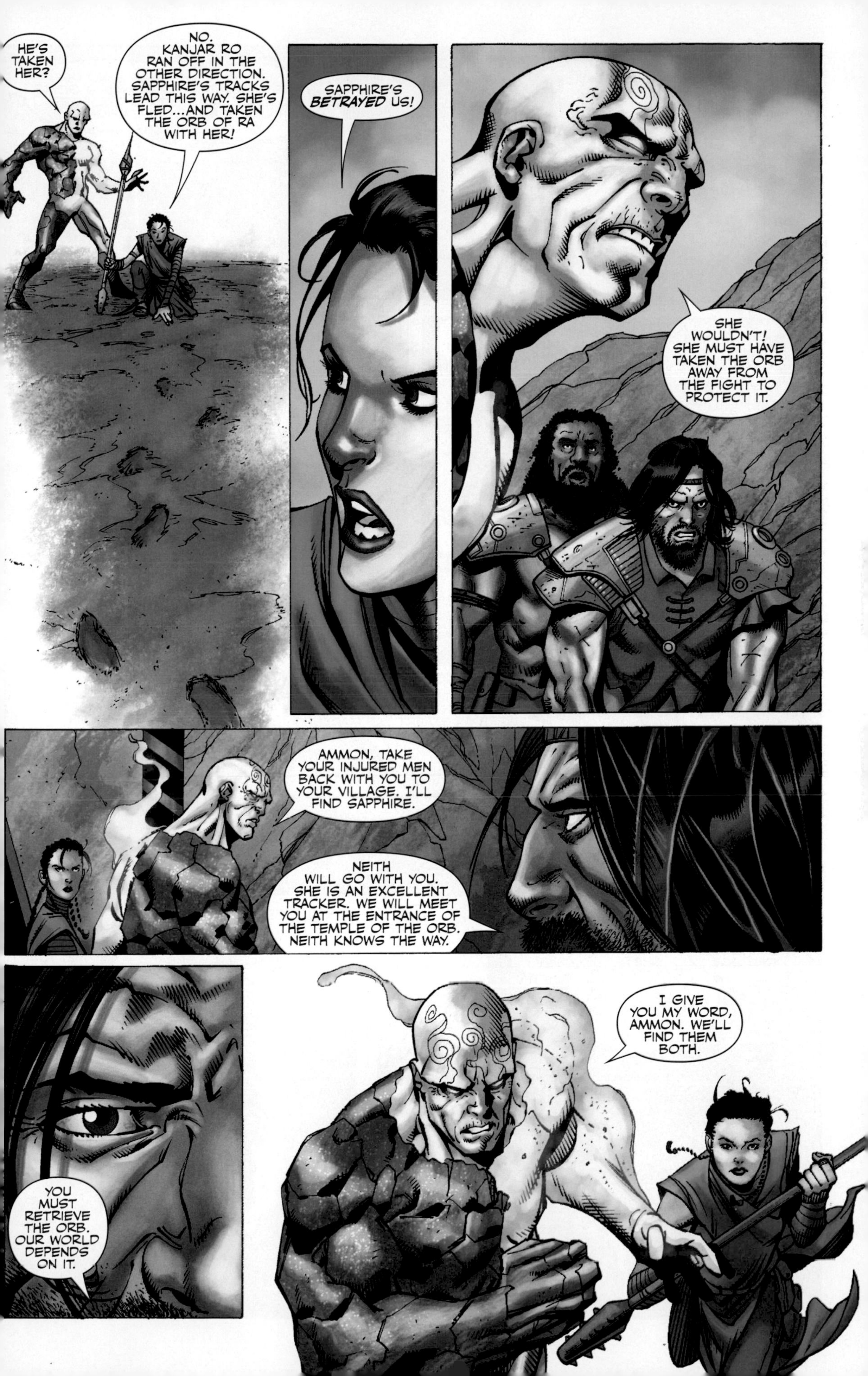
HE'S TAKEN HER?
NO. KANJAR RO RAN OFF IN THE OTHER DIRECTION. SAPPHIRE'S TRACKS LEAD THIS WAY. SHE'S FLED...AND TAKEN THE ORB OF RA WITH HER!
SAPPHIRE'S BETRAYED US!
SHE WOULDN'T! SHE MUST HAVE TAKEN THE ORB AWAY FROM THE FIGHT TO PROTECT IT.
AMMON, TAKE YOUR INJURED MEN BACK WITH YOU TO YOUR VILLAGE. I'LL FIND SAPPHIRE.
NEITH WILL GO WITH YOU. SHE IS AN EXCELLENT TRACKER. WE WILL MEET YOU AT THE ENTRANCE OF THE TEMPLE OF THE ORB. NEITH KNOWS THE WAY.
YOU MUST RETRIEVE THE ORB. OUR WORLD DEPENDS ON IT.
I GIVE YOU MY WORD, AMMON. WE'LL FIND THEM BOTH.

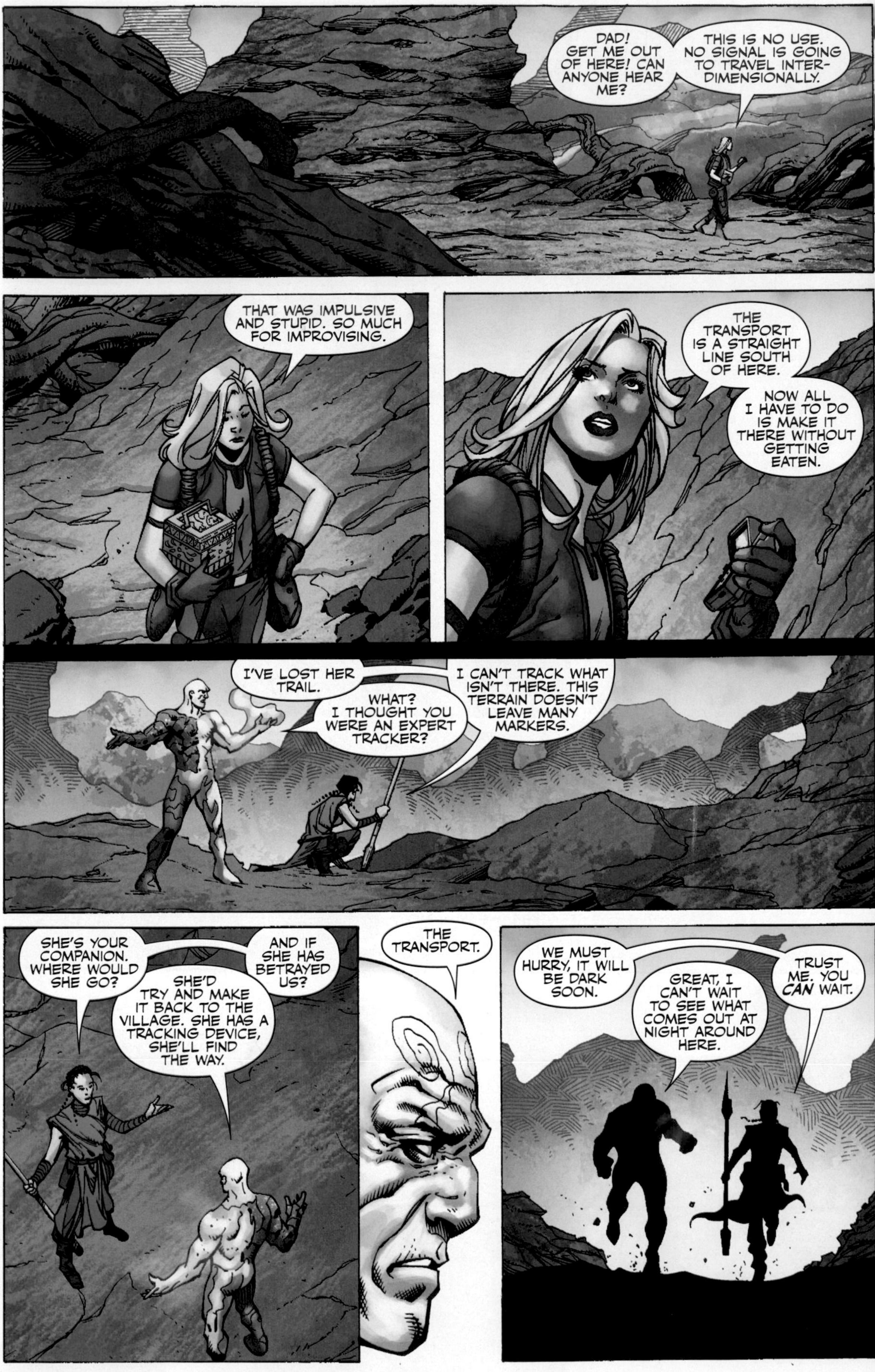
DAD! GET ME OUT OF HERE! CAN ANYONE HEAR ME?
THIS IS NO USE. NO SIGNAL IS GOING TO TRAVEL INTER-DIMENSIONALLY.
THAT WAS IMPULSIVE AND STUPID. SO MUCH FOR IMPROVISING.
THE TRANSPORT IS A STRAIGHT LINE SOUTH OF HERE.
NOW ALL I HAVE TO DO IS MAKE IT THERE WITHOUT GETTING EATEN.
I'VE LOST HER TRAIL.
WHAT? I THOUGHT YOU WERE AN EXPERT TRACKER?
I CAN'T TRACK WHAT ISN'T THERE. THIS TERRAIN DOESN'T LEAVE MANY MARKERS.
SHE'S YOUR COMPANION. WHERE WOULD SHE GO?
SHE'D TRY AND MAKE IT BACK TO THE VILLAGE. SHE HAS A TRACKING DEVICE, SHE'LL FIND THE WAY.
AND IF SHE HAS BETRAYED US?
THE TRANSPORT.
WE MUST HURRY, IT WILL BE DARK SOON.
GREAT, I CAN'T WAIT TO SEE WHAT COMES OUT AT NIGHT AROUND HERE.
TRUST ME. YOU CAN WAIT.

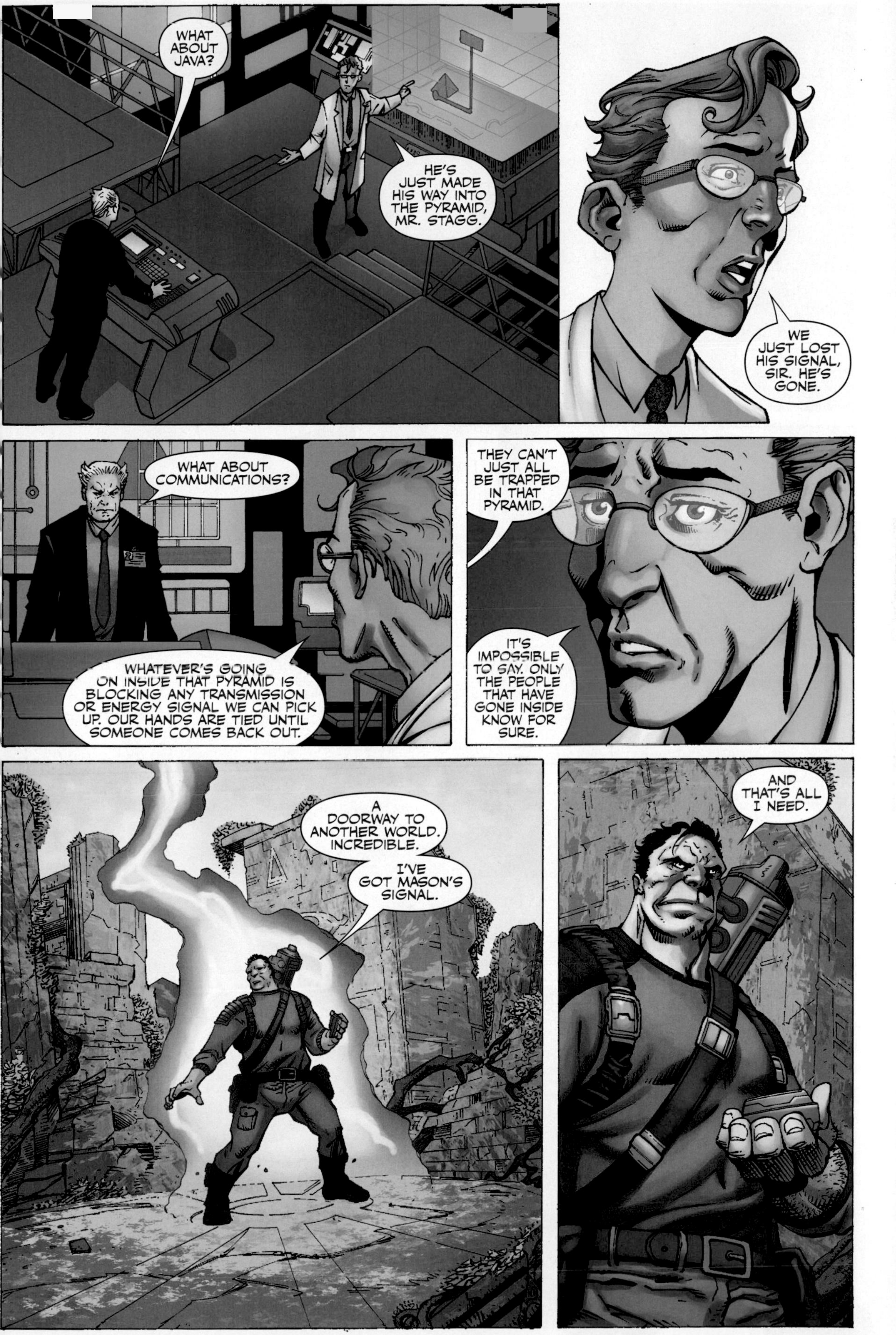
WHAT ABOUT JAVA?
HE'S JUST MADE HIS WAY INTO THE PYRAMID, MR. STAGG.
WE JUST LOST HIS SIGNAL, SIR. HE'S GONE.
WHAT ABOUT COMMUNICATIONS?
WHATEVER'S GOING ON INSIDE THAT PYRAMID IS BLOCKING ANY TRANSMISSION OR ENERGY SIGNAL WE CAN PICK UP. OUR HANDS ARE TIED UNTIL SOMEONE COMES BACK OUT.
THEY CAN'T JUST ALL BE TRAPPED IN THAT PYRAMID.
IT'S IMPOSSIBLE TO SAY. ONLY THE PEOPLE THAT HAVE GONE INSIDE KNOW FOR SURE.
A DOORWAY TO ANOTHER WORLD. INCREDIBLE.
I'VE GOT MASON'S SIGNAL.
AND THAT'S ALL I NEED.

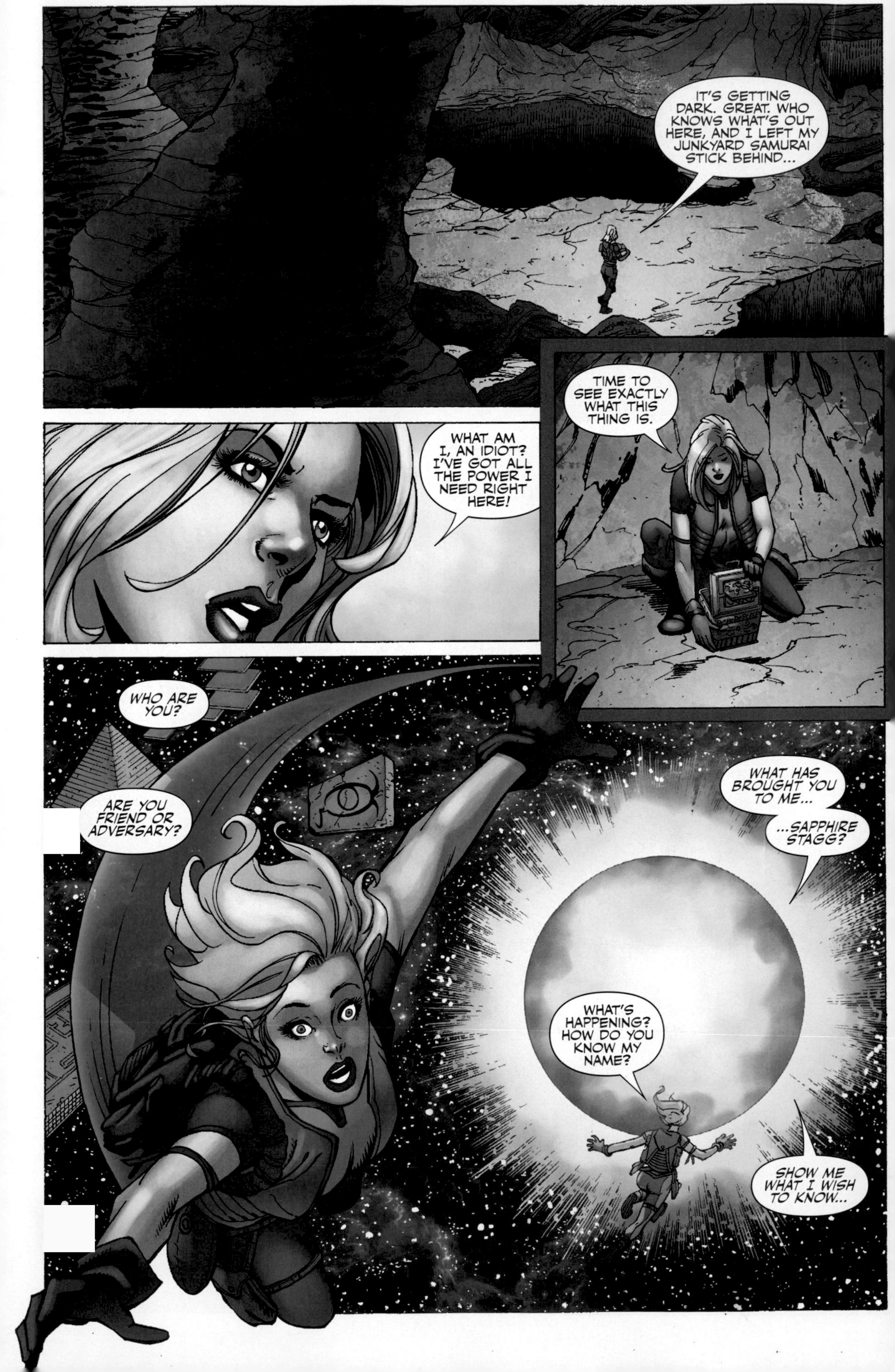
IT'S GETTING DARK. GREAT. WHO KNOWS WHAT'S OUT HERE, AND I LEFT MY JUNKYARD SAMURAI STICK BEHIND...
WHAT AM I, AN IDIOT? I'VE GOT ALL THE POWER I NEED RIGHT HERE!
TIME TO SEE EXACTLY WHAT THIS THING IS.
WHO ARE YOU?
ARE YOU FRIEND OR ADVERSARY?
WHAT HAS BROUGHT YOU TO ME...
...SAPPHIRE STAGG?
WHAT'S HAPPENING? HOW DO YOU KNOW MY NAME?
SHOW ME WHAT I WISH TO KNOW...

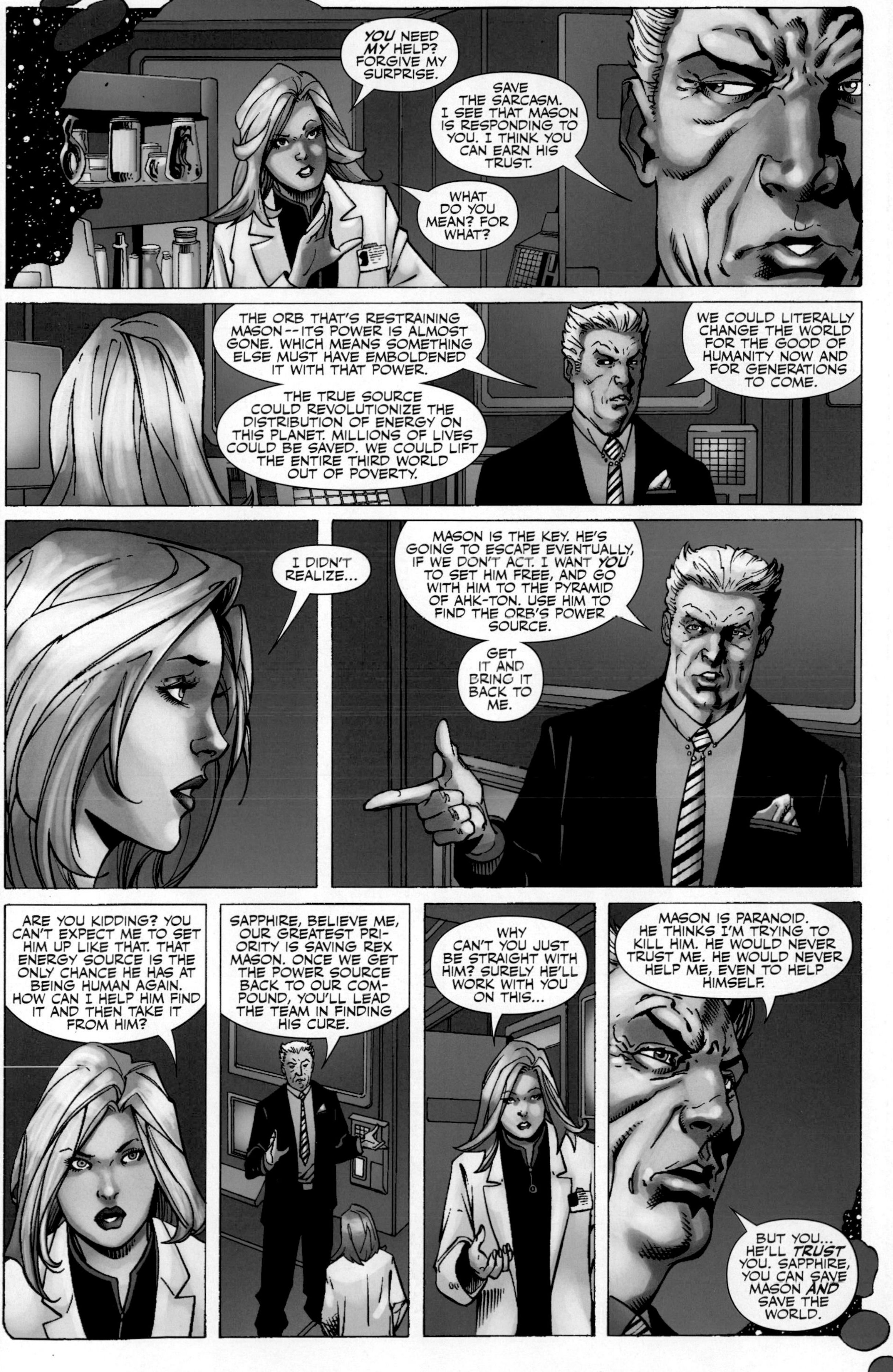
YOU NEED MY HELP? FORGIVE MY SURPRISE.
SAVE THE SARCASM. I SEE THAT MASON IS RESPONDING TO YOU. I THINK YOU CAN EARN HIS TRUST.
WHAT DO YOU MEAN? FOR WHAT?
THE ORB THAT'S RESTRAINING MASON--ITS POWER IS ALMOST GONE. WHICH MEANS SOMETHING ELSE MUST HAVE EMBOLDENED IT WITH THAT POWER.
THE TRUE SOURCE COULD REVOLUTIONIZE THE DISTRIBUTION OF ENERGY ON THIS PLANET. MILLIONS OF LIVES COULD BE SAVED. WE COULD LIFT THE ENTIRE THIRD WORLD OUT OF POVERTY.
WE COULD LITERALLY CHANGE THE WORLD FOR THE GOOD OF HUMANITY NOW AND FOR GENERATIONS TO COME.
I DIDN'T REALIZE...
MASON IS THE KEY. HE'S GOING TO ESCAPE EVENTUALLY, IF WE DON'T ACT. I WANT YOU TO SET HIM FREE, AND GO WITH HIM TO THE PYRAMID OF AHK-TON. USE HIM TO FIND THE ORB'S POWER SOURCE.
GET IT AND BRING IT BACK TO ME.
ARE YOU KIDDING? YOU CAN'T EXPECT ME TO SET HIM UP LIKE THAT. THAT ENERGY SOURCE IS THE ONLY CHANCE HE HAS AT BEING HUMAN AGAIN. HOW CAN I HELP HIM FIND IT AND THEN TAKE IT FROM HIM?
SAPPHIRE, BELIEVE ME, OUR GREATEST PRIORITY IS SAVING REX MASON. ONCE WE GET THE POWER SOURCE BACK TO OUR COMPOUND, YOU'LL LEAD THE TEAM IN FINDING HIS CURE.
WHY CAN'T YOU JUST BE STRAIGHT WITH HIM? SURELY HE'LL WORK WITH YOU ON THIS...
MASON IS PARANOID. HE THINKS I'M TRYING TO KILL HIM. HE WOULD NEVER TRUST ME. HE WOULD NEVER HELP ME, EVEN TO HELP HIMSELF.
BUT YOU... HE'LL TRUST YOU. SAPPHIRE, YOU CAN SAVE MASON AND SAVE THE WORLD.

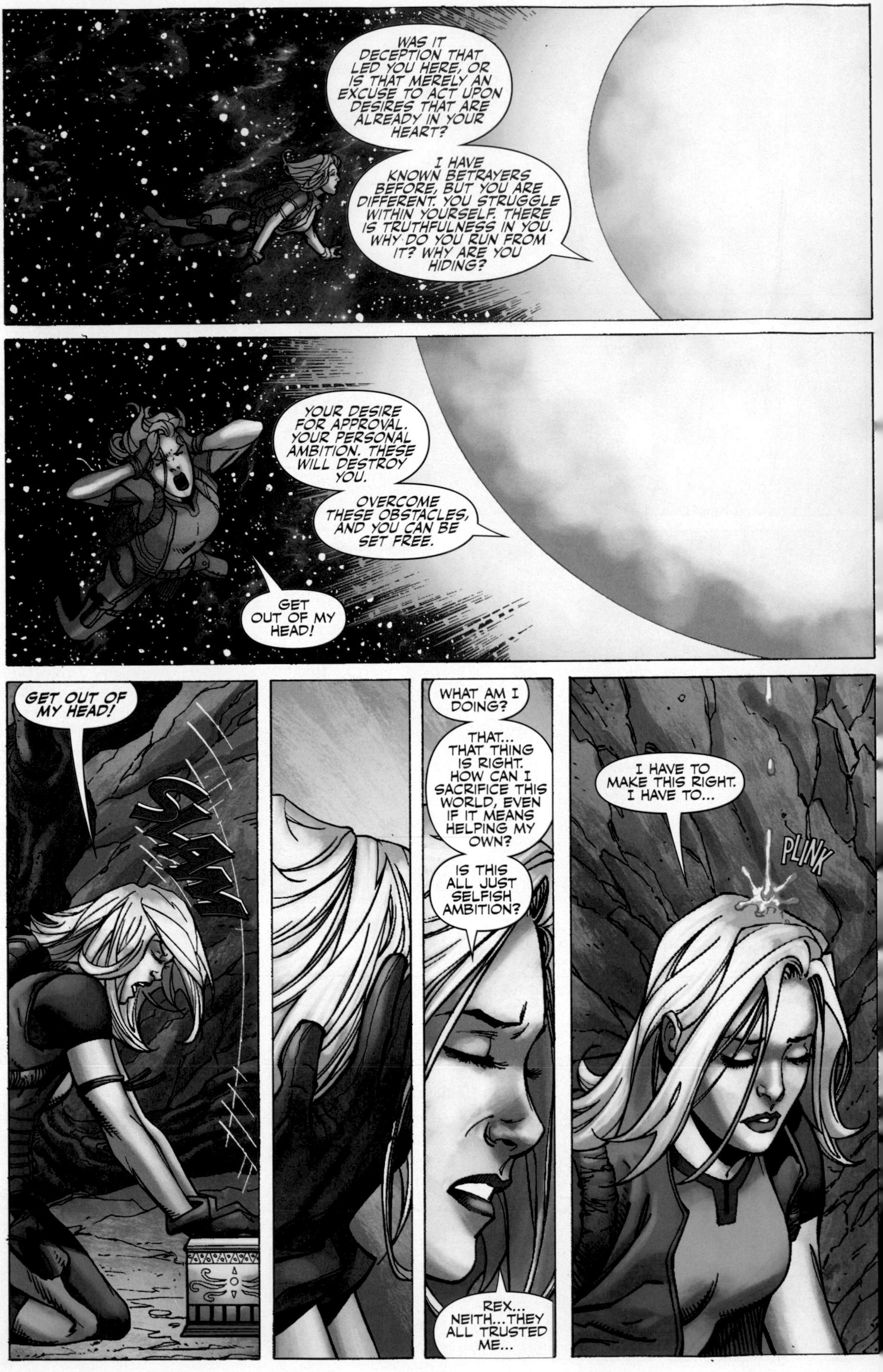
WAS IT DECEPTION THAT LED YOU HERE, OR IS THAT MERELY AN EXCUSE TO ACT UPON DESIRES THAT ARE ALREADY IN YOUR HEART?
I HAVE KNOWN BETRAYERS BEFORE, BUT YOU ARE DIFFERENT. YOU STRUGGLE WITHIN YOURSELF. THERE IS TRUTHFULNESS IN YOU. WHY DO YOU RUN FROM IT? WHY ARE YOU HIDING?
YOUR DESIRE FOR APPROVAL. YOUR PERSONAL AMBITION. THESE WILL DESTROY YOU.
OVERCOME THESE OBSTACLES, AND YOU CAN BE SET FREE.
GET OUT OF MY HEAD!
GET OUT OF MY HEAD!
SLAM
WHAT AM I DOING?
THAT... THAT THING IS RIGHT. HOW CAN I SACRIFICE THIS WORLD, EVEN IF IT MEANS HELPING MY OWN?
IS THIS ALL JUST SELFISH AMBITION?
REX... NEITH...THEY ALL TRUSTED ME...
I HAVE TO MAKE THIS RIGHT. I HAVE TO...
PLINK

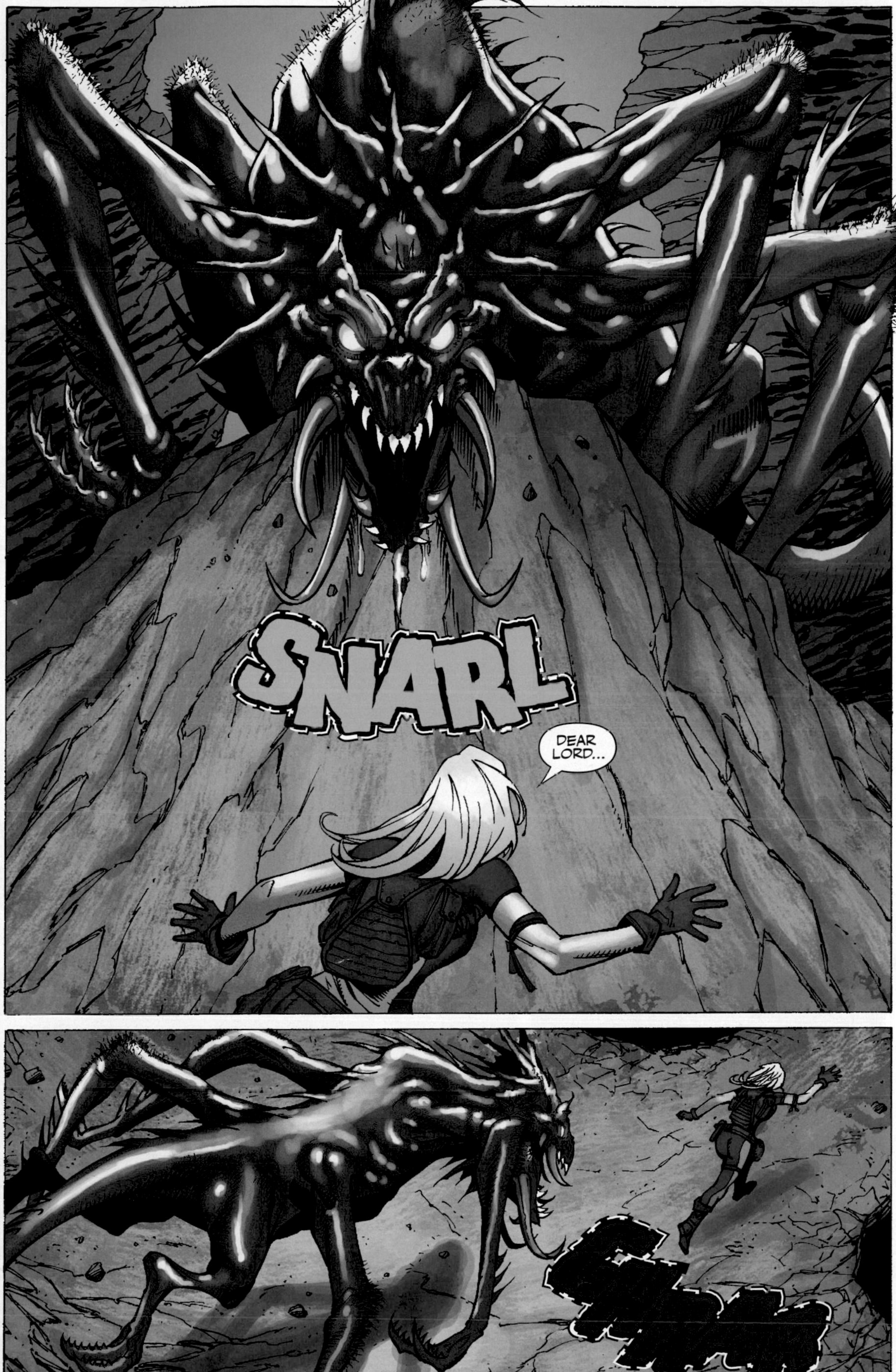
SNARL
DEAR LORD...

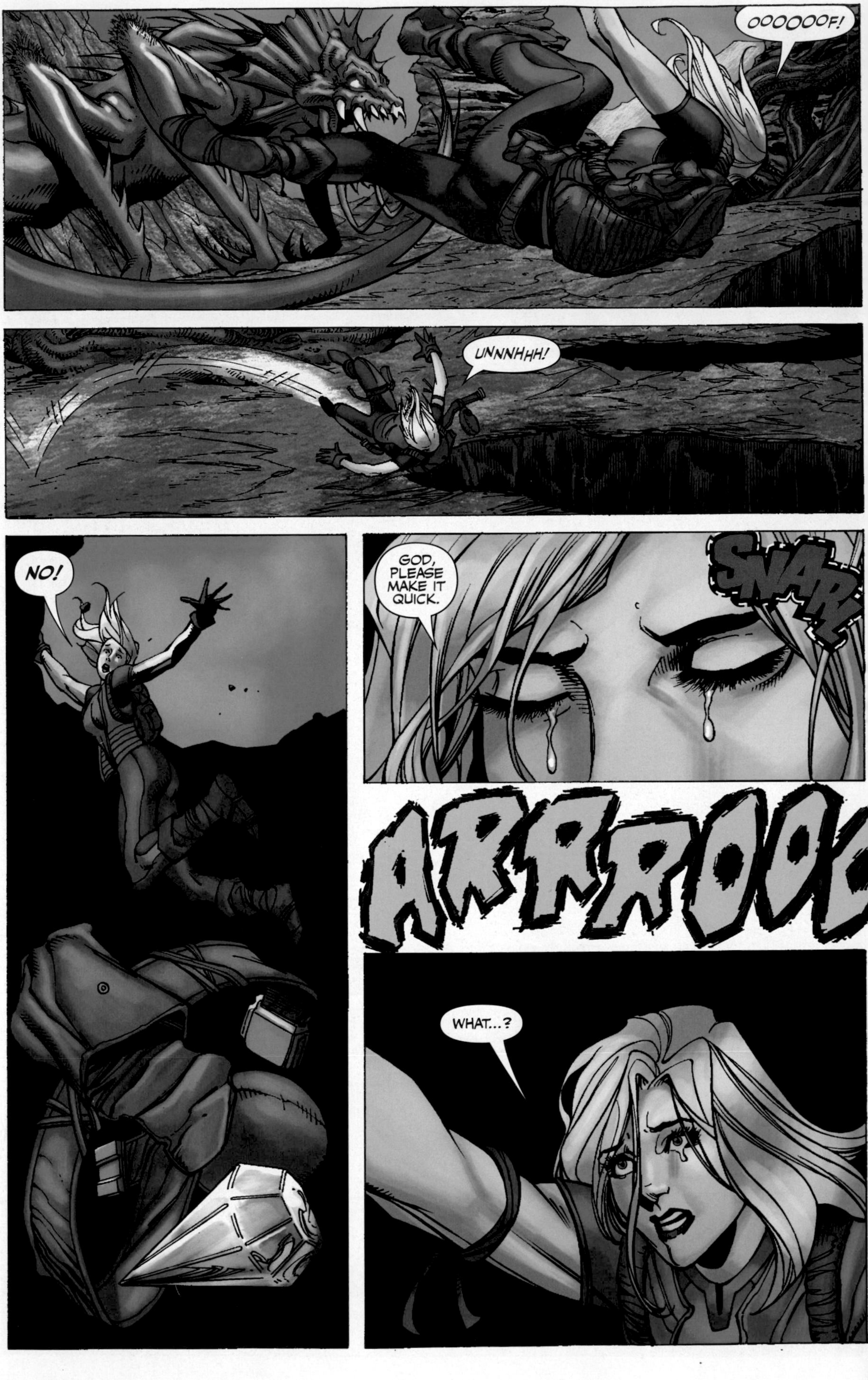
OOOOOOF!
UNNNHHH!
NO!
GOD, PLEASE MAKE IT QUICK.
SNAR
ARRROO
WHAT...?

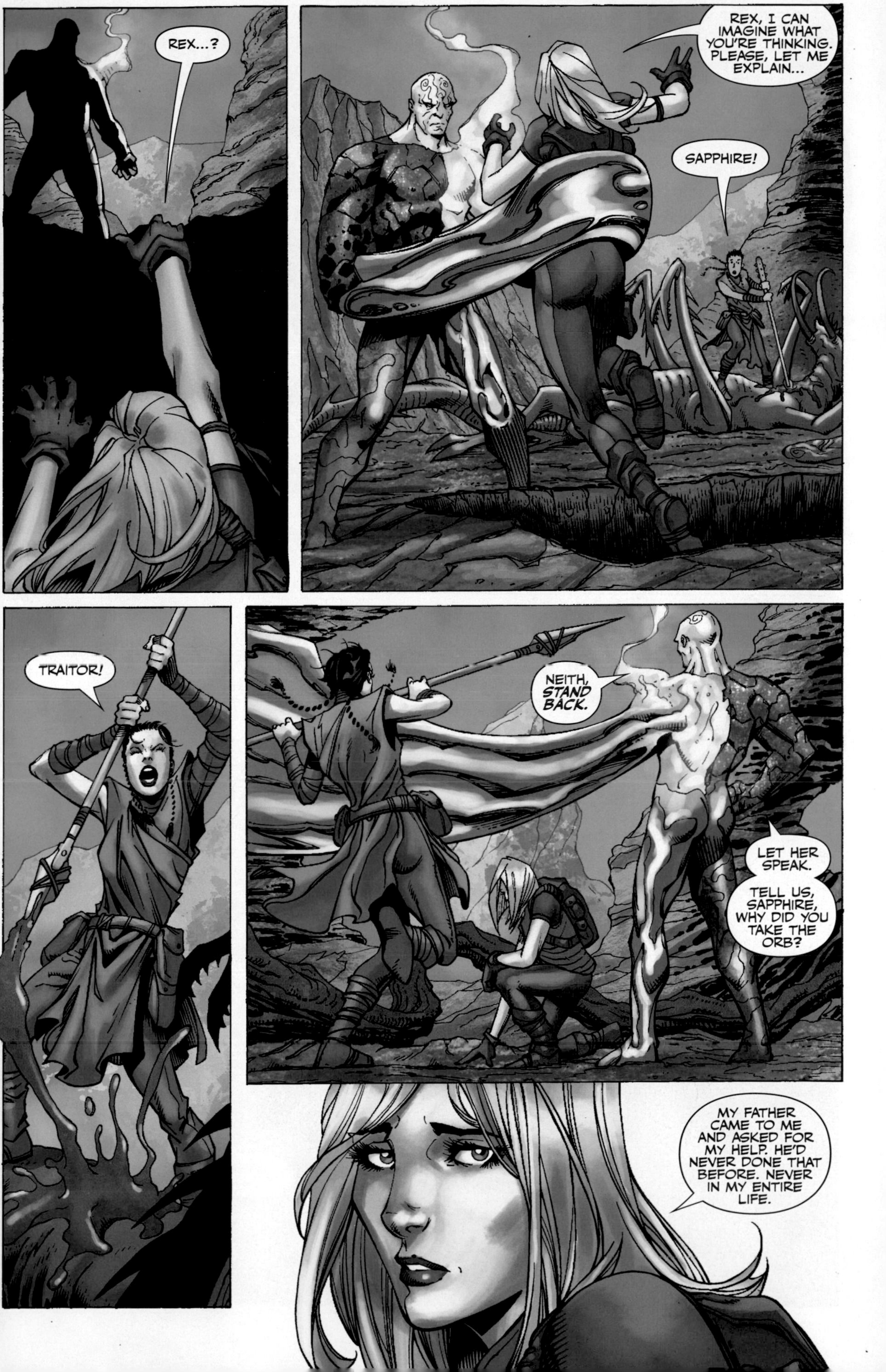
REX...?
REX, I CAN IMAGINE WHAT YOU'RE THINKING. PLEASE, LET ME EXPLAIN...
SAPPHIRE!
TRAITOR!
NEITH, STAND BACK.
LET HER SPEAK.
TELL US, SAPPHIRE, WHY DID YOU TAKE THE ORB?
MY FATHER CAME TO ME AND ASKED FOR MY HELP. HE'D NEVER DONE THAT BEFORE. NEVER IN MY ENTIRE LIFE.

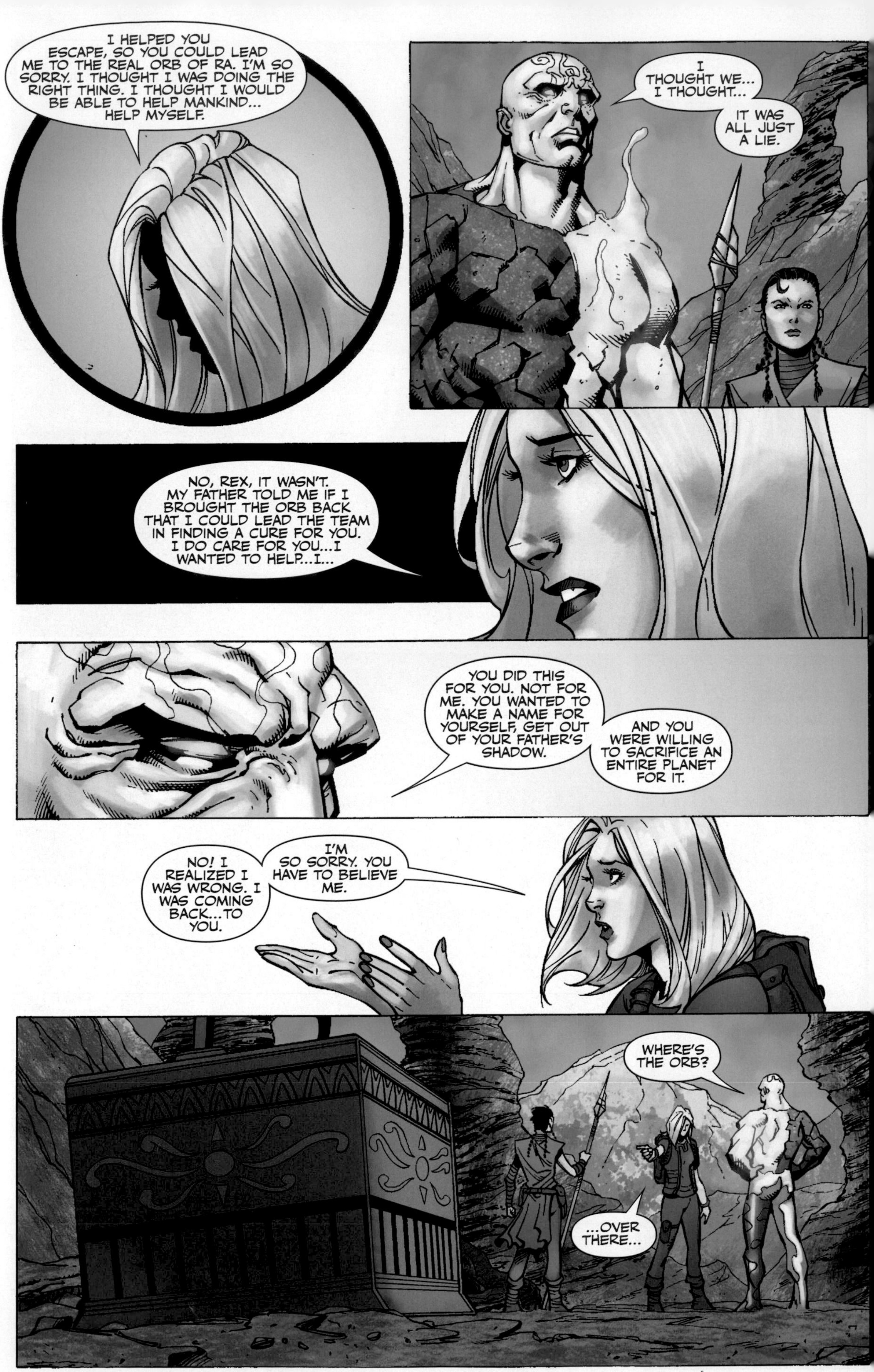
I HELPED YOU ESCAPE, SO YOU COULD LEAD ME TO THE REAL ORB OF RA. I'M SO SORRY. I THOUGHT I WAS DOING THE RIGHT THING. I THOUGHT I WOULD BE ABLE TO HELP MANKIND... HELP MYSELF.
I THOUGHT WE... I THOUGHT...
IT WAS ALL JUST A LIE.
NO, REX, IT WASN'T. MY FATHER TOLD ME IF I BROUGHT THE ORB BACK THAT I COULD LEAD THE TEAM IN FINDING A CURE FOR YOU. I DO CARE FOR YOU...I WANTED TO HELP...I...
YOU DID THIS FOR YOU. NOT FOR ME. YOU WANTED TO MAKE A NAME FOR YOURSELF, GET OUT OF YOUR FATHER'S SHADOW.
AND YOU WERE WILLING TO SACRIFICE AN ENTIRE PLANET FOR IT.
NO! I REALIZED I WAS WRONG. I WAS COMING BACK...TO YOU.
I'M SO SORRY. YOU HAVE TO BELIEVE ME.
WHERE'S THE ORB?
...OVER THERE...

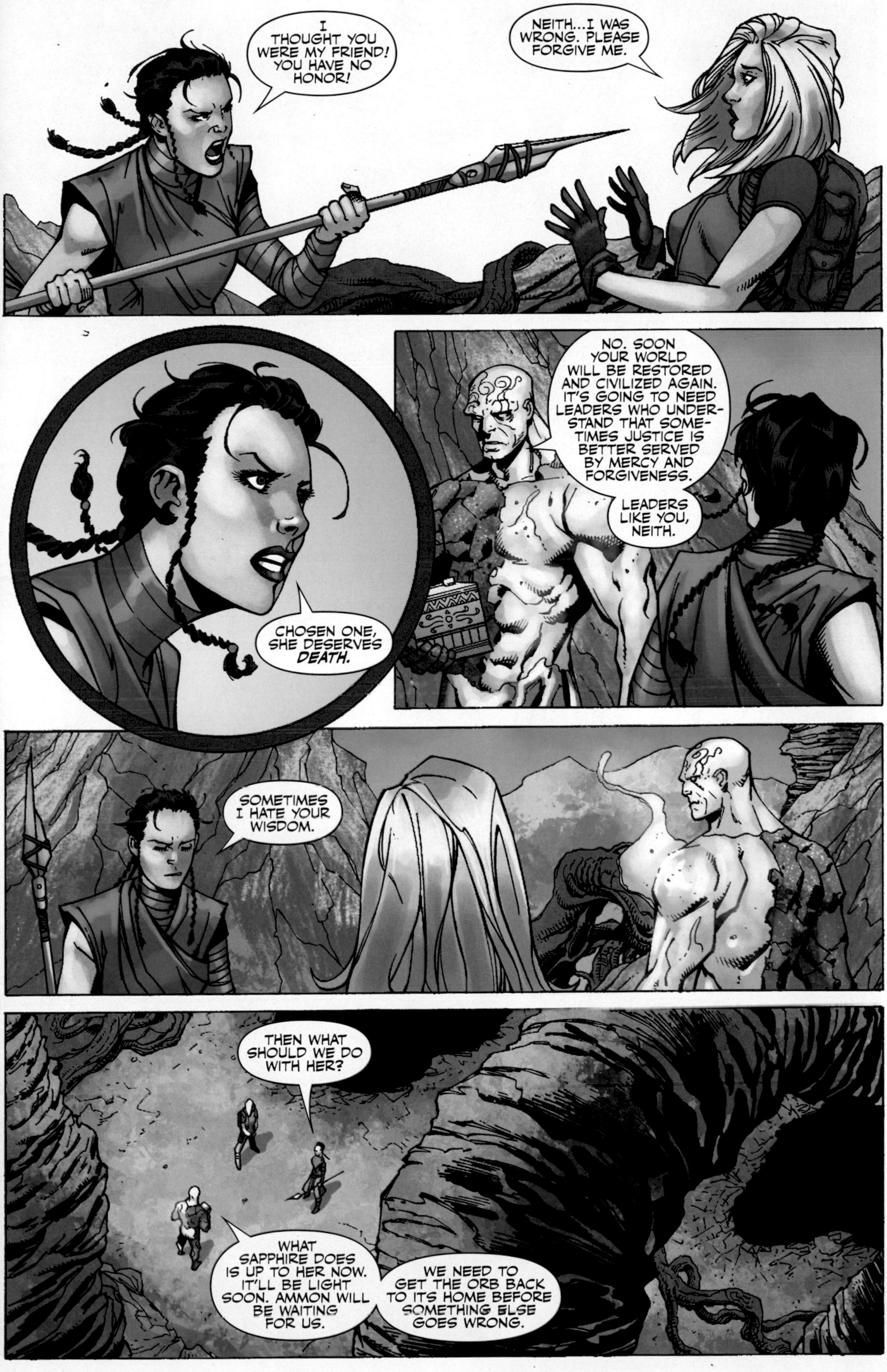
I THOUGHT YOU WERE MY FRIEND! YOU HAVE NO HONOR!
NEITH...I WAS WRONG. PLEASE FORGIVE ME.
CHOSEN ONE, SHE DESERVES *DEATH.*
NO. SOON YOUR WORLD WILL BE RESTORED AND CIVILIZED AGAIN. IT'S GOING TO NEED LEADERS WHO UNDER-STAND THAT SOME-TIMES JUSTICE IS BETTER SERVED BY MERCY AND FORGIVENESS.
LEADERS LIKE YOU, NEITH.
SOMETIMES I HATE YOUR WISDOM.
THEN WHAT SHOULD WE DO WITH HER?
WHAT SAPPHIRE DOES IS UP TO HER NOW. IT'LL BE LIGHT SOON. AMMON WILL BE WAITING FOR US.
WE NEED TO GET THE ORB BACK TO ITS HOME BEFORE SOMETHING ELSE GOES WRONG.

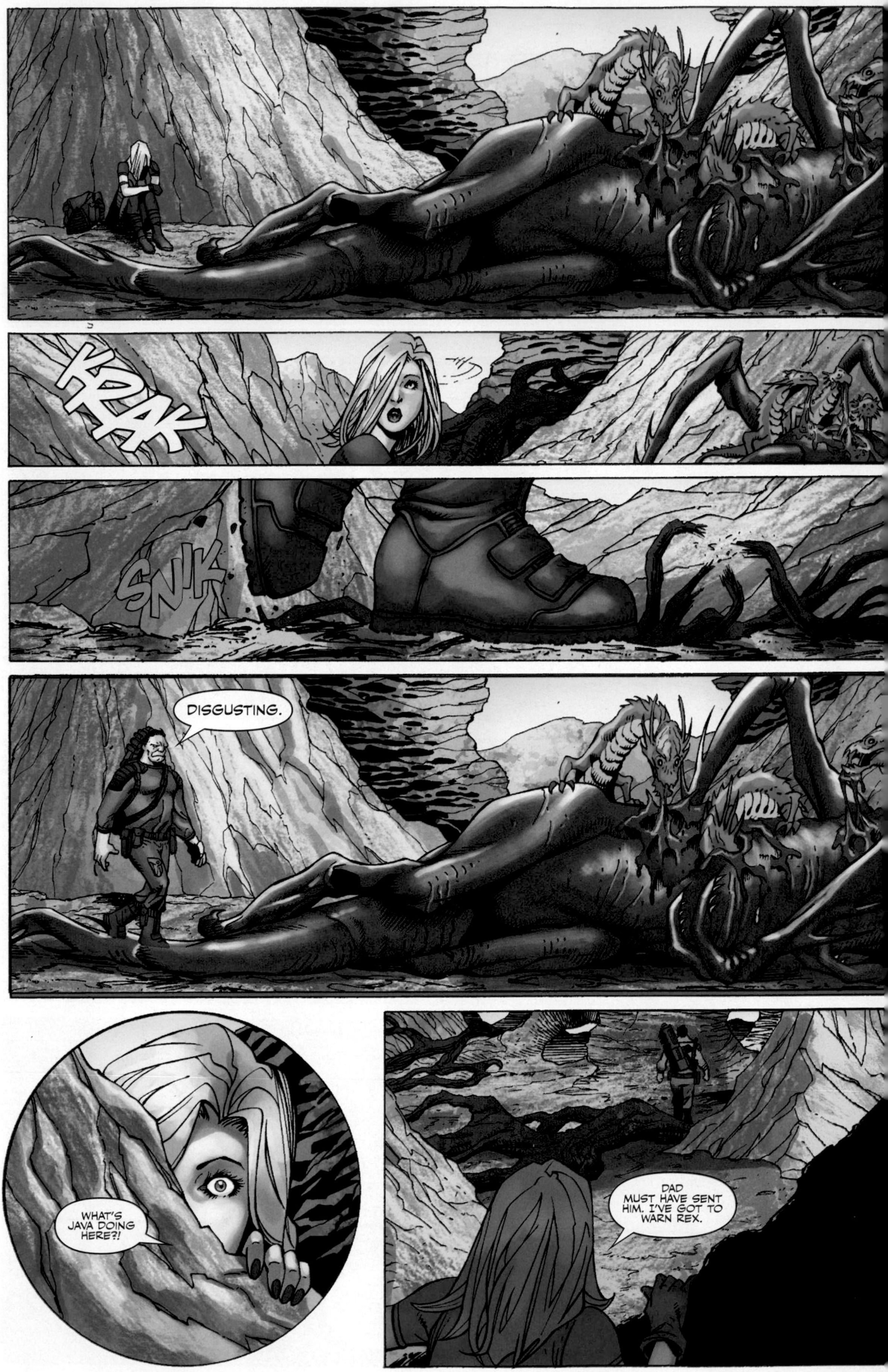
KRAK
SNIK
DISGUSTING.
WHAT'S JAVA DOING HERE?!
DAD MUST HAVE SENT HIM. I'VE GOT TO WARN REX.

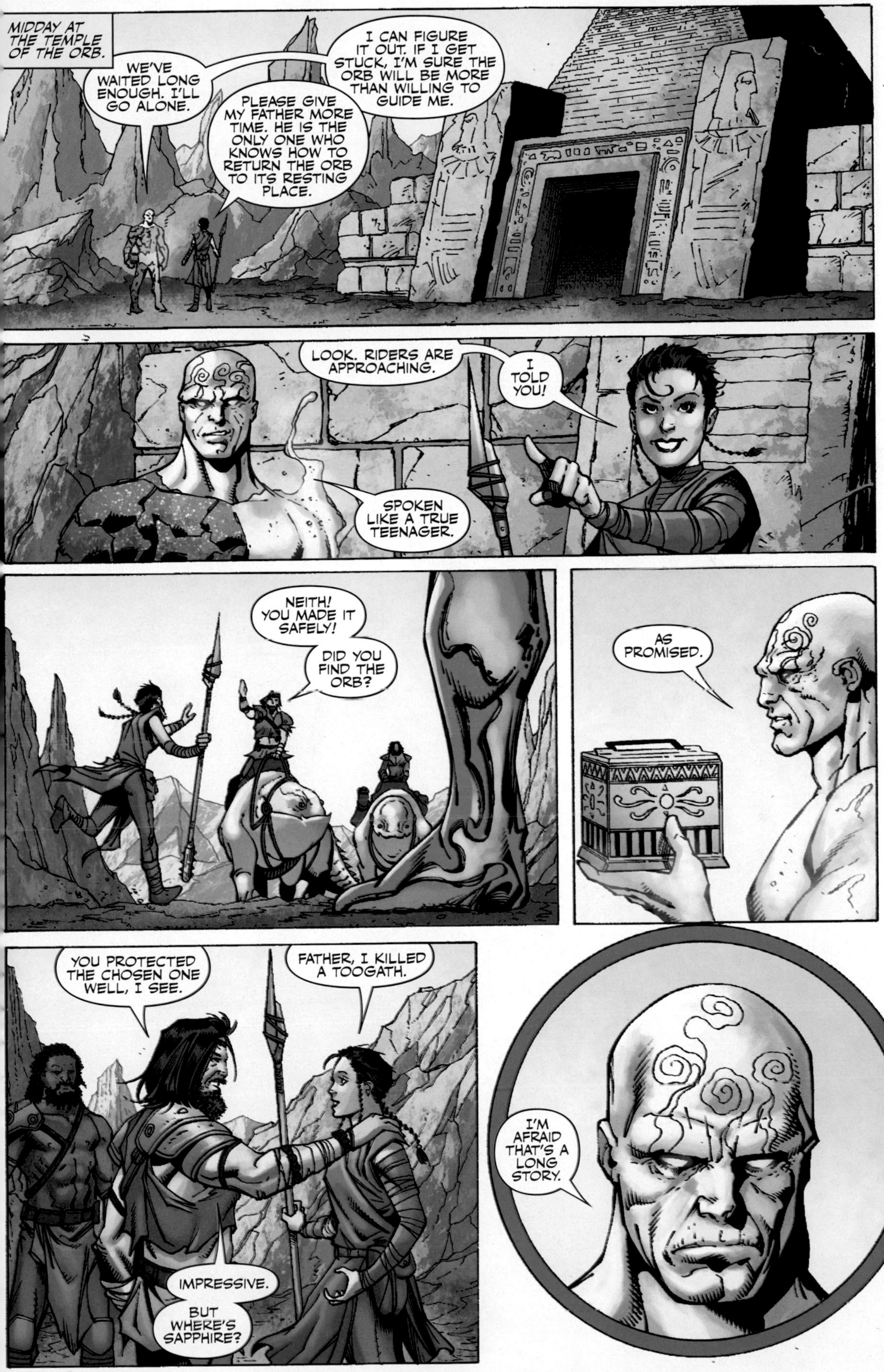
MIDDAY AT THE TEMPLE OF THE ORB.
WE'VE WAITED LONG ENOUGH. I'LL GO ALONE.
PLEASE GIVE MY FATHER MORE TIME. HE IS THE ONLY ONE WHO KNOWS HOW TO RETURN THE ORB TO ITS RESTING PLACE.
I CAN FIGURE IT OUT. IF I GET STUCK, I'M SURE THE ORB WILL BE MORE THAN WILLING TO GUIDE ME.
LOOK. RIDERS ARE APPROACHING.
I TOLD YOU!
SPOKEN LIKE A TRUE TEENAGER.
NEITH! YOU MADE IT SAFELY!
DID YOU FIND THE ORB?
AS PROMISED.
YOU PROTECTED THE CHOSEN ONE WELL, I SEE.
FATHER, I KILLED A TOOGATH.
IMPRESSIVE.
BUT WHERE'S SAPPHIRE?
I'M AFRAID THAT'S A LONG STORY.

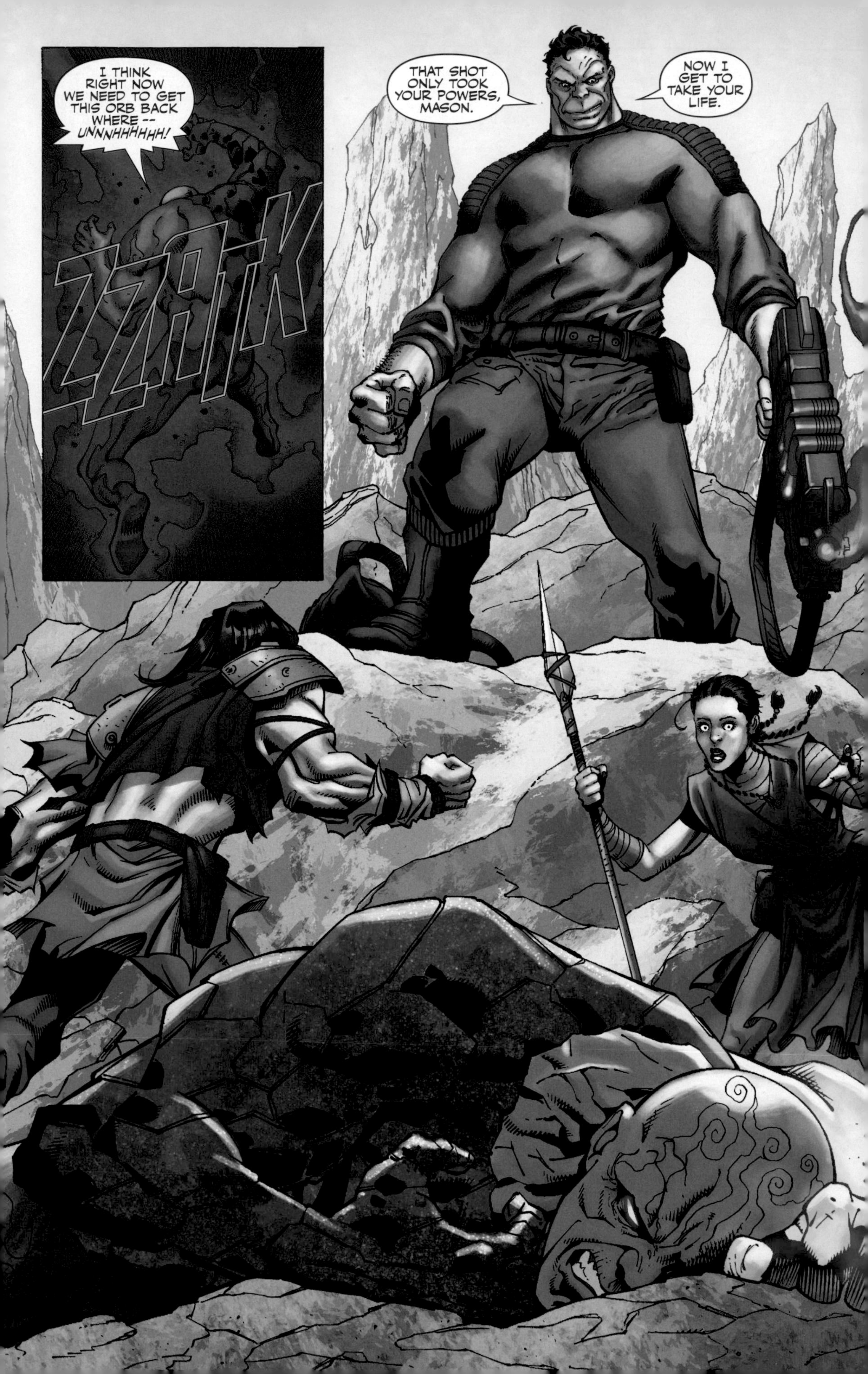

I THINK RIGHT NOW WE NEED TO GET THIS ORB BACK WHERE -- UNNNHHHHHH!
ZZZRTK
THAT SHOT ONLY TOOK YOUR POWERS, MASON.
NOW I GET TO TAKE YOUR LIFE.

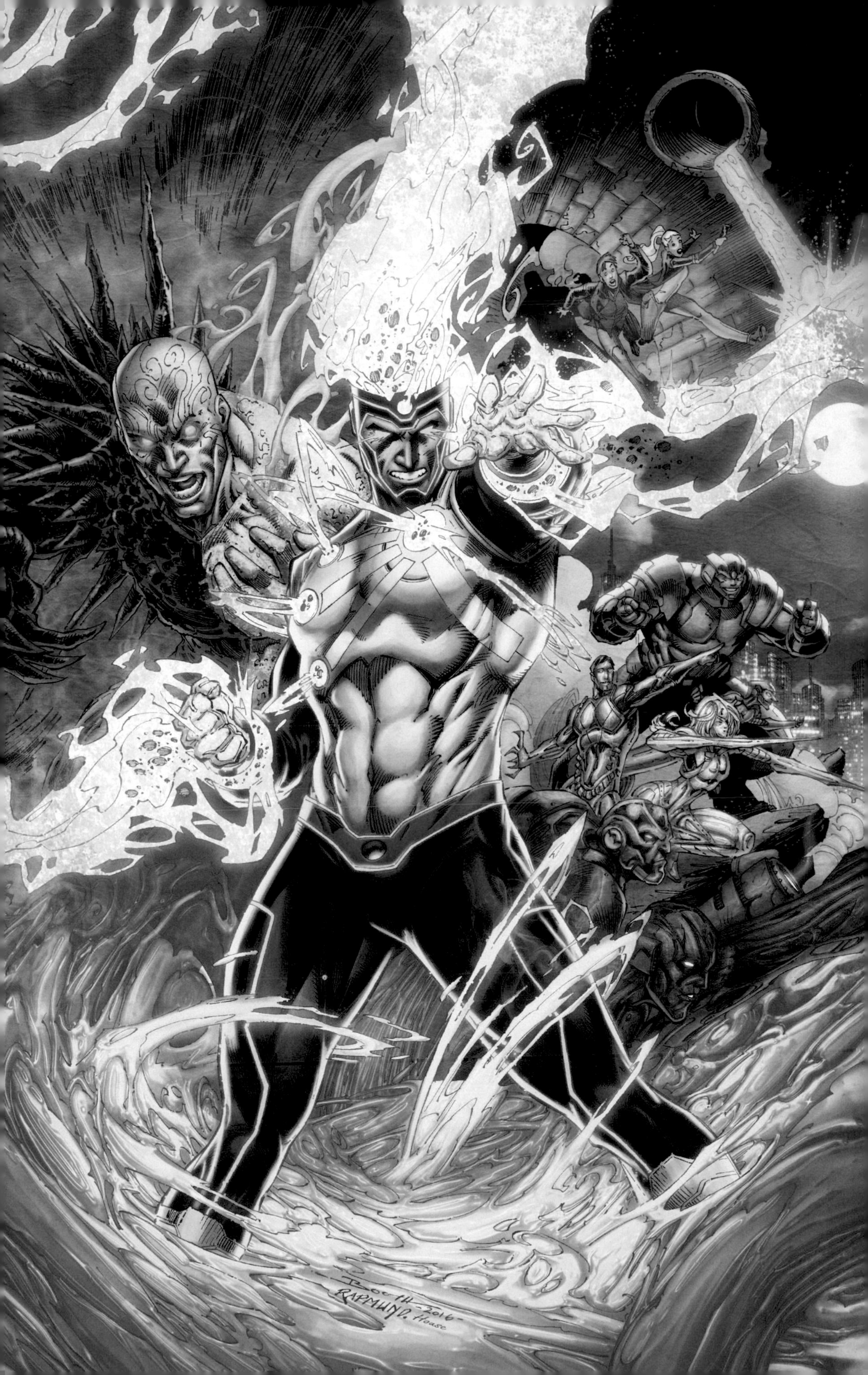
BOOTH-2016-
RAPMUND. Hoase

REBIRTH AND REDEMPTION

AARON LOPRESTI writer/penciller LIVESAY inker CHRIS SOTOMAYOR colorist MICHAEL HEISLER letterer

BRETT BOOTH and NORM RAPMUND with ANDREW DALHOUSE cover

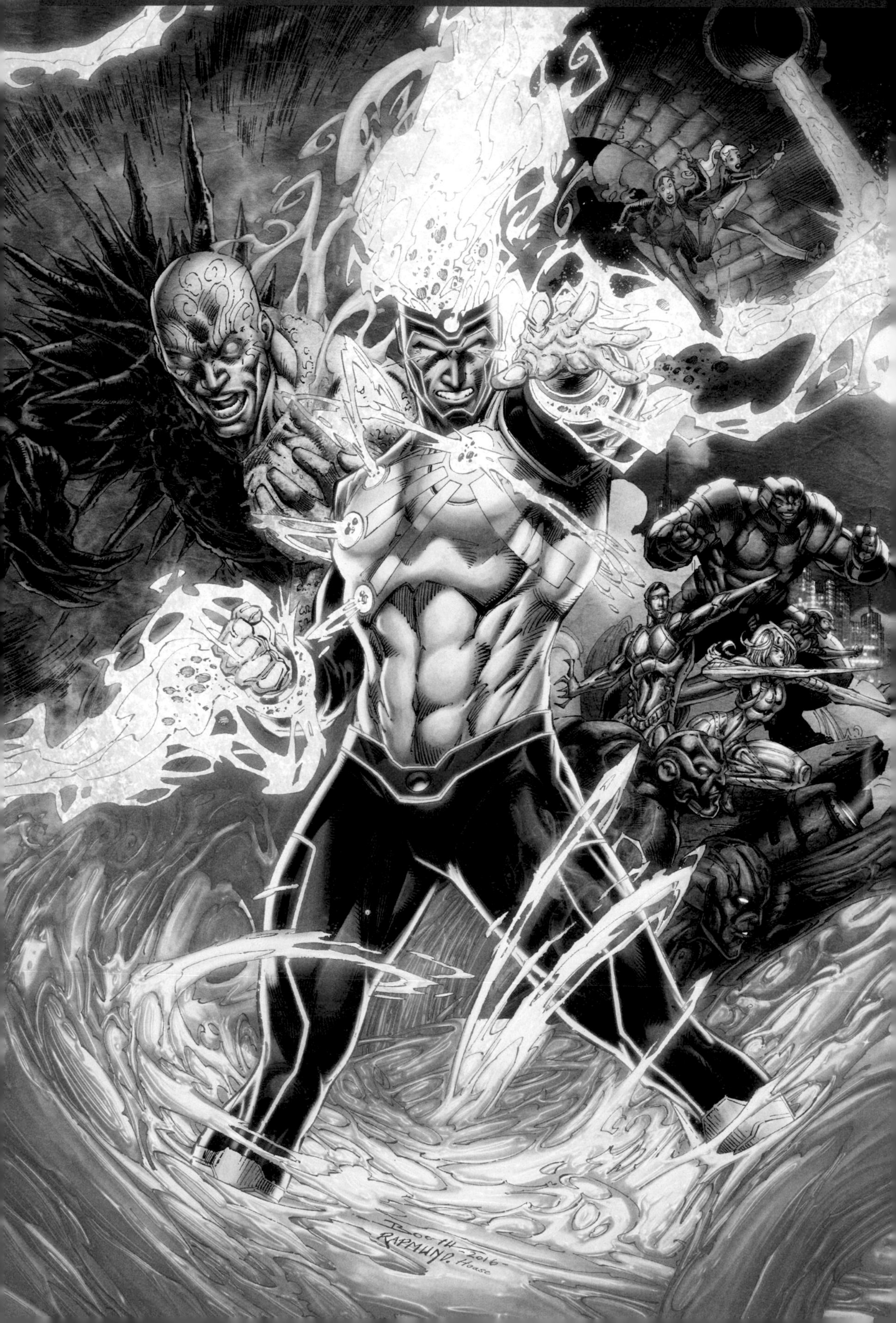
BOOTH -2016-
RAPMUND. House

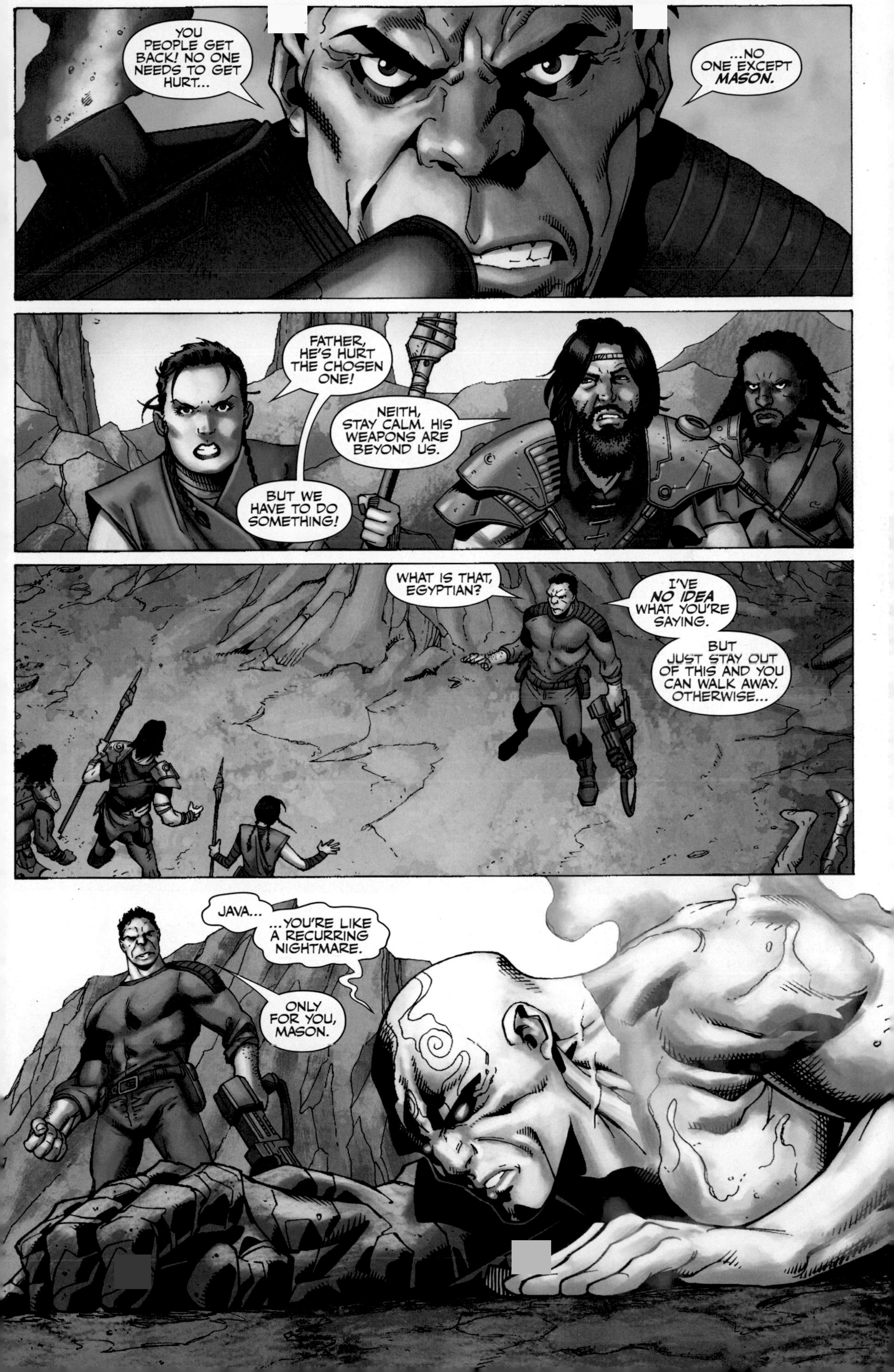
YOU PEOPLE GET BACK! NO ONE NEEDS TO GET HURT...
...NO ONE EXCEPT MASON.
FATHER, HE'S HURT THE CHOSEN ONE!
NEITH, STAY CALM. HIS WEAPONS ARE BEYOND US.
BUT WE HAVE TO DO SOMETHING!
WHAT IS THAT, EGYPTIAN?
I'VE NO IDEA WHAT YOU'RE SAYING.
BUT JUST STAY OUT OF THIS AND YOU CAN WALK AWAY. OTHERWISE...
JAVA...
...YOU'RE LIKE A RECURRING NIGHTMARE.
ONLY FOR YOU, MASON.

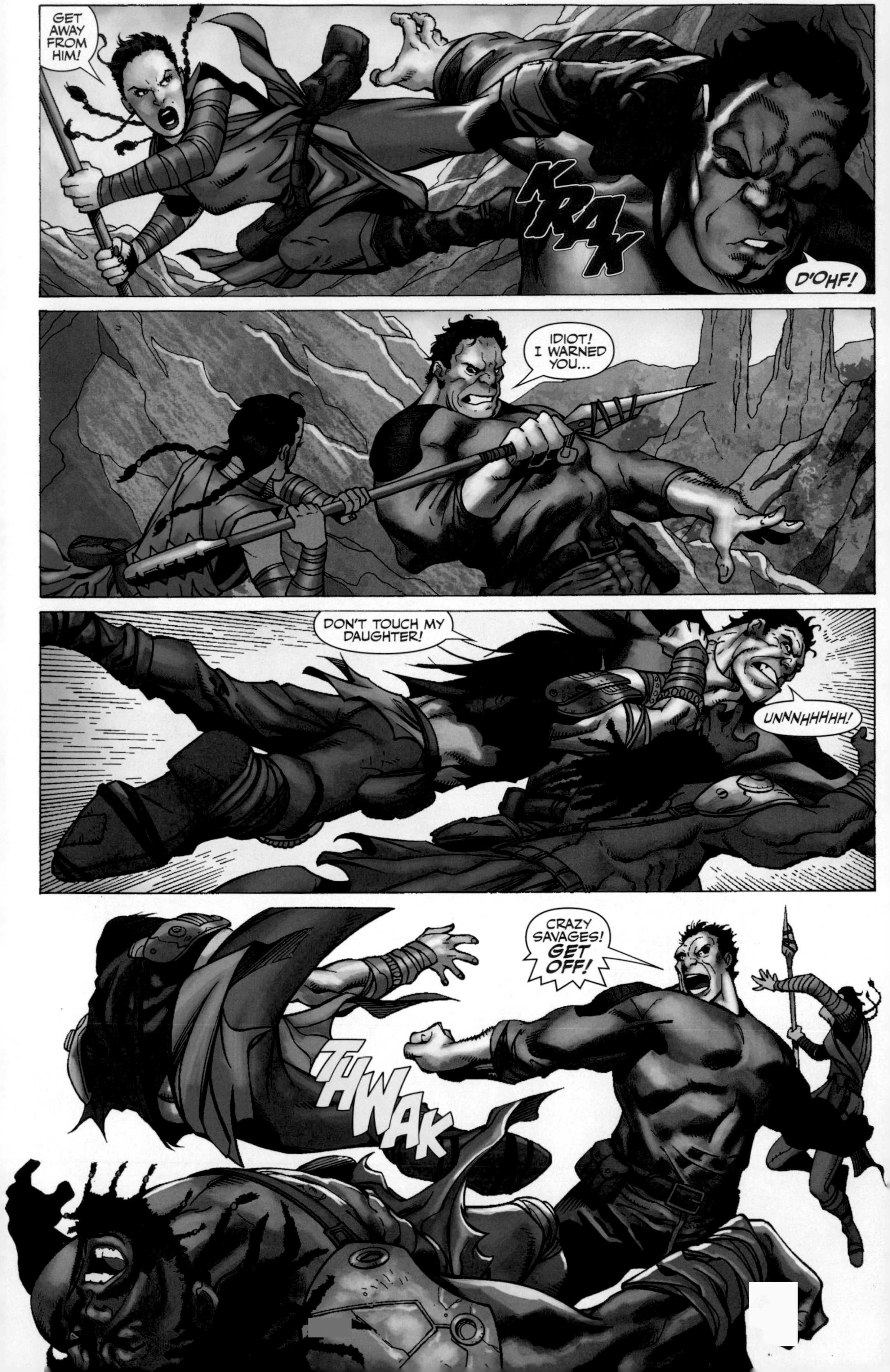
GET AWAY FROM HIM!
KRAK
D'OHF!
IDIOT! I WARNED YOU...
DON'T TOUCH MY DAUGHTER!
UNNNHHHHH!
CRAZY SAVAGES! GET OFF!
THWAK

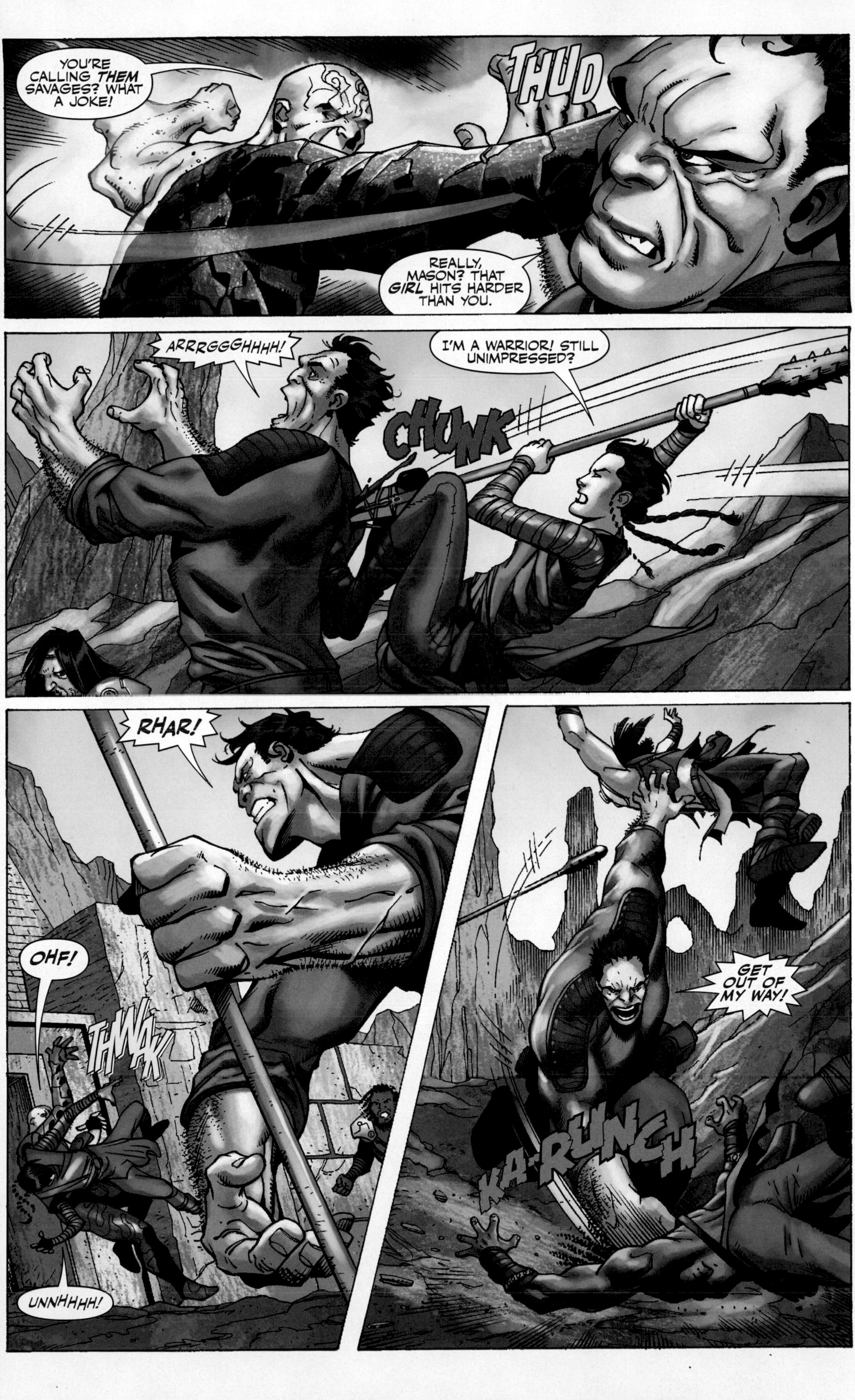
YOU'RE CALLING THEM SAVAGES? WHAT A JOKE!
THUD
REALLY, MASON? THAT GIRL HITS HARDER THAN YOU.
ARRRGGGHHHH!
I'M A WARRIOR! STILL UNIMPRESSED?
CHUNK
RHAR!
OHF!
THWAK
UNNHHHH!
GET OUT OF MY WAY!
KA-RUNCH

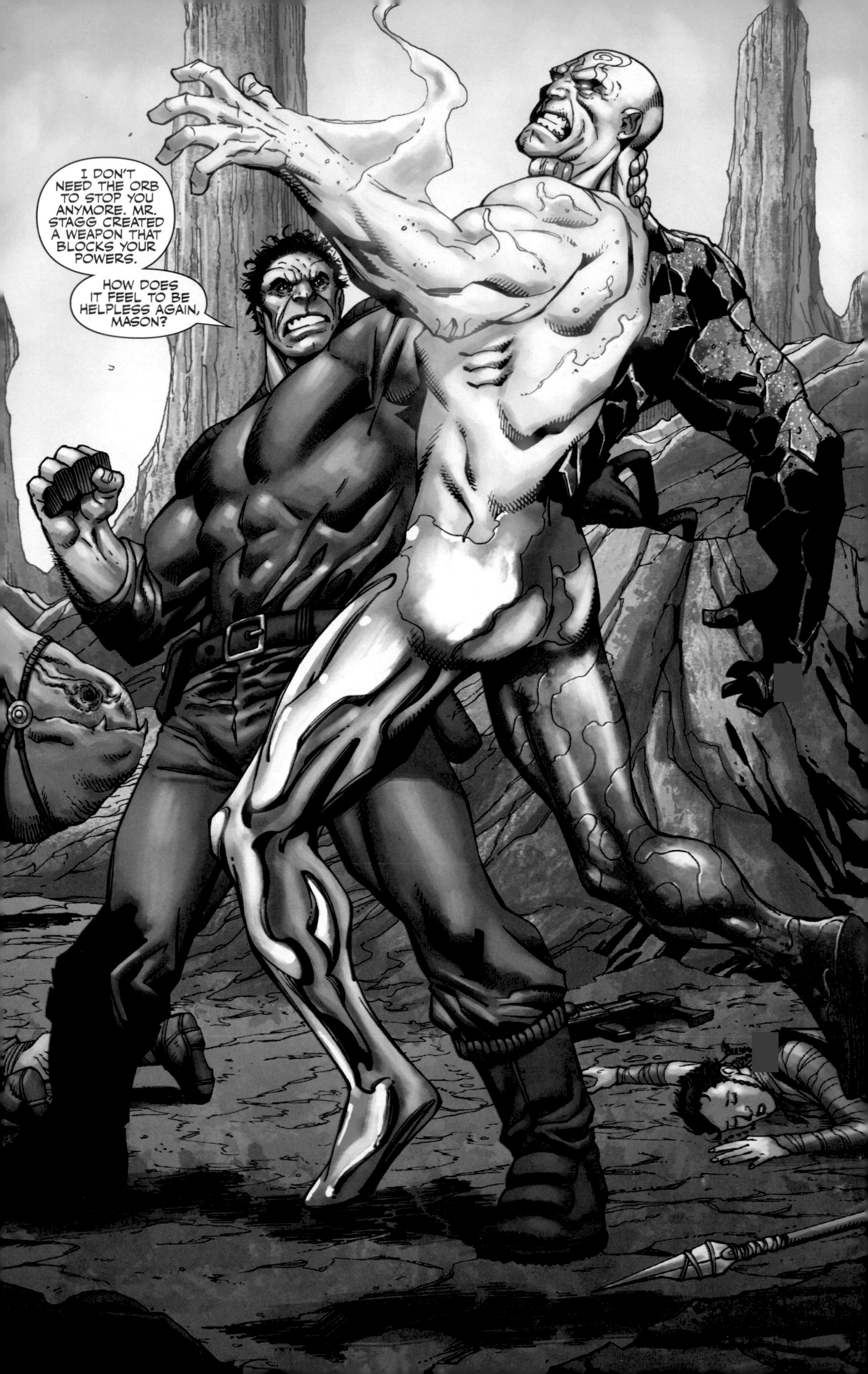
I DON'T NEED THE ORB TO STOP YOU ANYMORE. MR. STAGG CREATED A WEAPON THAT BLOCKS YOUR POWERS.
HOW DOES IT FEEL TO BE HELPLESS AGAIN, MASON?

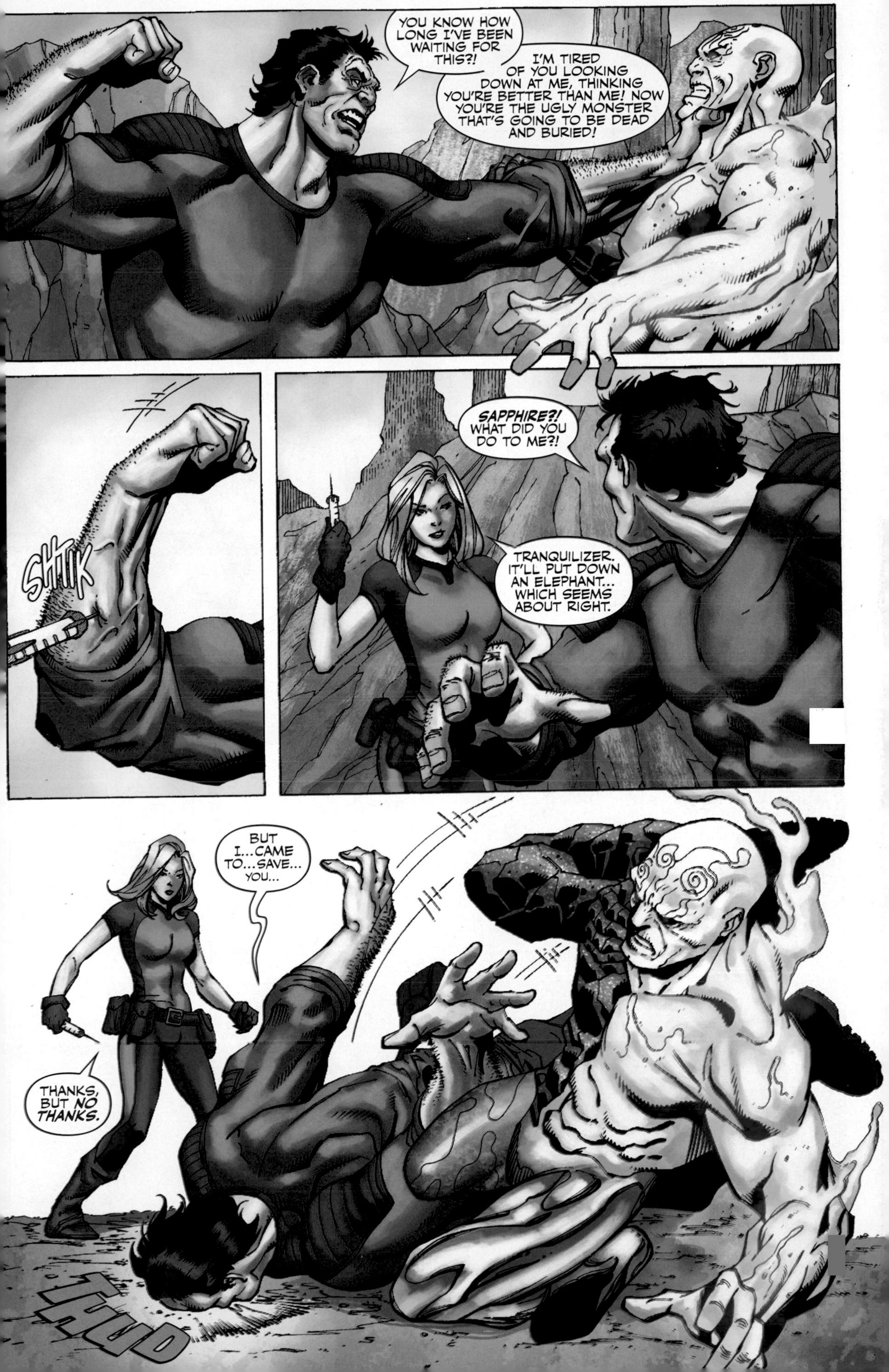
YOU KNOW HOW LONG I'VE BEEN WAITING FOR THIS?!
I'M TIRED OF YOU LOOKING DOWN AT ME, THINKING YOU'RE BETTER THAN ME! NOW YOU'RE THE UGLY MONSTER THAT'S GOING TO BE DEAD AND BURIED!
SHTIK
SAPPHIRE?! WHAT DID YOU DO TO ME?!
TRANQUILIZER. IT'LL PUT DOWN AN ELEPHANT... WHICH SEEMS ABOUT RIGHT.
BUT I...CAME TO...SAVE... YOU...
THANKS, BUT NO THANKS.
THUD

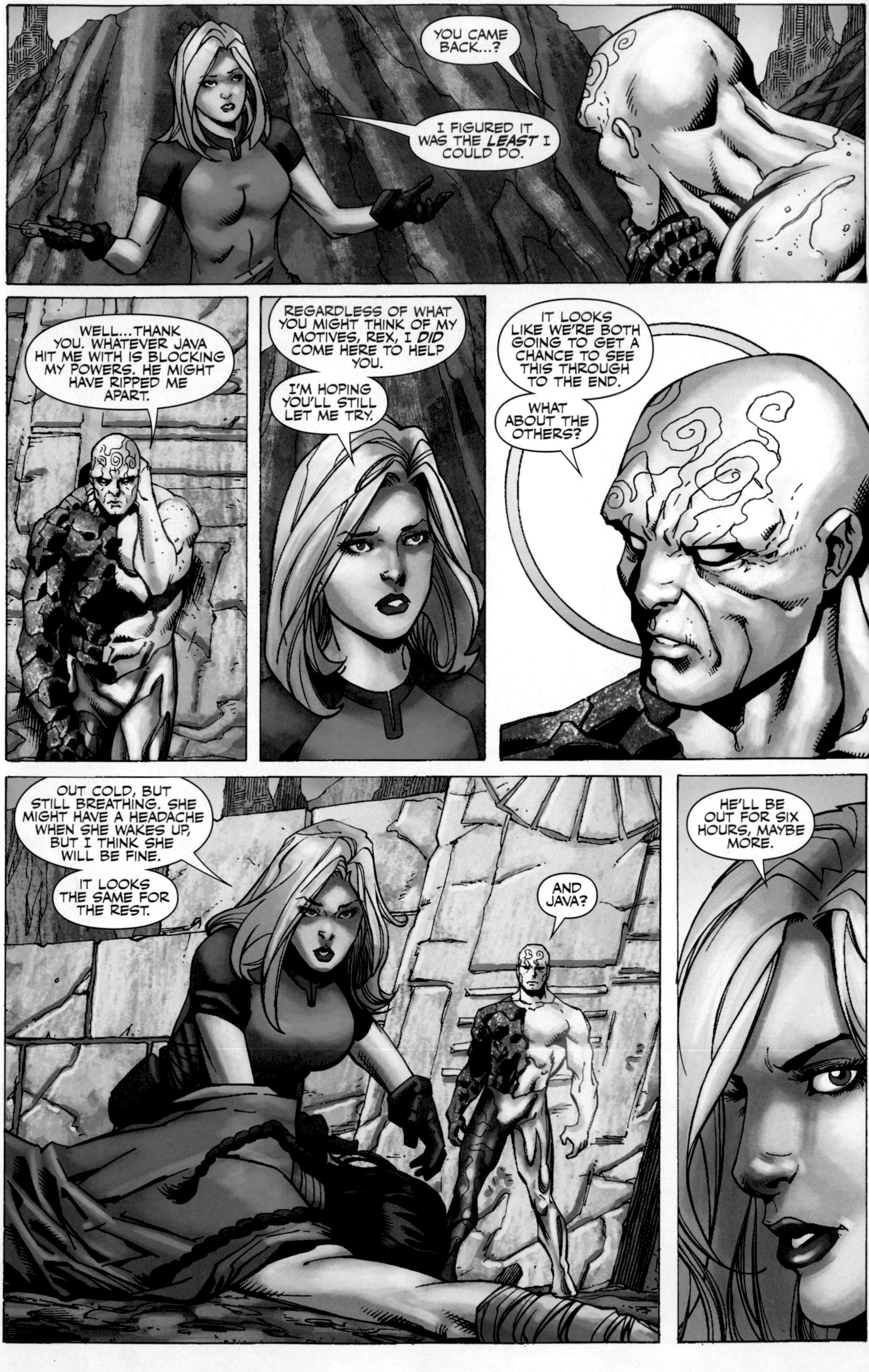
YOU CAME BACK...?
I FIGURED IT WAS THE *LEAST* I COULD DO.
WELL...THANK YOU. WHATEVER JAVA HIT ME WITH IS BLOCKING MY POWERS. HE MIGHT HAVE RIPPED ME APART.
REGARDLESS OF WHAT YOU MIGHT THINK OF MY MOTIVES, REX, I *DID* COME HERE TO HELP YOU.
I'M HOPING YOU'LL STILL LET ME TRY.
IT LOOKS LIKE WE'RE BOTH GOING TO GET A CHANCE TO SEE THIS THROUGH TO THE END.
WHAT ABOUT THE OTHERS?
OUT COLD, BUT STILL BREATHING. SHE MIGHT HAVE A HEADACHE WHEN SHE WAKES UP, BUT I THINK SHE WILL BE FINE.
IT LOOKS THE SAME FOR THE REST.
AND JAVA?
HE'LL BE OUT FOR SIX HOURS, MAYBE MORE.

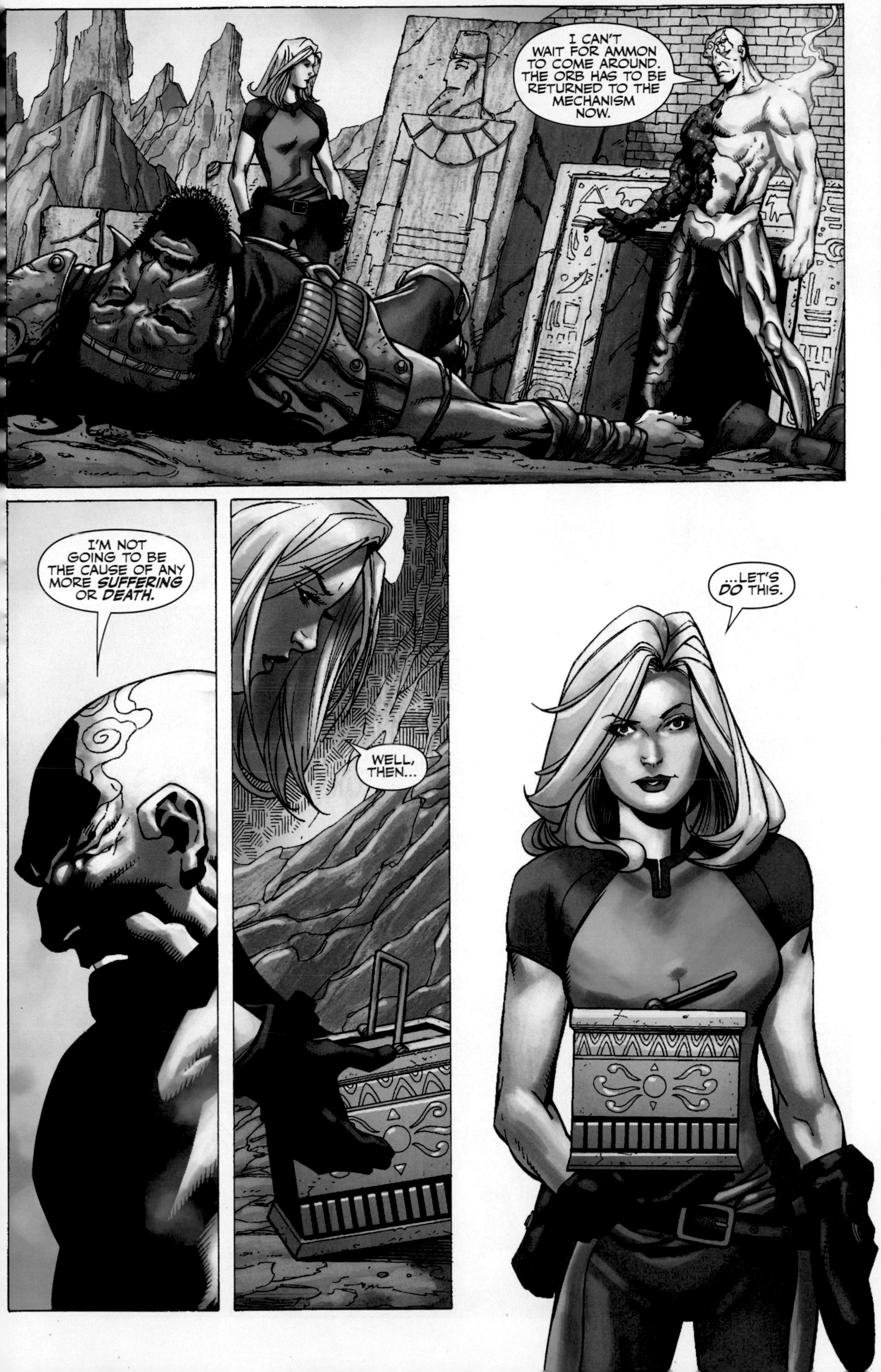
I CAN'T WAIT FOR AMMON TO COME AROUND. THE ORB HAS TO BE RETURNED TO THE MECHANISM NOW.
I'M NOT GOING TO BE THE CAUSE OF ANY MORE SUFFERING OR DEATH.
WELL, THEN...
...LET'S DO THIS.

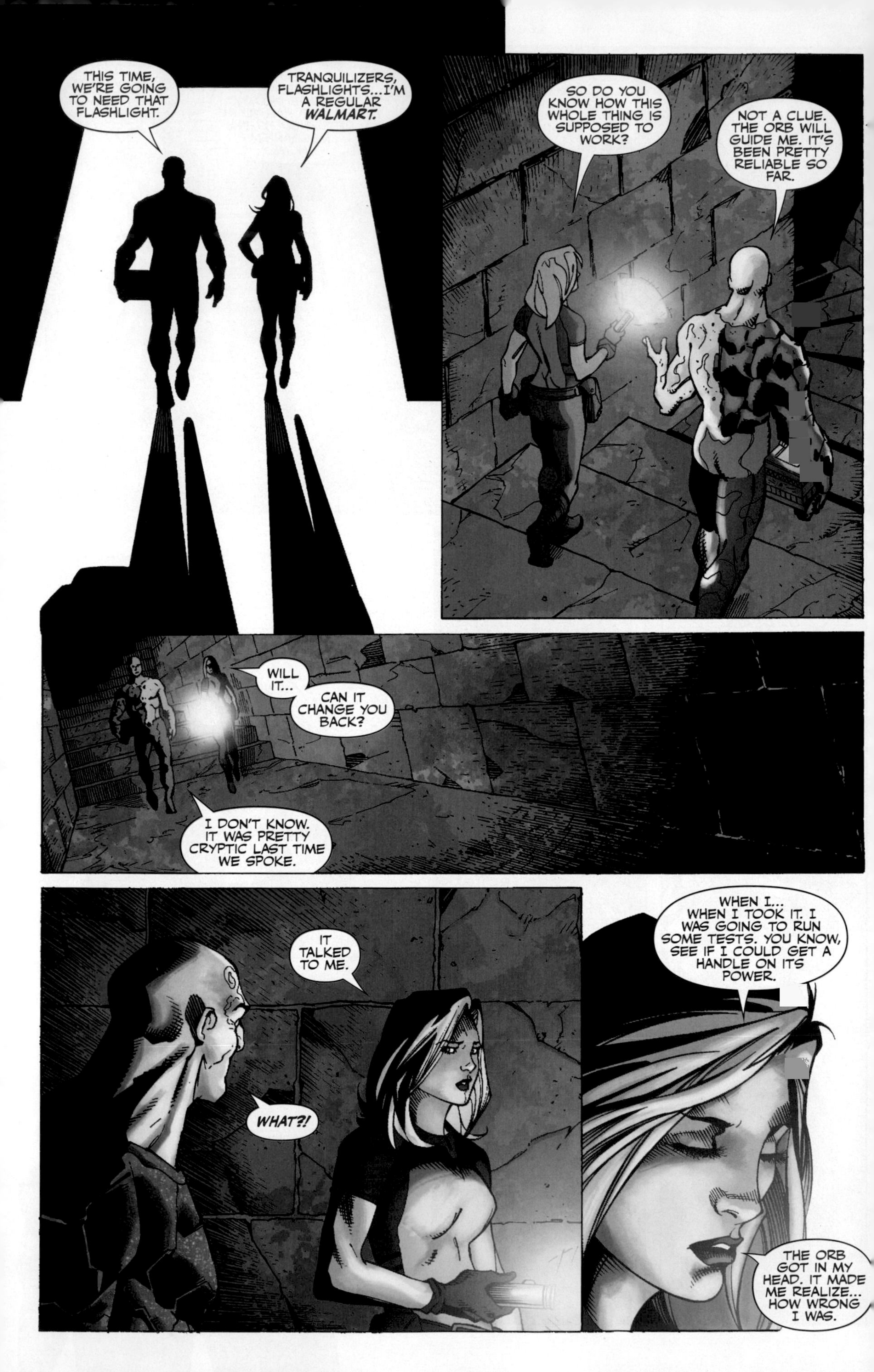
THIS TIME, WE'RE GOING TO NEED THAT FLASHLIGHT.
TRANQUILIZERS, FLASHLIGHTS...I'M A REGULAR *WALMART.*
SO DO YOU KNOW HOW THIS WHOLE THING IS SUPPOSED TO WORK?
NOT A CLUE. THE ORB WILL GUIDE ME. IT'S BEEN PRETTY RELIABLE SO FAR.
WILL IT...
CAN IT CHANGE YOU BACK?
I DON'T KNOW. IT WAS PRETTY CRYPTIC LAST TIME WE SPOKE.
IT TALKED TO ME.
WHAT?!
WHEN I... WHEN I TOOK IT. I WAS GOING TO RUN SOME TESTS. YOU KNOW, SEE IF I COULD GET A HANDLE ON ITS POWER.
THE ORB GOT IN MY HEAD. IT MADE ME REALIZE... HOW WRONG I WAS.

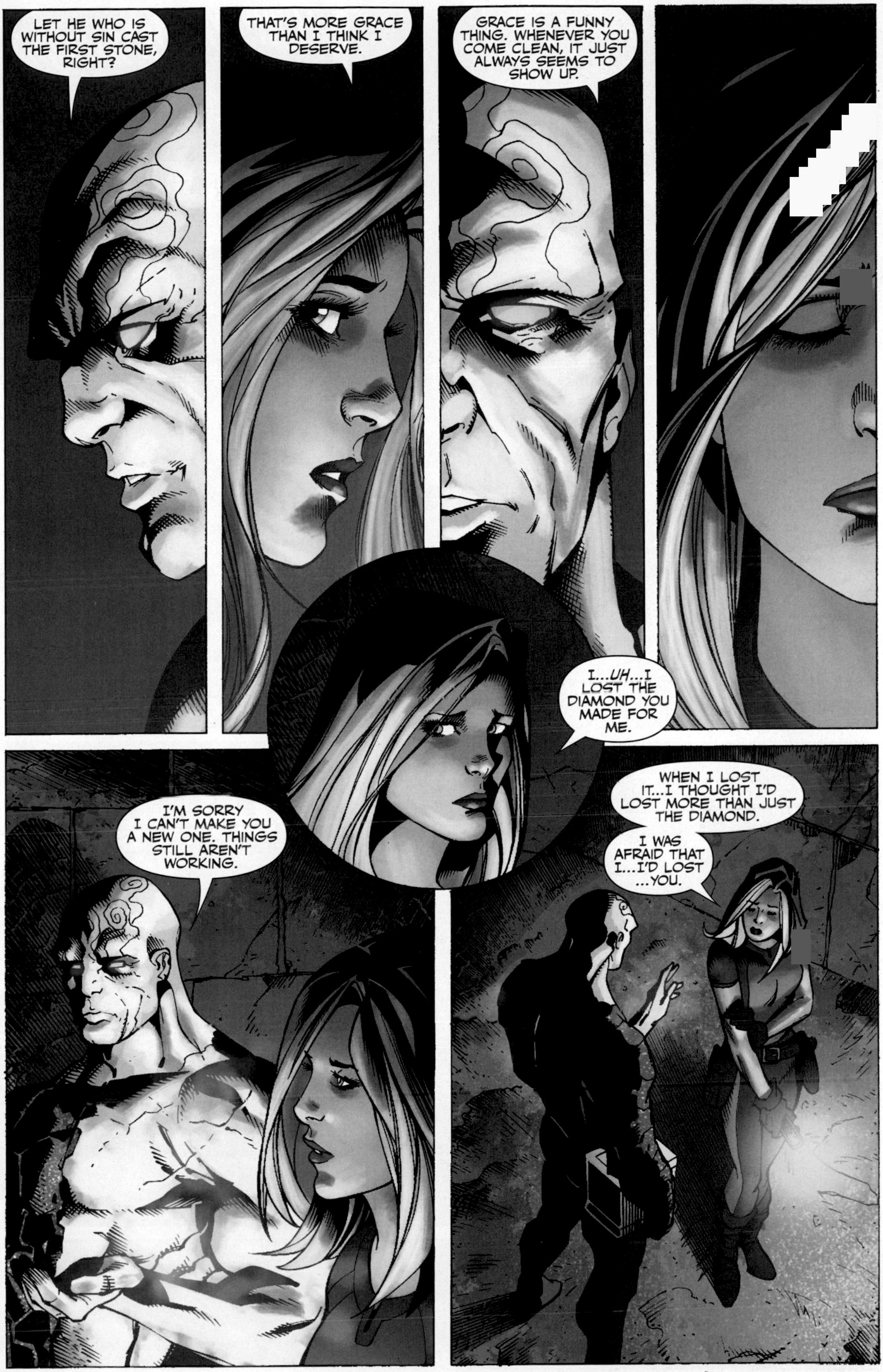
LET HE WHO IS WITHOUT SIN CAST THE FIRST STONE, RIGHT?
THAT'S MORE GRACE THAN I THINK I DESERVE.
GRACE IS A FUNNY THING. WHENEVER YOU COME CLEAN, IT JUST ALWAYS SEEMS TO SHOW UP.
I...UH...I LOST THE DIAMOND YOU MADE FOR ME.
I'M SORRY I CAN'T MAKE YOU A NEW ONE. THINGS STILL AREN'T WORKING.
WHEN I LOST IT...I THOUGHT I'D LOST MORE THAN JUST THE DIAMOND.
I WAS AFRAID THAT I...I'D LOST ...YOU.

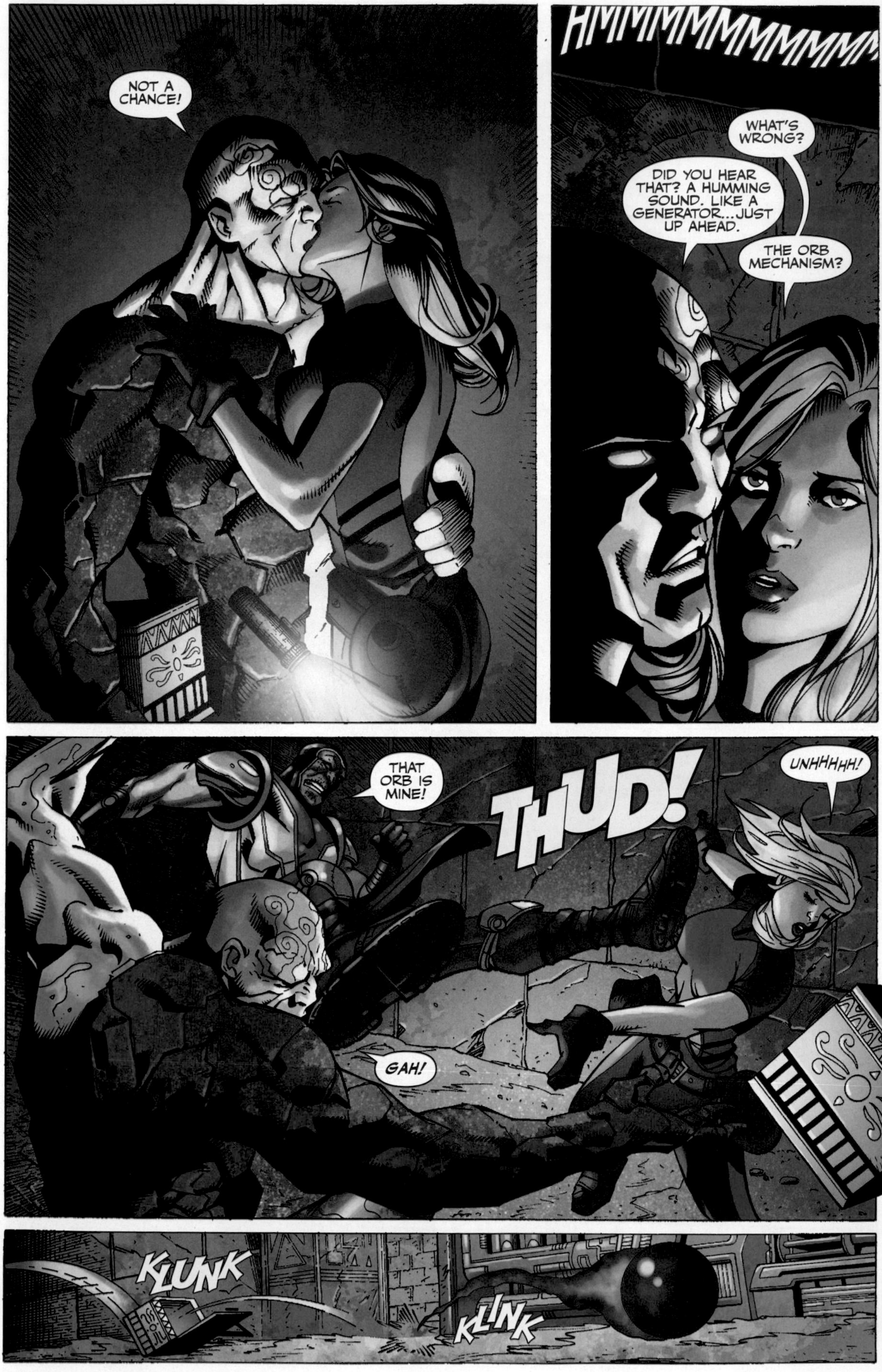
NOT A CHANCE!
HMMMMMMMMMMM
WHAT'S WRONG?
DID YOU HEAR THAT? A HUMMING SOUND. LIKE A GENERATOR...JUST UP AHEAD.
THE ORB MECHANISM?
THAT ORB IS MINE!
THUD!
UNHHHHH!
GAH!
KLUNK
KLINK

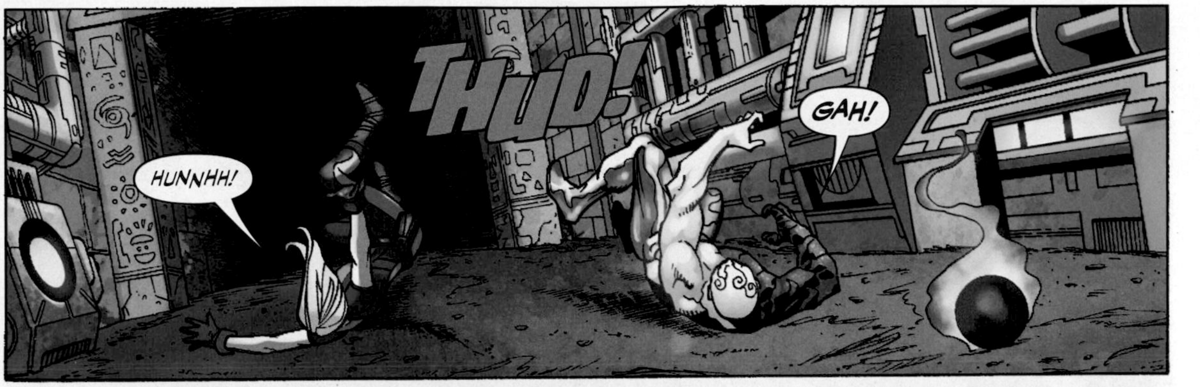
THUD!
HUNNHH!
GAH!

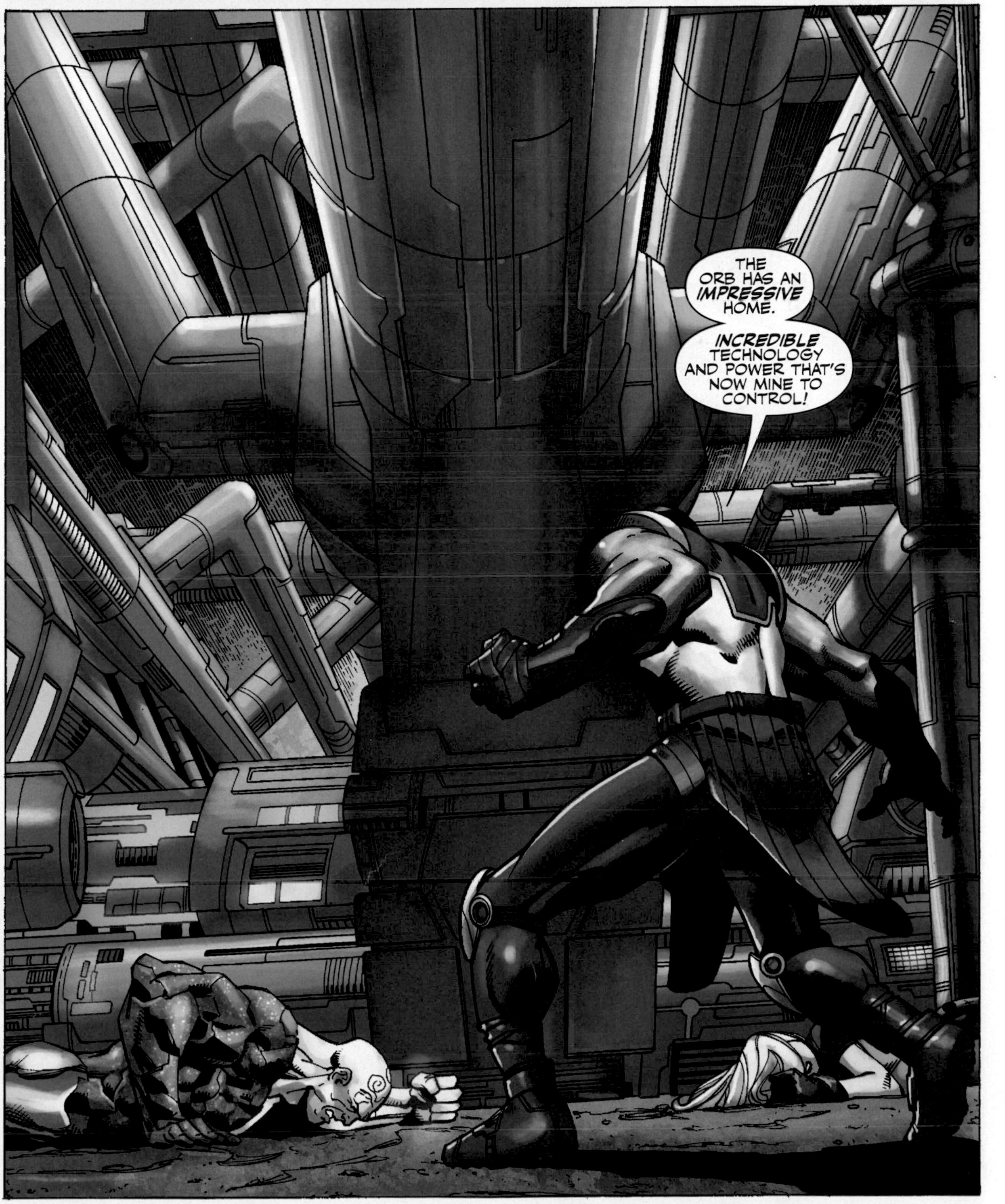
THE ORB HAS AN IMPRESSIVE HOME.
INCREDIBLE TECHNOLOGY AND POWER THAT'S NOW MINE TO CONTROL!

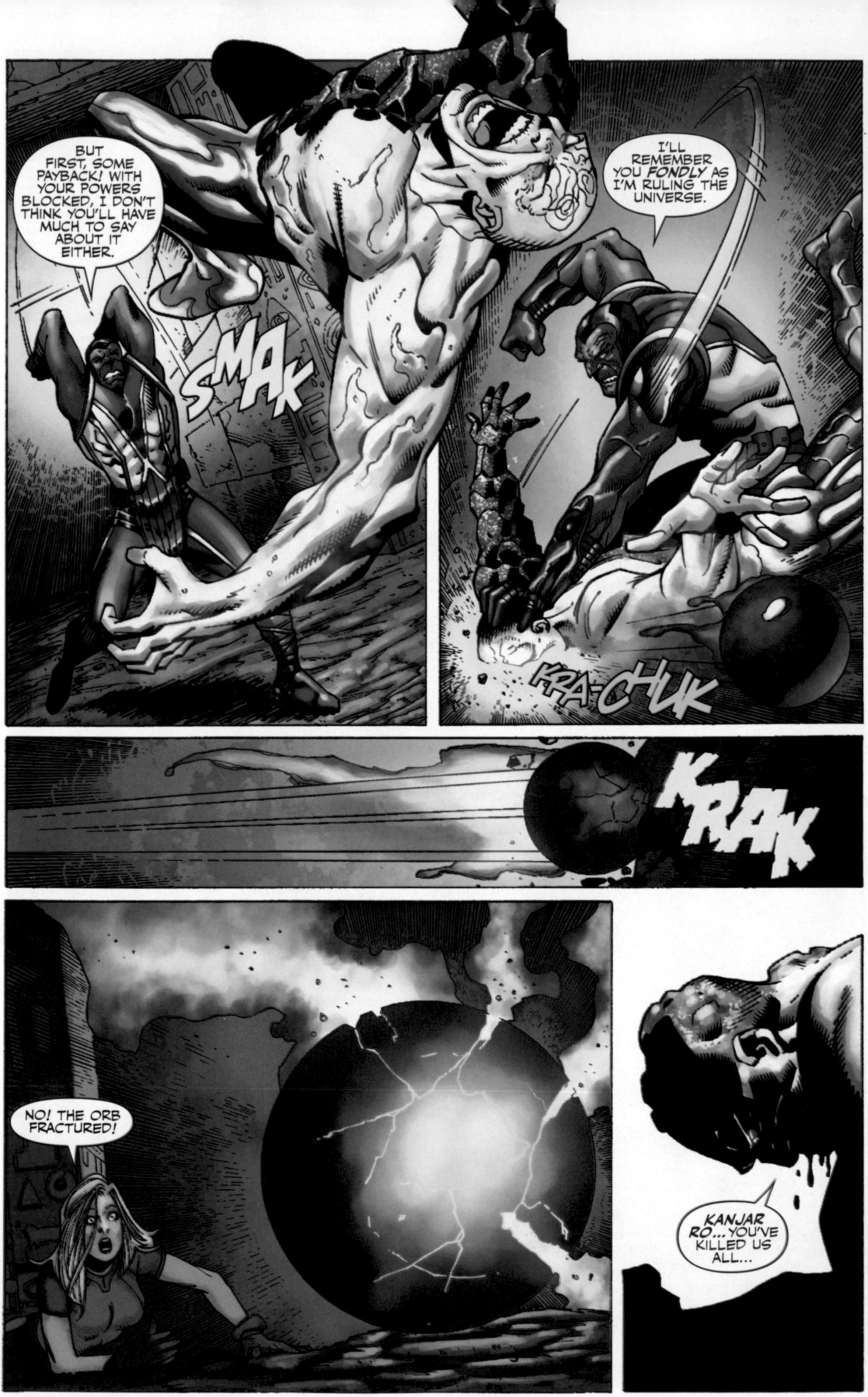
BUT FIRST, SOME PAYBACK! WITH YOUR POWERS BLOCKED, I DON'T THINK YOU'LL HAVE MUCH TO SAY ABOUT IT EITHER.
SMAK
I'LL REMEMBER YOU FONDLY AS I'M RULING THE UNIVERSE.
KRA-CHUK
KRAK
NO! THE ORB FRACTURED!
KANJAR RO... YOU'VE KILLED US ALL...

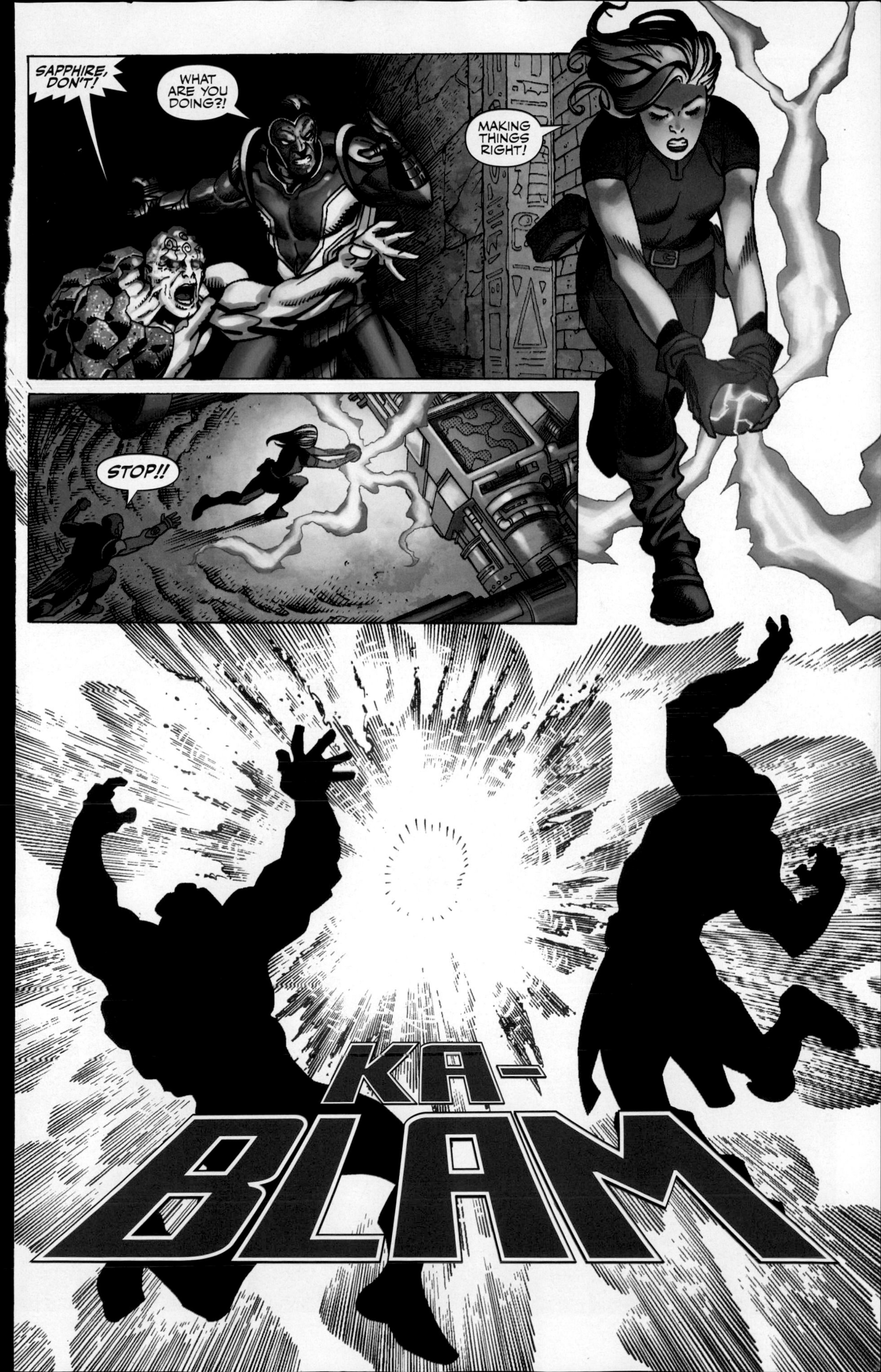
SAPPHIRE, DON'T!
WHAT ARE YOU DOING?!
MAKING THINGS RIGHT!
STOP!!
KA-BLAM

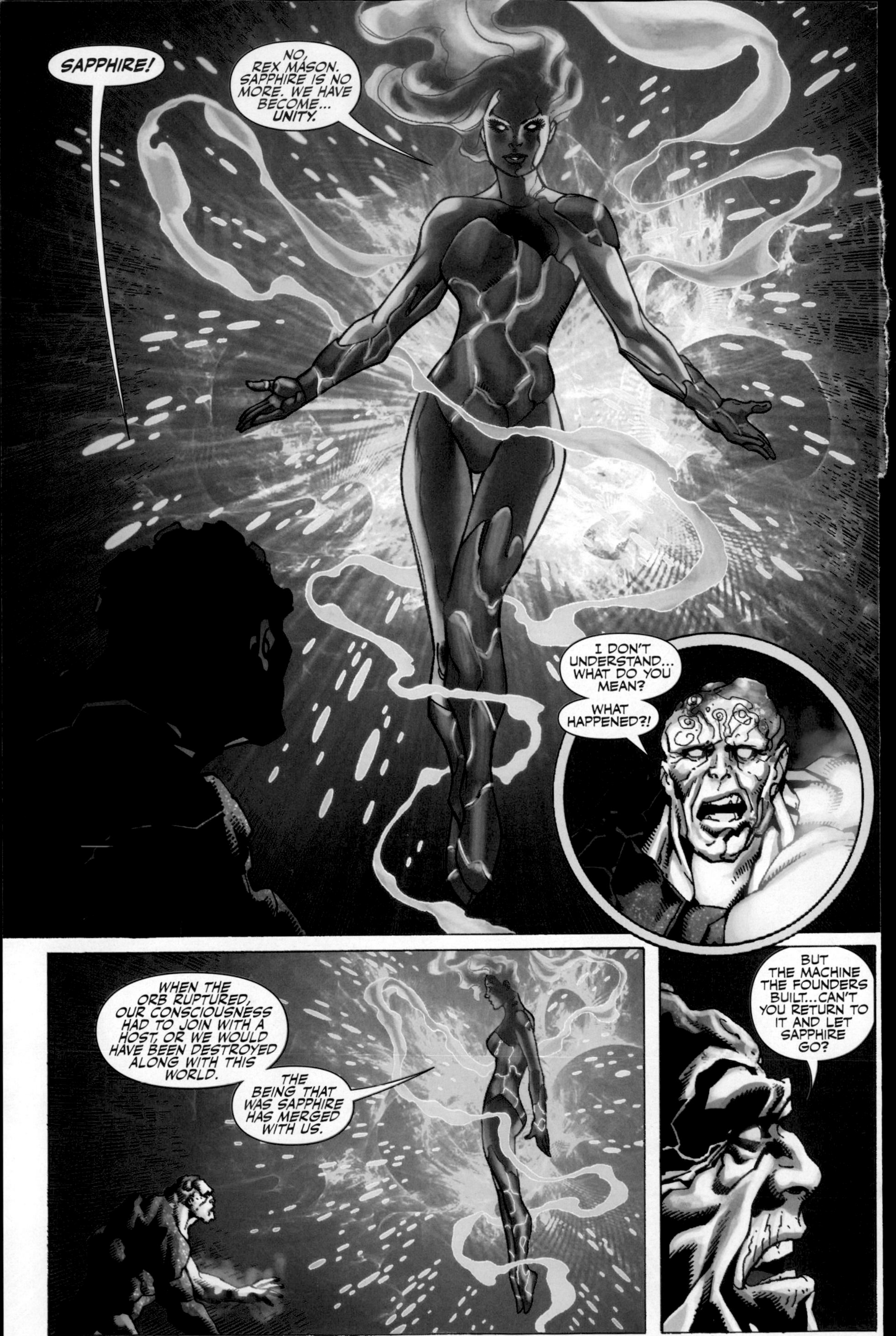
SAPPHIRE!
NO, REX MASON. SAPPHIRE IS NO MORE. WE HAVE BECOME... UNITY.
I DON'T UNDERSTAND... WHAT DO YOU MEAN?
WHAT HAPPENED?!
WHEN THE ORB RUPTURED, OUR CONSCIOUSNESS HAD TO JOIN WITH A HOST, OR WE WOULD HAVE BEEN DESTROYED ALONG WITH THIS WORLD.
THE BEING THAT WAS SAPPHIRE HAS MERGED WITH US.
BUT THE MACHINE THE FOUNDERS BUILT...CAN'T YOU RETURN TO IT AND LET SAPPHIRE GO?

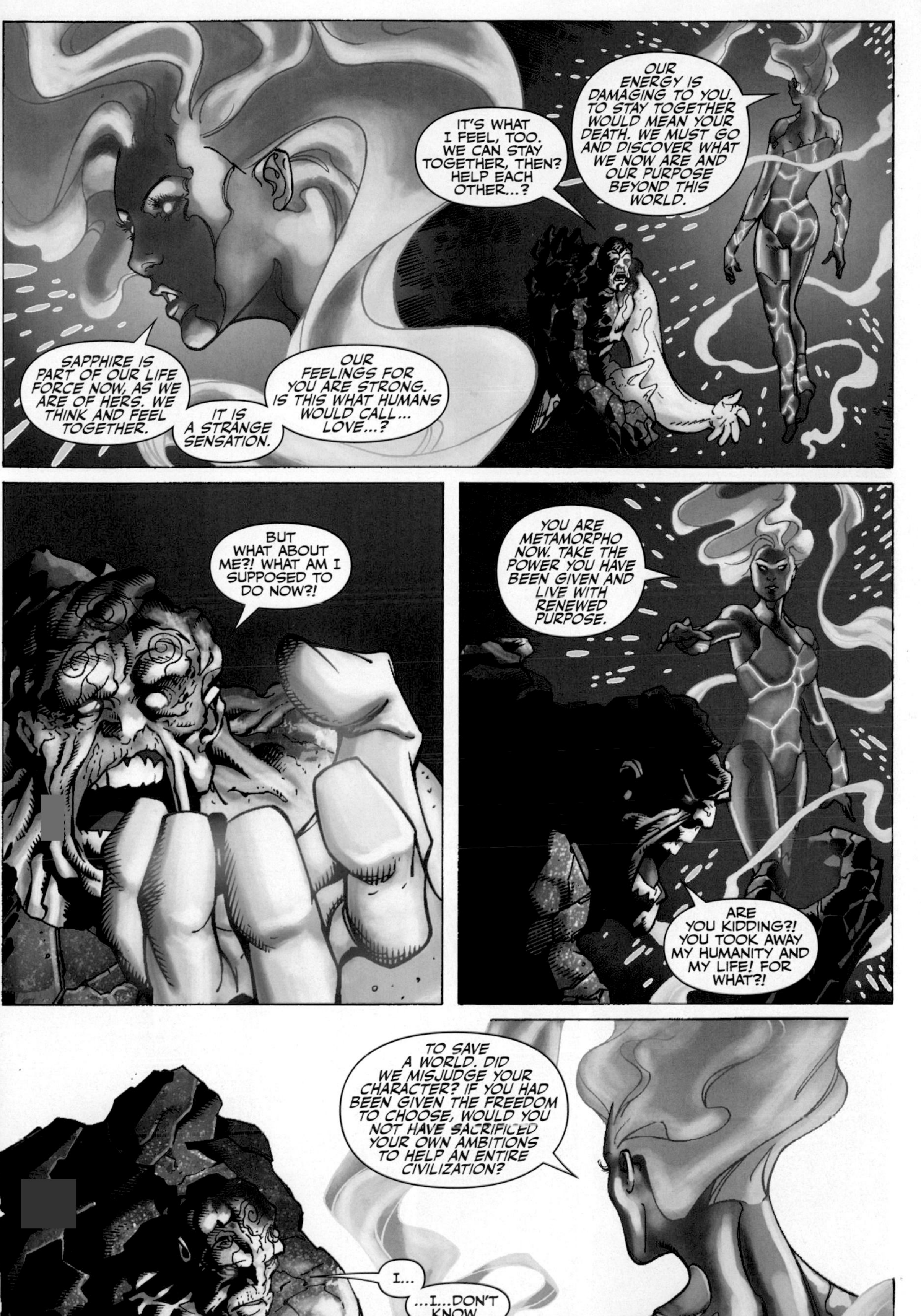
SAPPHIRE IS PART OF OUR LIFE FORCE NOW, AS WE ARE OF HERS. WE THINK AND FEEL TOGETHER.
IT IS A STRANGE SENSATION.
OUR FEELINGS FOR YOU ARE STRONG. IS THIS WHAT HUMANS WOULD CALL... LOVE...?
IT'S WHAT I FEEL, TOO. WE CAN STAY TOGETHER, THEN? HELP EACH OTHER...?
OUR ENERGY IS DAMAGING TO YOU. TO STAY TOGETHER WOULD MEAN YOUR DEATH. WE MUST GO AND DISCOVER WHAT WE NOW ARE AND OUR PURPOSE BEYOND THIS WORLD.
BUT WHAT ABOUT ME?! WHAT AM I SUPPOSED TO DO NOW?!
YOU ARE METAMORPHO NOW. TAKE THE POWER YOU HAVE BEEN GIVEN AND LIVE WITH RENEWED PURPOSE.
ARE YOU KIDDING?! YOU TOOK AWAY MY HUMANITY AND MY LIFE! FOR WHAT?!
TO SAVE A WORLD. DID WE MISJUDGE YOUR CHARACTER? IF YOU HAD BEEN GIVEN THE FREEDOM TO CHOOSE, WOULD YOU NOT HAVE SACRIFICED YOUR OWN AMBITIONS TO HELP AN ENTIRE CIVILIZATION?
I...
...I...DON'T KNOW.

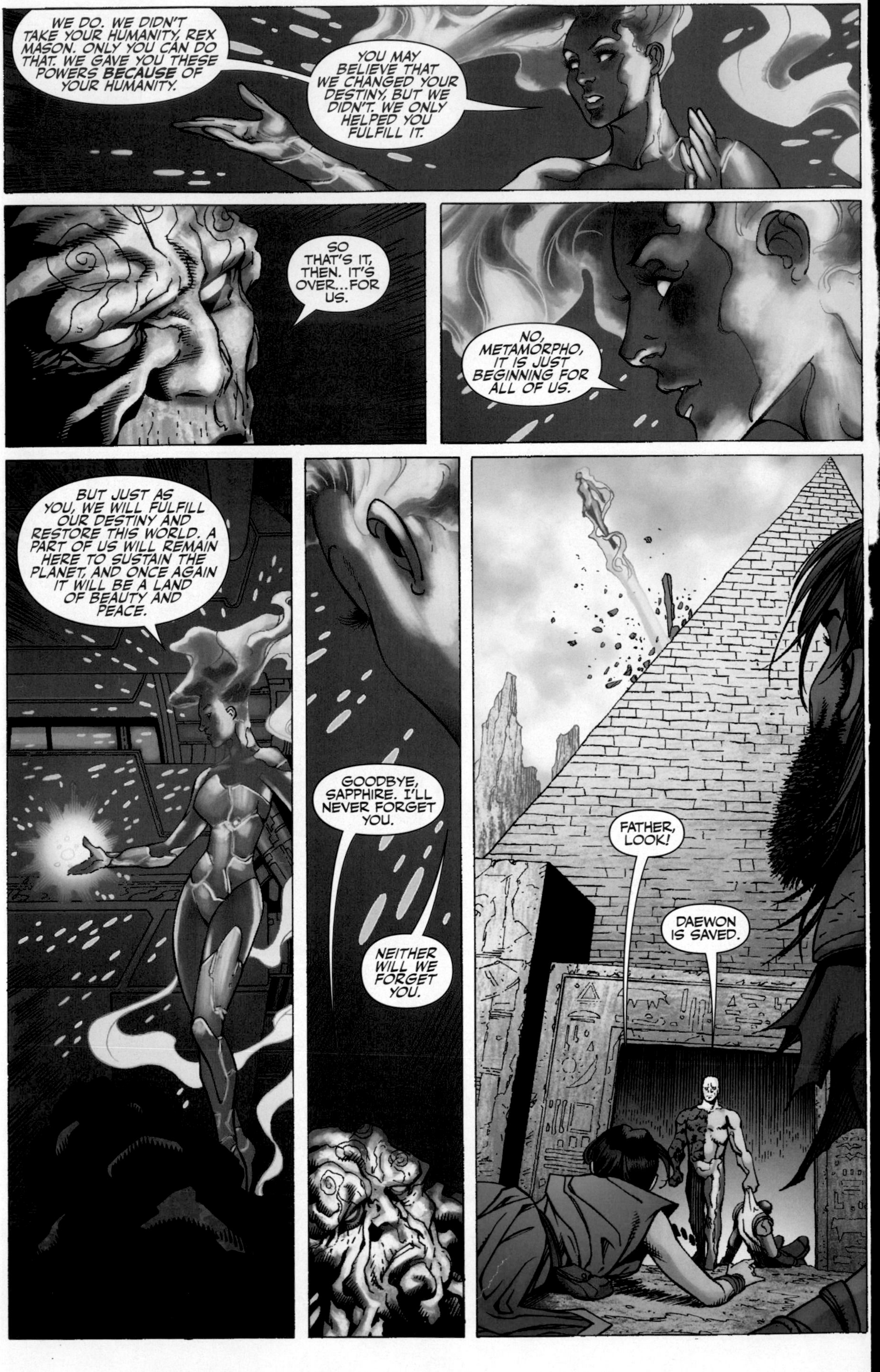
WE DO. WE DIDN'T TAKE YOUR HUMANITY, REX MASON. ONLY YOU CAN DO THAT. WE GAVE YOU THESE POWERS BECAUSE OF YOUR HUMANITY.
YOU MAY BELIEVE THAT WE CHANGED YOUR DESTINY, BUT WE DIDN'T. WE ONLY HELPED YOU FULFILL IT.
SO THAT'S IT, THEN. IT'S OVER...FOR US.
NO, METAMORPHO, IT IS JUST BEGINNING FOR ALL OF US.
BUT JUST AS YOU, WE WILL FULFILL OUR DESTINY AND RESTORE THIS WORLD. A PART OF US WILL REMAIN HERE TO SUSTAIN THE PLANET, AND ONCE AGAIN IT WILL BE A LAND OF BEAUTY AND PEACE.
GOODBYE, SAPPHIRE. I'LL NEVER FORGET YOU.
NEITHER WILL WE FORGET YOU.
FATHER, LOOK!
DAEWON IS SAVED.

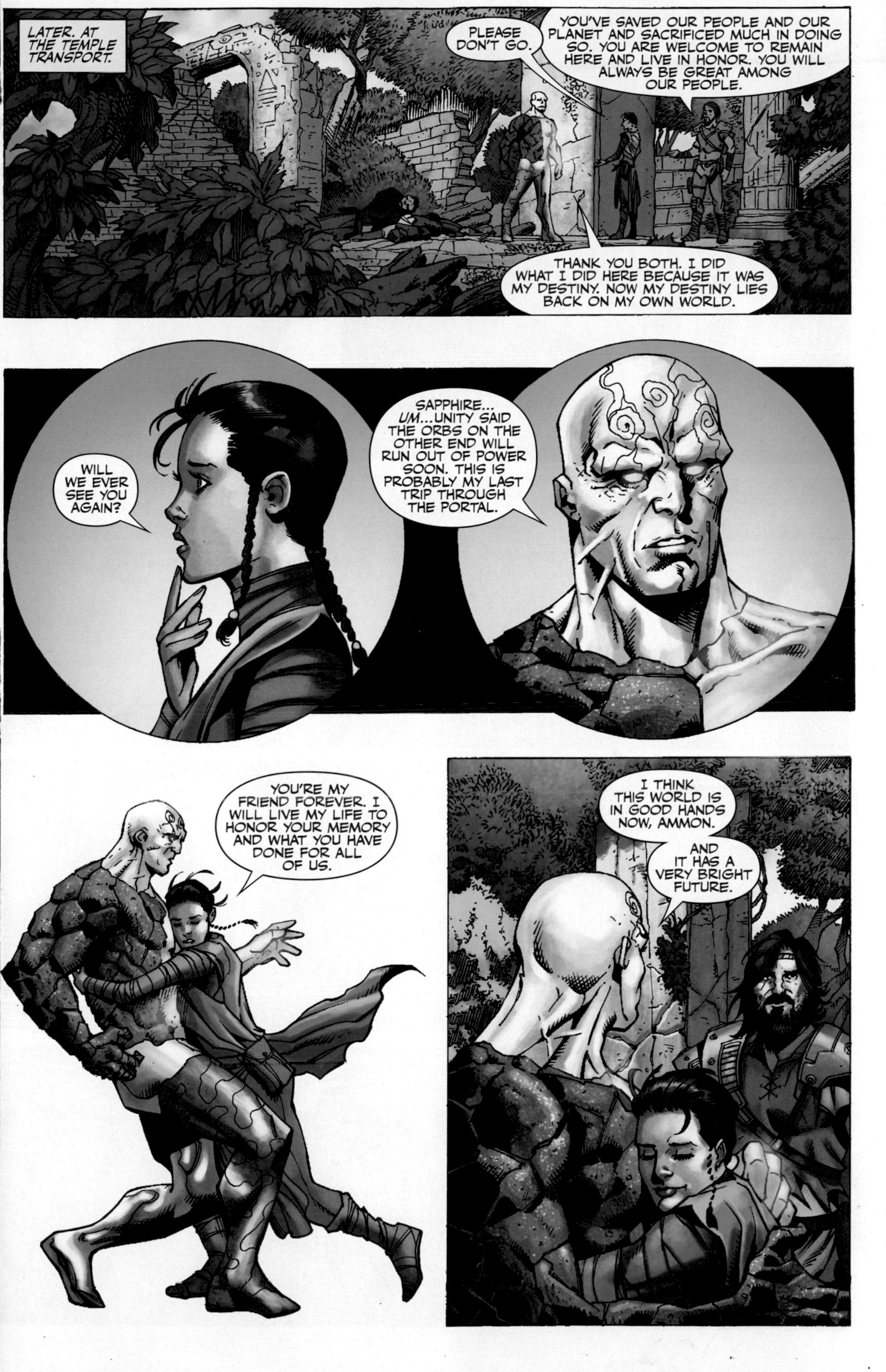
LATER. AT THE TEMPLE TRANSPORT.
PLEASE DON'T GO.
YOU'VE SAVED OUR PEOPLE AND OUR PLANET AND SACRIFICED MUCH IN DOING SO. YOU ARE WELCOME TO REMAIN HERE AND LIVE IN HONOR. YOU WILL ALWAYS BE GREAT AMONG OUR PEOPLE.
THANK YOU BOTH. I DID WHAT I DID HERE BECAUSE IT WAS MY DESTINY. NOW MY DESTINY LIES BACK ON MY OWN WORLD.
WILL WE EVER SEE YOU AGAIN?
SAPPHIRE... UM...UNITY SAID THE ORBS ON THE OTHER END WILL RUN OUT OF POWER SOON. THIS IS PROBABLY MY LAST TRIP THROUGH THE PORTAL.
YOU'RE MY FRIEND FOREVER. I WILL LIVE MY LIFE TO HONOR YOUR MEMORY AND WHAT YOU HAVE DONE FOR ALL OF US.
I THINK THIS WORLD IS IN GOOD HANDS NOW, AMMON.
AND IT HAS A VERY BRIGHT FUTURE.

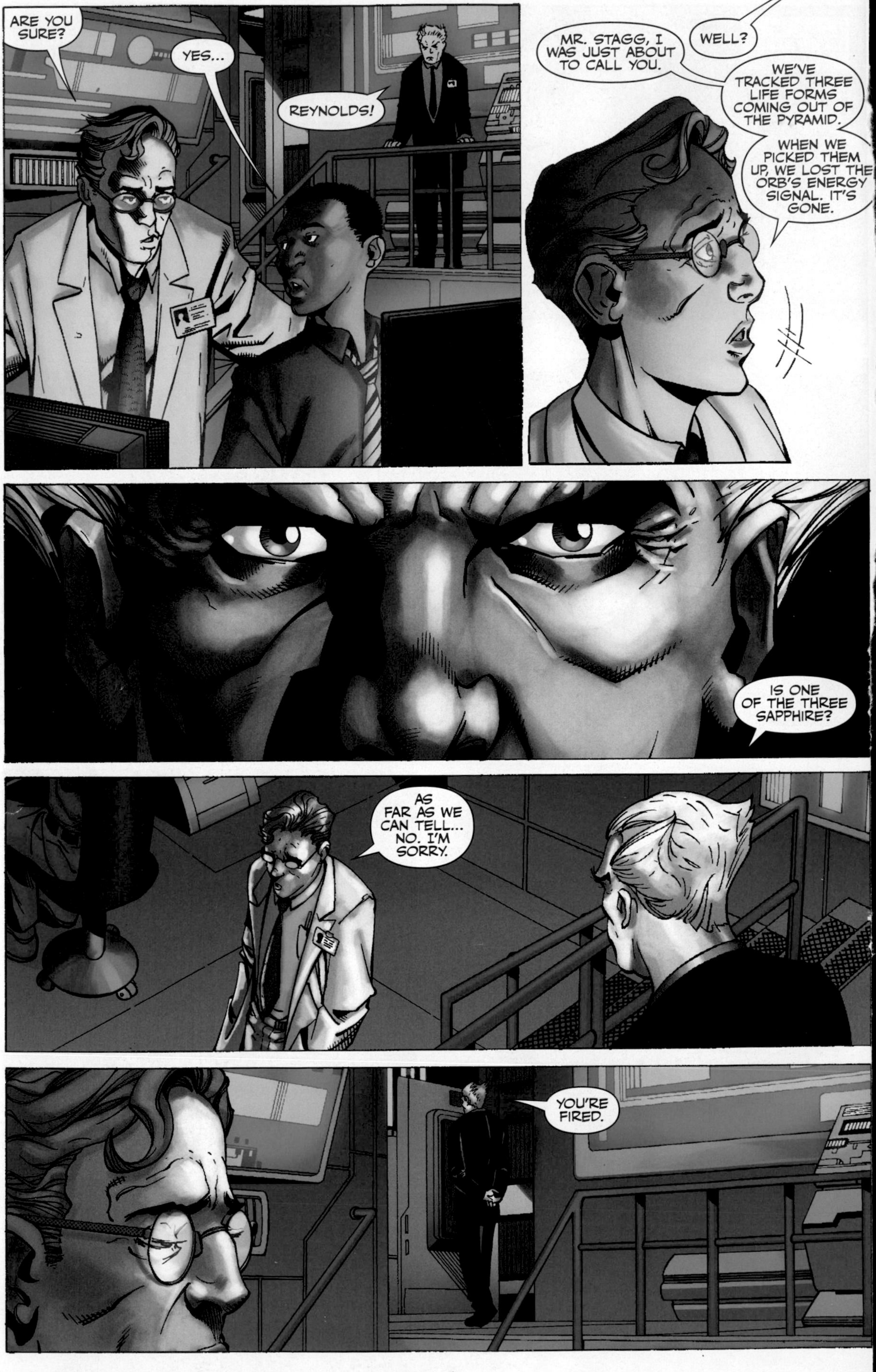
ARE YOU SURE?
YES...
REYNOLDS!
MR. STAGG, I WAS JUST ABOUT TO CALL YOU.
WELL?
WE'VE TRACKED THREE LIFE FORMS COMING OUT OF THE PYRAMID.
WHEN WE PICKED THEM UP, WE LOST THE ORB'S ENERGY SIGNAL. IT'S GONE.
IS ONE OF THE THREE SAPPHIRE?
AS FAR AS WE CAN TELL... NO. I'M SORRY.
YOU'RE FIRED.

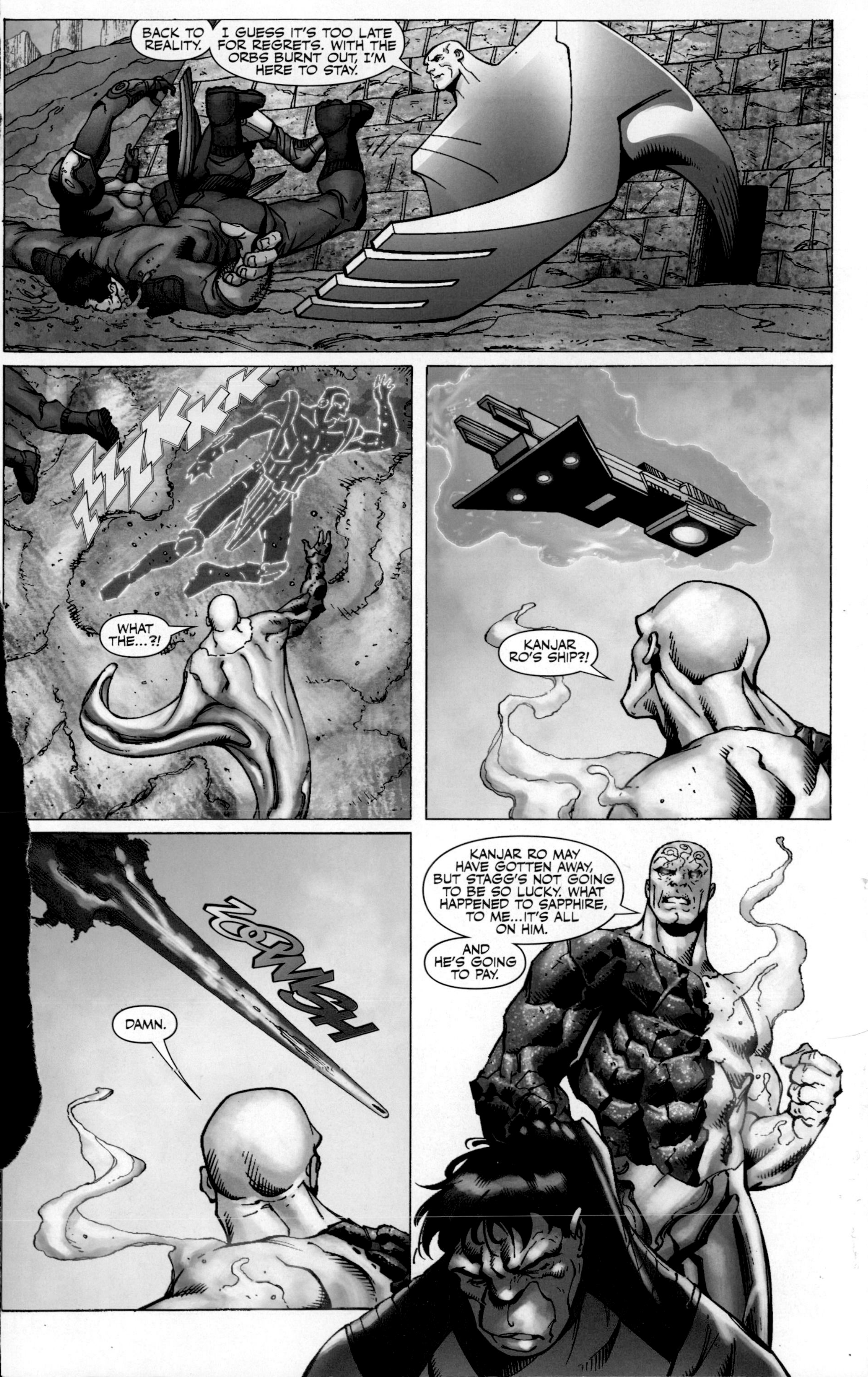
BACK TO REALITY.
I GUESS IT'S TOO LATE FOR REGRETS. WITH THE ORBS BURNT OUT, I'M HERE TO STAY.
WHAT THE...?!
KANJAR RO'S SHIP?!
DAMN.
KANJAR RO MAY HAVE GOTTEN AWAY, BUT STAGG'S NOT GOING TO BE SO LUCKY. WHAT HAPPENED TO SAPPHIRE, TO ME...IT'S ALL ON HIM.
AND HE'S GOING TO PAY.

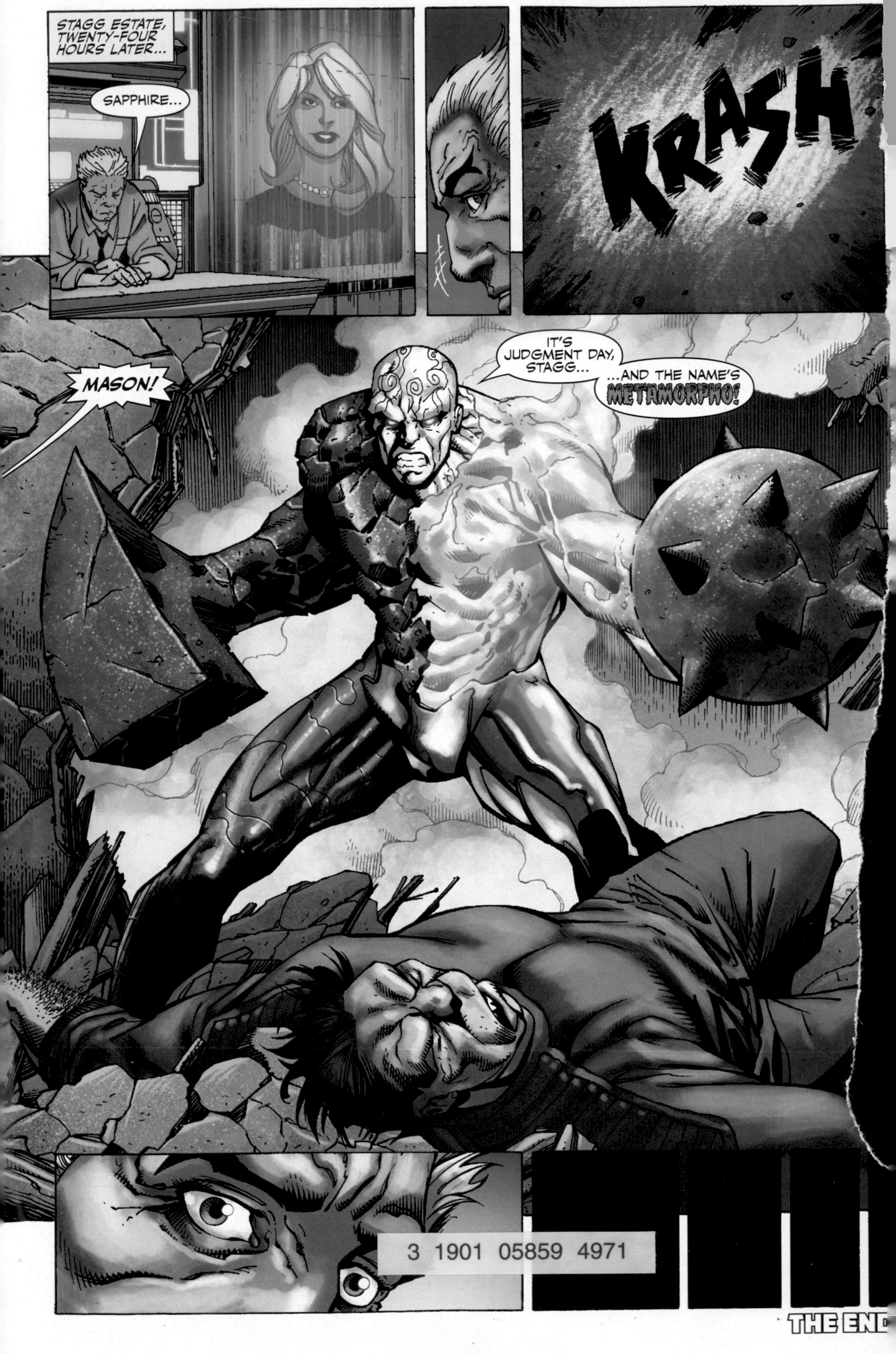
STAGG ESTATE, TWENTY-FOUR HOURS LATER...
SAPPHIRE...
KRASH
MASON!
IT'S JUDGMENT DAY, STAGG...
...AND THE NAME'S METAMORPHO!
THE END